VIETNAM AND AMERICAN FOREIGN POLICY

Problems in American Civilization

VIETNAM
and
AMERICAN
Foreign Policy

EDITED WITH AN INTRODUCTION BY

John R. Boettiger
HAMPSHIRE COLLEGE

D. C. HEATH AND COMPANY
Lexington, Massachusetts

INTRODUCTION

COULD THE AGONY of Vietnam herald the end of the Cold War? Few would put the question in such apocalyptic terms, and few would think it susceptible to unqualified answer. One cannot assume today, as one could a decade ago, a common understanding of the phrase "Cold War." Many factors other than Vietnam will influence the continuing evolution of great power relationships, and the historical significance of any current episode may be magnified by the pain and finiteness of one's own moment in history. Still, the issue has been widely raised: if the deep American engagement in Vietnam is a natural outgrowth of common policy perceptions and preferences of the post-World War II period, may it not also be true that the struggle over Vietnam will lead to the first truly strategic shift in United States foreign policy in over two decades?

Those inclined to answer such a question affirmatively tend to differ widely on the nature of the shift they anticipate and the relationship between current American policy in Vietnam and that which is likely to succeed it. Some believe that the transition to a less conflicted, more collaborative chapter in international relations hinges on U. S. determination to deny South Vietnam to the communists. Others are more impressed with the dangers of renewed isolationism: if the United States abandons Vietnam, Americans would react with such revulsion to the waste and frustration of the war that they would also abandon all efforts to promote the growth and stability of Asia. Still others, while perhaps sharing something of the same apprehension, fear the consequences of perseverance more than those of withdrawal; they hope to build, out of the bankruptcy of the perspective that has led to Vietnam, a less oppressive and more humane foreign policy. Whatever the source, there is considerable speculation that — in W. W. Rostow's words — "Vietnam could be made the closing of one chapter in modern history and the opening of another."

In any event, the very existence of such speculation by serious analysts suggests the order of importance widely attributed to the nation's conduct in Vietnam. As the dimensions of conflict grew in 1965 and 1966, questioning of American strategy and the legitimacy of the American presence in Vietnam occurred with greater sharpness and frequency. By the autumn of 1967 the war appeared to most observers to be in a state of costly irresolution. For the United States, with one-half million men and approximately two billion dollars a month committed to Vietnam, the war had become the focus of one of the most significant foreign policy debates in the nation's history. Widespread and increasingly demonstrative dissent from the Johnson administration's perspective and conduct seemed likely to make of United States policy in Vietnam the major issue in the Presidential campaign of 1968.

The President and his advisers, clearly apprehensive that the domestic ground of permissive popular mood was eroding and that the North Vietnamese would be encouraged by demonstrations of sizable popular opposition to official policy, spoke strongly of the responsibility for sustained determination. "I think it is time," said Vice President Hubert Humphrey, "that all Americans realized that we are in the midst of a protracted, costly struggle — a struggle in which we are making slow but steady progress — which nevertheless will probably not end until [North Vietnam] comes to believe that we have the will, the determination, the perseverance, patience and strength to see it through. We must know that the enemy's hope for victory is not in his military power but in our division, our weariness, our uncertainty."

From the administration's perspective, three key points seemed clear:

1. A "just and peaceful settlement" was unlikely so long as North Vietnam held to its uncompromising posture. In President Johnson's words, "Those who began the war are not willing to explore ways to end it. . . . Peace and stability will come to Asia only when the aggressors know that they cannot take another people's land by force."

So long as massive United States military action was necessary to sustain a non-communist South Vietnam — and the duration of that necessity was widely viewed as indefinite — American national interests demanded such unequivocal commitment on two related grounds:

2. The United States has committed itself by treaty and repeatedly by pledged word to assist in the defense of South Vietnam against communist aggression. Secretary of State Rusk was most plain: ". . . those who would place in question the credibility of the pledged word of the United States under our mutual security treaties would subject this nation to mortal danger. If any who would be our adversary should suppose that our treaties are a bluff, or will be abandoned if the going gets tough, the result could be catastrophe for all mankind."

3. The threat of a militant China demanded, in the administration's view, exemplary and effective resistance to communist incursions in Asia generally. "Within the next decade or two," Secretary Rusk asserted, "there will be a billion Chinese on the mainland, armed with nuclear weapons, with no certainty about what their attitude toward the rest of Asia will be."

Opposition to administration policy took a wide variety of forms, from those who pronounced impatiently on the fainthearted restraint of the government's bombing of North Vietnamese port and residential areas to those who favored total and abrupt American withdrawal from a cruel and inhuman enterprise. The increasing *scope* of opposition reflected a common ground of opinion described by the New York Times: ". . . the unpleasant fact is that the American policy of military escalation, after nearly three years, has not succeeded. That failure is the essence of the problem in Vietnam." That the enemy was being *hurt,* as Administration spokesmen emphasized in justification of continued bombing of North Vietnam, was not really at issue. The costs to the United States of inflicting that hurt, however, seemed considerable — particularly the political costs entailed by incidental or accidental damage to civilians and their property. Furthermore, the enemy had neither been intimidated nor forced to operate with lower force levels; indeed, communist combat forces had virtually tripled since the American bombing program began in early 1965. And in the crucial competition for pacification and organization of the South Vietnamese countryside, progress on the government side was inordinately slow and meagre. Meanwhile, the critics added, the appalling human toll of the war continued to mount — the hundreds of soldiers and civilians killed each day in Vietnam, and the deprived elsewhere in the world (including the dispossessed of America's own urban and rural ghettos) denied adequate assistance while enormous American resources poured into a corner of Southeast Asia.

Finally, it was widely argued that the administration was both unwise in its exaggeration of Chinese aggressiveness in Asia and unduly optimistic about the likely deterrent impact of the American "example" in Vietnam. "The temptation," wrote Theodore Draper, "is almost overpowering to magnify the importance of the game, to try to retrieve one's fortunes with one more raise of the ante, to be prisoners of an ever-changing present because looking back at the past is too painful and peering into the future is too unpromising." And "raising the ante" had its own penultimate danger: that of provoking Chinese intervention and an Asian war of continental dimensions.

The lines of debate over the American role in Vietnam have not been drawn with anything approaching precision. Analysis has often suffered in the interest of polemic, and the knowledge on which policy recommendations or predictions should be based has as often been conspicuously thin. The stakes are large, and the emotions engaged are strong — a combination which has tended to polarize debate and lead to the rigidifying assumption that the "other side" really has nothing practical or legitimate to say. The available literature is vast and, on the whole, rather perishable. An attempt has been made here to compose a reasonably coherent and balanced collection of opinions on American policy in Vietnam and its possible results. In the one area where no satisfactory published material was available, an original essay was commissioned (Melvin Gurtov's "Hanoi on War and Peace").

This book has been designed to pro-vide some grounds for judging the nature and wisdom of American policy. Such a judgment cannot, of course, be fully secure, any more than the grounds here offered can be characterized as comprehensive. Much has yet to be unveiled; some interpretations here advanced will stand the test of time better than others; and no doubt there will prove to be some irreducible element of obscurity.

The initial historical section, Part I, deals primarily with the evolution of American interest and presence in Vietnam since World War II, with emphasis on the growing intensity and size of the American role. If, as several have claimed, why we are in Vietnam is today a question of mainly historical interest, it is an historical question with the deepest implications for the current and future thrust of American diplomacy. Surely, as Arthur Schlesinger writes, "we *are* there, for better or for worse, and we must deal with the situation that exists," but to assess whether "for better or for worse" is nonetheless a judgment of extraordinary importance, and one requiring the application of historical insight.

Part II, "The Objects of Containment," examines the forces against whom the efforts of the Government of South Vietnam (GVN) and its American ally have been directed. Much of the controversy and confusion that has characterized the debate on Vietnam is related to the nature of the enemy and his allies, their intentions, capabilities, and relationships to one another: the Vietcong, or South Vietnamese communists, and their political organization, the National Liberation Front (NLF or NLFSV); the Democratic Republic of Vietnam (DRV), or North Vietnamese communist regime; the Soviet Union; and China. The word "containment," coined by George F. Kennan over twenty years ago to characterize the need to restrain Soviet expansion in Europe, perhaps serves as well as a description of official American strategy vis-à-vis China. The wisdom of its applicability to Asian circumstances, and of the instruments employed in an effort to secure it, are addressed particularly by William Bundy, David Mozingo, and Lucian Pye.

Part III addresses most directly the central issue of the practicability and wisdom of United States policy in Vietnam and of proposed alternatives. It also raises some important aspects of context: the general post-World War II foreign policy posture of the United States from which the Vietnam enterprise has grown, the larger policy goals that enterprise is held to serve, and the challenges confronting those who would design or specify the goals and instruments of a post-Vietnam diplomacy.

CONTENTS

III. THE FUTURE – VIETNAM AND BEYOND

I. THE EVOLUTION OF AMERICAN POLICY

Joseph Buttinger: VIETNAM AT WAR

This selection, excerpted from Mr. Buttinger's enormously rich two-volume history of Vietnam, offers a careful account — as well as some forceful judgments — of the U. S.–Vietnamese relationship as it developed after World War II, through the Geneva Conference of 1954, concluding with the demise of Ngo Dinh Diem in 1963.

THE OUTBREAK of the Indochina War [in 1945–46] at a time when both Great Britain and the Netherlands were working toward a peaceful settlement of their colonial problems was generally deplored in the United States, but widespread sympathy with the aspirations of the Indochinese peoples did not prompt the Truman Administration to criticize the French policy of colonial reconquest. The almost proverbial "anti-colonialism" of the American people remained a platonic sentiment — too weak to overcome the many obstacles against a firm American policy in favor of independence for the three Indochinese states [Cambodia, Laos, Vietnam]. France was too important an ally in Europe to be officially rebuffed by Washington for her Indochinese policy, and the fear that a compromise with the Hanoi regime might create a Communist Vietnam was even then strong in the United States: Washington felt it could not urge France to seek such a solution. The United States remained officially "neutral." But when the hope for an early return of peace, expressed by Secretary of State Marshall in February, 1947, was killed by developments, Washington was gradually induced to drop its policy of detachment

and take an active part in the struggle for Indochina.

It is useless to speculate whether this change would have happened had it been possible to predict the extent to which the United States would one day be involved in Vietnam. The active role henceforth played by Washington in Indochinese affairs was not unanimously applauded, but nobody could foresee where the first modest steps would ultimately lead. . . . The nature of these first steps was determined by the country's traditional ideas that had long found expression in an unrecognized ideological "worldview," and the mounting preoccupations engendered by the Cold War, as the evolving conflict between the West and the Soviet bloc began to be called. The justifiable fear that a French defeat in Indochina might produce a Communist Vietnam was among these considerations. That changes in the *status quo* of many countries, particularly those still under colonial rule, were necessary, was part of the American worldview; but such changes had to conform to firm American notions about what kind of society should grow out of theoretically welcome "revolutions."

The men who formulated U. S. policy

Joseph Buttinger, *Vietnam: A Dragon Embattled,* Volume II (New York: Frederick A. Praeger, 1967), pp. 805–811, 818–821, 823, 838–844, 918–920, 924–927, 930, 933–942, 946, 949–950, 952, 960, 969–970, 972–974, 977, 981–985. Reprinted with the permission of Frederick A. Praeger, Inc. Copyright 1967 by Joseph Buttinger.

over the next few years, unaware of this strong ideological inclination, were convinced that they were faithful to the American ideals of political pragmatism. Was it not obvious, even before the victory of Communism in China, that the rise of a new Communist state in Asia would upset the existing balance of power in the world to the disadvantage of the West? That this must be prevented was not denied by even the fiercest enemies of French colonialism. The practical question was how this could be done without actually promoting French colonialism, which some at least knew to be one of the reasons for Communist strength in Vietnam. Here was a great but as yet still unrecognized new American dilemma: Would an active role by the United States in Indochinese affairs help to end colonialism? Was American aid for the French war effort in Indochina compatible with the need for evolution of strong non-Communist Indochinese states? And could Communism be prevented, particularly in Vietnam, if this meant helping the French, whose desire to maintain control over Indochina the United States did not wish to support? . . . The United States not only subscribed to the view that since Communism had to be defeated there must be no negotiations with Ho Chi Minh; it also accepted the French contention that this required a military victory over the Vietminh, and that if France lacked the means to achieve this victory, she had a right to appeal to the "free world" for aid. This meant that military aid would soon be extended for the fight against Vietnamese Communism, as the entire resistance movement against the French was henceforth called; and that this aid was not given to an independent anti-Communist government, which did not exist, but only to the French. It also meant that

Washington . . . accepted "independence within the French Union" as the answer to the problem of Vietnamese nationalism. For Washington, too, the struggle between Vietnamese nationalism and French colonialism was transformed into a local encounter in the world-wide struggle between Communism and the "free world."

However, overt U. S. support, both moral and financial, was still slow in coming and became an irreversible policy only after the victory of Communism in China. After Peking and Moscow extended diplomatic recognition to the Hanoi regime early in 1950, Secretary of State Dean Acheson said that this "should remove any illusions as to the 'nationalist' nature of Ho Chi Minh's aims and reveals Ho in his true colors as the mortal enemy of native independence in Indochina." . . .

On June 27, 1950, after the outbreak of the Korean War, President Truman announced that the United States would accelerate military assistance "to the forces of France and the Associated States in Indochina," and also dispatch a military mission "to provide close working relations with those forces." The gates were now open. Every new announcement about aid to Indochina disclosed another increase in the grants for military assistance to the French. These sums jumped from $119 million given through the Mutual Security program in summer, 1951, to $815 million for fiscal year 1954. Economic aid to the Associated States on the other hand still did not exceed $25 million. . . .

[A]lthough an informed and articulate minority of Americans — some senators and political writers, even some military men — opposed the policy of aiding France in the Indochina War as long as the Associated States were denied full independence, serious pressure to bring about a change in French policy was never applied. That colonialism should end was an American desire, often expressed but unfulfilled. . . . This was not only because, as some analysts of American policy in Southeast Asia have suggested, the pressure of events forced the United States to renounce the promotion of social and political reforms and that Washington, instead of insisting on reforms that might have inspired the Indochinese populations to fight against Communism relied more and more on superior military force. Nor was the main reason for lack of pressure on the French by Washington that the leadership of the United States, in spite of a predilection for verbal endorsements of "revolutions," always avoided political steps likely to produce drastic social and economic changes. Furthermore, Washington had no real reason to fear that France might be lost as an ally against Communism in Europe if the United States were to make true independence for Vietnam a condition for military aid. The failure of the United States to put real pressure on the French had a deeper and vastly more consequential reason, one that could not be publicly admitted, since it had not yet become a fully conscious motive of U. S. foreign policy. The great question facing Washington was: Would France continue the Indochina War if she lost control of Vietnam, Cambodia, and Laos, as seemed more and more likely, even if American aid enabled the Expeditionary Corps to defeat the Vietminh? The answer, unacceptable to the United States, was no. The French, no matter what they said in justification of their policy, would continue the war only so long as there was hope that its outcome would not mean the end of the French "presence" in Indochina. A milder form of colonial domination was still the aim France pursued through the Indochina War, an aim that Washington had no interest whatsoever in supporting for its own sake. . . . However, for the sake of preventing another Communist victory in Asia, Washington decided that continued French domination of Indochina was by far the lesser of two evils. Thus the Vietnamese, still effectively ruled by the French, were promoted to the status of a "free people" resisting "subversion by armed minorities or by outside pressure." Indeed, all the clichés that ten years later would be used to justify U. S. policy in Vietnam, were already coined when Washington decided to extend political and military support to the French halfway through the Indochina War. This is true even of the famous "domino theory." Based on ignorance of the fact that Communist strength in Vietnam was a unique and isolated case, this theory assumed that a refusal to defend French Indochina would necessarily lead to the triumph of Communist aggression all over Southeast Asia. The wish to contain Communism was infinitely stronger than the desire to see colonialism end, and as early as February, 1950, it produced the most dubious and yet most enduring of all propaganda claims, namely that the war was "fostered from abroad."

This American attitude explains why U. S. participation in the struggle for Indochina generated not a single new idea for advancing a political solution of the conflict, in no way modified the course pursued by the French, and contributed nothing to a better understanding of the political conditions for reducing Communist strength. On the contrary, it soon became evident that U. S. intervention multiplied the obstacles to a political settlement of the war. When, after eight years of useless effort, French determination to continue the struggle gave way to a desire to seek peace, if necessary through negotiations and a compromise with Ho Chi Minh, only the United States of all the countries concerned sought to prevent the calling of a conference toward this end. And at the conference, which came about against U.S. wishes, Washington refused to play an active role.

* * *

The first great crisis over conflicting allied aims in Indochina, which the boorish diplomacy of Dulles did nothing to mitigate, reached its climax in spring, 1954. On March 20, General Paul Ely, one of France's highest-ranking military men, arrived in Washington, on a mission decided on by the French Cabinet on March 11 — only a few days before the first blows against the garrison at Dien Bien Phu dramatically altered the military situation in Indochina. The original request of the French Government — that the United States should threaten direct military action if the Chinese intervened with their air force in the battle at Dien Bien Phu — had become pointless: After March 18, the French realized that Vietminh strength was sufficient for victory at Dien Bien Phu without direct Chinese intervention. Ely's mission was to make clear to Washington the full plight of the Expeditionary Corps, to press for immediate additional aid in the form of supplies, above all bombers, and auxiliary American personnel to increase the effectiveness of the French Air Force. But Ely was also instructed to leave no doubt about the unwillingness of France to continue the war. No longer was American military assistance requested in order to achieve victory over the Vietminh; its purpose now was merely to keep the Expeditionary Corps in the fight until the

Geneva conference had produced a settlement acceptable to France.

Since the Administration, the Congress, and the military leadership in the United States were deeply divided over the course to be adopted in this emergency, the reaction to Ely's rather modest demands and to his surprising pessimism was understandably mixed. The circles opposed to steps that might involve the United States in another Korea-type war in Asia — the vast majority of the Congress and even of the Joint Chiefs of Staff — were relieved. So was President Eisenhower, who gave Ely most emphatic assurances of speedy compliance with his demands for increased aid. But to the parties who had expected that American aid would enable the French eventually to defeat the Vietminh, the decision of France to fight for nothing more than an acceptable compromise came as a shock. Was this not another retreat by the West before Communist aggression in Asia? And had the Republican platform not promised that the United States would never again be a party to treaties sanctioning an extension of Communist rule? Not only did the so-called "China Lobby" and the Republican majority leader, Senator William Knowland, denounce the idea of a compromise solution in Indochina as a fresh betrayal of the cause of freedom. That such a compromise must be avoided, if necessary through direct U. S. military intervention, was also the position of Vice-President Nixon, Secretary Dulles, and the Chairman of the Joint Chiefs of Staff, Admiral Radford.

The plans and actions of these three powerful men, which, in the absence of Presidential leadership, remained uncoordinated from beginning to end, would probably have pushed the United States over the brink if wiser counsels had not prevailed in Paris and London, and to a lesser extent in the U. S. Congress.

The moves that Radford, Dulles, and Nixon made during April, 1954, to stop Communism in Indochina are among the saddest chapters of U.S. diplomacy. The first one to act, entirely on his own, to bring about direct American military intervention was Admiral Radford. He induced Ely, who was ready to leave for Paris on March 25, to stay an additional twenty-four hours, during which Radford persuaded the receptive French general that a massive strike by the U.S. Air Force could still save the French garrison at Dien Bien Phu. Radford assured Ely that Eisenhower would approve such action. The plan, which became known as Operation Vautour (Vulture), envisaged the use of planes stationed in the Philippines and on aircraft carriers in the Far East, which were later ordered to move into the Gulf of Tongking.

Radford's offer was submitted to the French Government by Ely on March 27. On March 29, a "war council" convened by the cabinet decided to send an officer to Hanoi, who, on April 2, informed the government of Navarre's belief that such an airstrike could destroy the Vietminh artillery positions around Dien Bien Phu and probably save the garrison, which otherwise would certainly be lost. Another meeting of the war council on April 4 thereupon decided, not without some misgivings, officially to request the intervention proposed by Admiral Radford.

If there is one particular day when the policy that would govern U.S.–Vietnamese relations for more than a decade was decided, it was April 5, 1954, the day Washington's answer to the French request for intervention was given to Ambassador Dillon in Paris. It was a downright refusal, which, understandably, came as a surprise and shock to both Ely and the cabinet. What had happened, they asked themselves, to bring about this apparent reversal of U. S. policy?

They learned only much later what had happened: The initiative in shaping policy to ward off the threatened loss of Indochina to Communism had passed from Admiral Radford to Secretary Dulles immediately after Ely's departure; and Dulles had an entirely different concept of the U. S. role at this historical juncture, a concept that could be pursued only with full Congressional support. He did not want a one-strike American intervention to save the French at Dien Bien Phu. He wanted more. Indochina — all of it — had to be saved from Communism. Dulles was not interested in U. S. intervention merely to improve the position of the French for a deal with the Communists at Geneva. He was opposed to any such deal; he did not want a compromise to end the war. He wanted the war to continue until Communism was defeated, and he did not want this war to be conducted under the old banner of the French, which was still tainted with colonialism. The war had to be truly internationalized, and the French, who still regarded it as exclusively their own business had to be replaced by a coalition of Western allies under the leadership of the United States. . . .

One notion only dominated the thinking of Dulles: that no time must be lost in preparing "united action," and that at least the threat of it had to become real before the opening of the Geneva conference. Preventing the conference had been his aim at Berlin; torpedoing it was his ill-concealed intention now. But French and British determination to steer clear of anything that might wreck the conference was precisely the reason why Dulles' project failed. . . .

To a great extent, Eisenhower's fear of

engaging U.S. ground forces in another Asian war caused the policy of Dulles, who insisted that U.S. intervention must have Allied support, to prevail in the end. Nixon's notion that "the United States would have to replace [the French] if necessary to prevent a Communist conquest of Southeast Asia" anticipated the future, but in April, 1954, the time was not yet ripe.

* * *

The Geneva agreements consisted of two parts. The first one was a lengthy document devoted exclusively to the implementation of the cease-fire and the regrouping of the French and Vietminh forces in their respective zones. The cease-fire accord was the only document signed at Geneva, and it was signed only by the military command of the French and the Vietminh. . . .

The cease-fire agreement provided for Vietnam's provisional division along the 17th parallel, with the French Union forces regrouped south of that line and the Vietminh forces north. For their withdrawal, different dates were set for different regions, but the regroupment in the two zones was to be completed within 300 days. These agreements also stipulated that any civilian who desired to move from one zone into the other should be allowed to do so within a fixed period of time, the cut-off date being May 18, 1955. Both parties pledged to refrain from reprisals against persons or organizations for acts committed during the hostilities and agreed to a ban on the introduction of fresh troops, military personnel, arms, munitions, and military bases. An International Control Commission (ICC) to supervise the execution of the cease-fire was set up; it consisted of representatives of India, Canada, and Poland. The chairman was to be an Indian.

The second document agreed upon at Geneva was the so-called Final Declaration. In a statement consisting of thirteen points, the participants at the conference took notice, in their final meeting on July 21, of the cease-fire concluded and signed by the two belligerents. But this declaration served also another purpose, one vastly more important than the formal endorsement of the stipulations for ending hostilities. It attempted to spell out the existing political differences, in particular the question of how and when the partition of Vietnam as set forth in the cease-fire agreement should come to an end. The document essentially contained the concessions on which the Communist powers had insisted as conditions for agreeing to a cease-fire. The most important of these conditions stated "that the military demarcation line is provisional and should in no way be interpreting a political or territorial boundary." . . . The date for general elections was set for July, 1956, with "consultations to be held on this subject between the competent authorities of the two zones from July 20, 1955 onwards." Since the State of Vietnam was not mentioned in this context, it remained open who these "competent representative authorities" might be — the French, the only non-Communist party that had signed anything at Geneva, or the government south of the 17th parallel, which had vigorously protested against the Geneva agreements? This unsettled question was surpassed only by the even stranger fact that the powers that concluded the agreement concerning elections expected it to be binding although it remained unsigned. It is indeed inappropriate to justify American rejection of certain stipulations of the Geneva agreements by reference to the fact the United States did not sign any of these agreements. With the exception of the cease-fire accords signed only by the French and Vietminh High Commands, nothing at all was signed by anyone at Geneva. A roll-call vote was taken to confirm acceptance of the agreements by all participants, and this was followed by a number of statements of delegations who desired to voice reservations or give their own interpretations of certain points, among them the representative of the United States, Bedell Smith. His government, he said, was not prepared to join in a declaration by the conference such as was submitted, but it would refrain from the threat or use of force to disturb the agreements. However, the warning addressed to the Communists that Smith added could be interpreted not only as acquiescence but also as qualified endorsement of the agreement. His government, he said, "would view any renewal of the aggression in violation of the aforesaid Agreements with grave concern and as seriously threatening international peace and security." Concerning the elections, Smith repeated a declaration by Washington made on June 29, 1954, which said: "In the case of nations now divided against their will, we shall continue to seek to achieve unity through free elections supervised by the United Nations to insure that they are conducted fairly." In a statement issued in Washington the same day, Bedell Smith's reservations were endorsed by President Eisenhower.

The only unambiguous protest came from the Foreign Minister of the State of Vietnam. In a cable to Premier Diem dated July 22, Tran Van Don said: "We fought desperately against partition and for a neutral zone in the Catholic area of North Vietnam. Absolutely impossible to surmount the hostility of our enemies and the perfidy of false friends. We express our deepest sorrows in this total failure of our mission. We respectfully submit our resignation." On July 23, Diem, in a broadcast from Saigon, raised "a most solemn protest" against the "iniquity which hands over to the Communists the entire North of the country and more than four provinces of the Center." All flags were ordered to be flown at half-mast for three days.

However, more important for the future relations between the State of Vietnam (which henceforth was generally referred to as South Vietnam) and the Democratic Republic of Vietnam (or North Vietnam) was a statement delivered by Tran Van Don in the name of his government before the conclusion of the conference. "Vietnam," he declared, "reserves to itself the entire freedom of action to safeguard the sacred right of the Vietnamese people to territorial unity, independence, and freedom."

This was a formal announcement of nonconcurrence with the Geneva agreements on the part of Ngo Dinh Diem's Government of South Vietnam. Although this government was then even in the South one in name only, as early as August 3 it called on the people of the North "to rally to the South in order to continue the struggle for independence and liberty."

Dulles, too, had a postscript to Geneva, delivered at a news conference on July 23. What he said was of infinitely greater significance for the future of Vietnam that Diem's empty threat to rally the South against the North. Dulles acknowledged that the Geneva negotiations "reflected the military developments in Indochina," adding that "the French people did not desire to prolong the war." These "basic facts" led to the settlement which "contains many features which we do not like." But "the important thing" for Dulles was "not to mourn the past but to seize the future opportunity to prevent the loss in northern Vietnam from leading to the extension of Communism throughout Southeast Asia and the Southwest Pacific." In spelling out this "future opportunity," Dulles implied once more that French colonialism had been an obstacle in the fight against the Vietminh. "One lesson is that resistance to Communism needs popular support, and this in turn means that the people should feel that they are defending their own national institutions." . . .

There was another reason for Dulles' belief in the "future opportunity" to halt any further Communist advance: The obstacles to "united action" were at last removed. "Prompt steps will be taken in this direction," he announced, having secured both British and French consent to proceed in preparing what on September 8, 1954, became, via the so-called Manila Pact, the Southeast Asia Treaty Organization (SEATO). . . .

In spite of Vietminh dissatisfaction, the Communists had every reason to be content: A Communist-led national movement of armed resistance had defeated the armies of one of the oldest and greatest Western colonial powers; France, as Ho Chi Minh had predicted, had lost the Indochina War; and the West was forced to become reconciled to the existence of another Communist state.

Whatever shortcomings and seeds of future trouble critics have found in the Geneva agreements, their great historical importance cannot be denied. They ended the longest and most senseless attempt of this century to defeat an anticolonial movement of national liberation by military means — the Indochina War, which destroyed French presence in Southeast Asia and Vietnamese national unity. They ended almost one hundred years of French colonial rule in Indochina and produced the two Vietnams that have become known to the world as the Communist North and the anti-Communist South.

This second result of the Indochina War — the division of Vietnam into two states with hostile regimes — received some sort of international sanction from the powers than concluded the Geneva agreements. But as for the conflict between the Vietminh and their nationalist opponents, the Geneva conference failed to produce a workable solution. As a consequence, the promise of national unity — a mere by-product of the Geneva cease-fire accords between the French and the Vietminh — remained unfulfilled. Even as the Final Declaration was read and taken exception to by the governments of South Vietnam and the United States, it could have been predicted that the promised elections would never be held. As a consequence, it could also have been foreseen that the peace that came to the country as the only blessing of the Geneva bargain would last no longer than a few anxiety-filled years. The antagonism of the two Vietnam regimes would ultimately prove irreconcilable. Both sides would be hardened in their attitudes by the support promised them by their respective big allies, the Western and Eastern power blocs engaged in the Cold War. Far from considering any compromise solution, the government in Hanoi and its sworn enemies ruling South Vietnam could be expected to continue to move farther apart. Soon both would become convinced that unity was possible only if one side succeeded in destroying the other, and both would start working toward this end. Since under prevailing conditions the regime in the South could not have survived general elections, it was predictable that it would oppose the holding of such elections, while the Communists, deprived of this peaceful means for extending their control over the whole of Vietnam, would again resort to force. When they unleashed their insurrection against the regime of Ngo Dinh Diem, the loss of peace, like the loss of unity before, reminded a troubled world how dangerously imperfect the Geneva settlement had been. Ten years after the Geneva conference, a new armed conflict, truly a second Indochina War, reached dimensions and produced international involvements that posed an even greater threat to world peace than the first Indochina War briefly did in spring, 1954.

Finally, the Geneva settlement, along with its failure to bring unity and lasting peace, also failed to open the road to political freedom in both the North and South. In the North, as expected, the struggle for economic survival and industrial progress barred any retreat from the hard Communist dictatorship into which the regime of Ho Chi Minh had developed during the last years of the war. In the South, where the civil war reinforced the leaders' innate tendency toward authoritarian rule, the sacrifice of freedom demanded of the people also turned the anti-Communist regime into a ruthless dictatorship, which, however, failed to produce what was supposed to be its *raison d'être* — administrative efficiency and military strength. Ten years after achieving independence, the people of Vietnam still did not have free institutions adapted to their way of life, were still deprived of the national unity essential for rapid economic progress, and, subjected to the brutalities of the new Indochina War, were once more in danger of losing what they had fought for during the entire colonial period: a truly independent national existence.

*   *   *

The story of U.S. policy toward the Diem regime richly illustrates the power of wishful political thinking, the shortcomings of U.S. diplomacy, and the fact that the United States still does not know the most effective methods of fighting Communism. But it is not an entirely negative story. In principle, there was nothing wrong with the decision that South Vietnam should be helped to survive as a non-Communist state — if it turned out that this was what its people wanted. . . .

What makes this story, which for many years was expected to have a happy ending, so tragic is that not only did the prospects for building a viable South Vietnam, for breaking the hold of the Communists on the people, and for avoiding another dreadful war exist, but they were in fact excellent. Despite the ravages of the war and the problems created for the South's economy through partition of the country and withdrawal of the [French] Expeditionary Corps, the South was economically in better shape than the North. It had assets that could be effectively exploited in the political competition with the North. One of these was the potential for a large food surplus. . . . Vietnam's coal and mineral deposits, cement production, and the larger part of her industry remained in the North. But the South had all of its rubber plantations, which had suffered surprisingly little during the war. As expected, rubber soon became the South's major export.

But much more important, for obvious political reasons, was another advantage the South had over its rival in the North. There was plenty of land available for distribution among peasants who owned none or very little. This meant that the millions of poor, exploited peasants and tenants, who still expected the victory of the Vietminh to put an end to their plight, could be turned into a class of politically satisfied landowners and grateful supporters of a non-Communist regime. This, however, required not only the recultivation and distribution of the almost 1 million acres of rice land that had been abandoned during the war, but above all a radical program of agrarian reform.

* * *

Survival, therefore, required economic, social, and political achievements designed to win the loyalty of the vast majority of the people, a loyalty strong enough to make them determined to defend the regime against armed rebellion.

It was never easy, and still is not, to measure the extent to which the Diem regime enjoyed popular, even though not enthusiastic, support. There is no doubt that between 1955 and 1957, Diem made some efforts to advance on this promising road. . . .

If the reality and strength of the support Diem received from his people is somewhat uncertain, no doubt exists in regard to the support he enjoyed in the United States, without whose aid he would have had little chance of gaining his people's loyalty. American aid, indispensable for the accomplishment of deeds designed to get the people behind Diem, was quite rightly regarded as vital for the survival of South Vietnam. . . . That he would use American aid to achieve this end was taken for granted.

How mistaken an assumption this was had become obvious by 1960. But up to the end of 1957, the belief that the doors to a better future for the people of South Vietnam were still open was by no means mere wishful thinking. There was a period in the history of Diem's rise and decline when it seemed as if under his guidance, anti-Communist nationalism might yet become a force capable of

breaking the attraction of the Vietminh. It is clear that in the end Diem failed because the harvest of his policy was not popular support but deep popular discontent. But why, years after his political inadequacy had become apparent, did he succeed in keeping the firm support of the United States Government? And more puzzling still: Why, for so many years, was he defended by so many well-informed and politically mature Americans who on the whole were deeply concerned with the fate of the Vietnamese people and anxious to advance democracy in Vietnam? . . .

In retrospect, it is quite easy to see why doubts about the viability of Diem's regime began to disappear after 1955. Programs for solving what were considered military and administrative requirements of survival were energetically pursued during 1955 and 1956. When it came to questions of power, Diem rarely indulged his propensity for delaying decisions. . . .

Diem's triumph in 1955 over his anti-Communist rivals, after months of near disaster, had had a profound effect both on his admirers and on his (more numerous) critics, whose prediction had been that he could not possibly succeed. For the admirers, who were relieved of much anxiety, Diem was henceforth a hero, whose faults, if seen at all, had to be forgiven a man who had secured the survival of a non-Communist Vietnam. For the critics, whose pessimism Diem had confounded, Diem turned into a figure whom it was safer henceforth to treat with circumspection. . . .

[M]uch of Diem's success in retaining popularity in the United States must be ascribed to organized propaganda. As early as the end of 1955, a group of mostly selfless and highly motivated citizens founded the American Friends of Vietnam, an organization that enlisted the support of the most diverse representatives of American political life. The spokesmen of the American Friends of Vietnam became Diem's most effective defenders. They were valuable for his regime not only because they volunteered their services, but also because they spoke with the authority of experts (which some of them actually were), and because they were in a better position than any Vietnamese agent to convince the American public and government that Diem's achievements were real, that under him the South would become prosperous and eventually also democratic, and that Diem's critics made the mistake of regarding the minor flaws of his regime as omens of failure.

In this American propaganda, the gap between Diem's claims and his actual performance was filled with the praise of achievements that, necessary and welcome though they were, failed to remove the colonial heritage of social injustice, administrative evils, and political backwardness.

* * *

It seemed that American optimism in regard to the Diem regime was nourished chiefly by the very need for it: Only good news from Saigon could sustain the belief that the miracle of Vietnam was real and not a mirage. This need for good news continually prompted all worried anti-Communist observers to overlook, or at least play down, the shortcomings of Diem that threatened to make his achievements politically worthless.

An early instance of this tendency to overlook Diem's shortcomings was the reluctance of most of his supporters to admit that the regime's approach to the problem of agrarian reform was politically disastrous. When the slightness of Diem's plans was revealed, he was not blamed for the inadequacy of his program, but rather was praised for the careful manner in which he tackled the delicate task of agrarian reform. What he proposed was widely considered as only a beginning. This at least was the hope of those Diem supporters who regarded a radical land reform as the most urgent measure in the struggle against the Vietminh, and therefore regretted that he had acted so late, set his goal so low, and worked toward it with such exasperating slowness.

The land-reform program was inadequate in several respects. It was started too late and was carried out too slowly; it did not go far enough, particularly in regard to land distribution; and its provisions for payment by the peasants who received land created an unnecessary hardship and were a serious political blunder.

* * *

The narrow scope and the fragmentary execution of the agrarian reform, so fateful for the country's political evolution, reveal a great deal about Diem's political philosophy and the hollowness of his claim that his was a revolutionary regime. Diem was unable to see that Vietnam's national revolution could be completed and all remnants of colonialism wiped out only through radical economic and social reforms. For the peasant masses, exploitation under a feudal land regime had been the dominant reality of colonialism. Colonialism, therefore, would not end for them until landlordism was abolished.

Far from being eliminated by a thorough agrarian reform, the landlords, for decades the associates of the colonial regime, were in fact the group that, more than any other, succeeded in asserting its interests under Diem. . . .

"Lack of serious interested administrators" was given as the cause for the slow progress of the reform by American advisers. "Government officials, beginning with the Minister of Agrarian Reform, have divided loyalties, being themselves landholders." Of the Minister of Agrarian Reform it was reported that he had not "signed leases with his tenants as provided by the land reform decrees, and he is most certainly not interested in land distribution which would divest him of much of his property." . . .

If Diem had been convinced that a more radical reform was necessary, respect for the property of the landlord would not have prevented him from pursuing it; and he could have mobilized the forces he needed to break landlord opposition. Moreover, he certainly possessed the moral courage required had he decided that the interests of its small upper class had to be sacrificed to save the country. . . .

Diem was a highly complex political man: His modern authoritarian ideas, his almost medieval principles of monarchism, and his professed adherence to some form of democracy, which together made up his politics, resist definition. Yet the answer to the question of why he failed as a social reformer could hardly be more simple: Measured against the needs of his country and the spirit of his time, Diem simply was too much of a conservative to discharge his historical mission.

The banality of this explanation makes it difficult to realize that here lies the key to Diem's failure. Diem was radical only as a nationalist and anti-Communist. His nationalism aimed at removing foreign rule, at reestablishing a genuine Vietnamese regime, not at changing the social structure that colonialism had created in Vietnam. Diem's concept of a "free" Vietnam was not concerned with the social aspirations of the masses, and, as it turned out, was also hostile to the political aspirations of the elite. Once the French were out and the Communists kept at bay, South Vietnam was, as far as Diem was concerned, "free" by definition. His nationalism, therefore, had little social content, and his anti-Communism none at all. Had Diem understood that mass support for his regime was indispensable in his struggle against Communism, he would probably have done away with landlordism completely and turned all tenants into landowners at no cost to them at all. The political gains of such a land reform would have been worth an even higher price. But Diem, the conservative, rejected revolutionary social change as a means of reducing the attraction of Communism, and it was this which gradually led him to rely more and more on antidemocratic measures and naked force. . . .

While after 1956, disenchantment with Diem at home turned rapidly into enmity toward his regime, his American support continued to grow for some years. Not only did the Americans lack the sad experience of the Vietnamese people, but by and large they remained unaware of the slowly emerging evidence that the social and political aspirations of both the masses and the elite were of steadily diminishing concern to the Diem regime. What continued to matter to most Americans was that Diem fought the West's battle against Communism on a threatened front. He had turned from a hopeless prospect into an apparent success. He had saved the South. . . .

In the United States, the then Senator John F. Kennedy in June, 1956, expressed concisely what would have to be done if Communism in South Vietnam was to be defeated: "What we must offer [the Vietnamese people] is a revolution — a political, economic, and social revolution far superior to anything the Communists can offer — far more peaceful, far more democratic, and far more locally controlled."

Yet Kennedy, and even people with fewer illusions about Diem, supported his regime long after disturbing news from Vietnam made them fear that the chance for the survival of the South was being wasted. One line of arguments in support of this misguided attitude rested upon the perfectly plausible assumption that profound social and political changes required not only time but also an end of conditions under which the Communists would have benefited from certain reforms, as Diem was constantly pointing out. . . . Perhaps Diem was too timid and moving too slowly; perhaps he was not as yet sufficiently aware of the need for certain reforms. But once the time was ripe, it was held, he would take whatever action was required to make the South's survival permanent. Had he not himself repeatedly recognized the necessity of radical social reforms, and proclaimed his intention to build "democratic institutions"? And was the word revolution not "a constant part of the Vietnamese Government's vocabulary"? As early as 1949, Diem had specified that this revolution must also be "a social revolution for the economic independence of the Vietnamese farmer and laborer," and as late as 1960, he accused his anti-Communist critics of "trying to crush the social revolution" which his regime allegedly carried out. At the time, Diem's reputation for integrity made it almost impossible for his American admirers to assume that he might not believe what he said. Some suspected that he did not go along with the generally accepted meaning of the words "democracy" and "revolution," but most of his defenders were inclined to believe that objective conditions, not Diem himself, continued to prevent the realization of his true aims. . . .

Popular disaffection, it was admitted, seemed to be increasing, but there was no sign of an organized opposition strong enough to replace Diem and to promise the establishment of a more democratic, more effective, and more popular regime. Withdrawal of support from Diem, it was felt, would very likely lead to chaotic conditions favorable to a Communist strike for power. Unless it was decided that there was no hope for South Vietnam, Diem had to be supported. Those who realized that this was a perilous course but thought that it could not be changed eased their conscience by demanding greater pressure on Diem for reforms.

There were of course also those to whom the question of whether or not to continue the support of Diem posed no dilemma at all, people who remained convinced that Diem followed the only course that promised success. Democracy, these people asserted, was impossible under existing conditions, and reforms simply had to wait until the battle against the Communists was won. Diem needed more aid, particularly military aid. All else for the time being was unimportant. Making difficulties for Diem could only be of help to the Communists, against whom only force could prevail. If it was necessary to establish a tough dictatorship in order to deal effectively with the Communist threat, then the United States had to support Diem, even if he were a dictator. Those who held this position were not aware that they were accepting the discredited Communist dictum that the end justifies the means.

An official policy based on this dictum became America's greatest political improbity in regard to Vietnam. Those who claim to fight Communism on behalf of democracy and social justice can subscribe to the notion that the end justifies the means only at the risk of betraying their own cause. In doing so, they show not only a lack of integrity but a lack of political understanding as well: It was precisely this betrayal of democracy, the cause in whose name Communism was fought, which brought about the defeat of Diem by the Communists. To be sure, under certain conditions the naked force of a dictatorial or even an openly fascist regime, can temporarily contain Communism — all the while adding to its potential strength. In Vietnam, force alone could not secure even such a limited and deceptive success.

The history of the Diem regime, from its unexpected early triumphs to its inglorious end, had a lasting effect on American political thinking, an effect which in turn continued to determine the fate of Vietnam. The real lesson to be learned from it is not that the policy of supporting Diem beyond the first two or three years of his rule was a mistake. Much more important is the realization that the decision to withdraw support from Diem signified no break with this policy. Diem was dropped not because he was a dictator. As long as there was hope that his policies could prevent Communism in South Vietnam, his dictatorship enjoyed full American support. He was dropped because the dictatorship he created proved to be ineffective. There was, and still is, little or no awareness of the fact that this failure in the struggle against Communism was caused not by his personal shortcomings as a dictator but by the reactionary character of his regime.

The attempt to fight Communism by building a more democratic and socially more progressive state for South Vietnam would no doubt have meant taking risks and struggling against enormous obstacles. What condemns Diem is that the attempt was never made, that in spite of his verbal commitment to some measure of democracy he deliberately chose the opposite path.

*　*　*

[T]he Diem regime, as Robert Scigliano, its least biased and most effective American critic put it, "transformed itself into a light image of its rival," the meaning of "light" obviously being that the Diem regime lacked the strength to deprive the people of freedom as effectively as the North. It would of course be absurd to say that there was no difference between the regimes of Ngo Dinh Diem and Ho Chi Minh. Their aims were irreconcilable, their ideologies as different as day and night, and their positions in the twentieth-century political world could hardly have been farther apart. What is true, however, is that Diem pursued his intended total negation of Communism with means that were either close copies of, or indeed identical with, those employed by the Communists. Diem's republic, says Scigliano, was "for practical purposes a one-party state," which had "its political re-education camps, its Communist denunciation rallies, its ubiquitous propaganda extolling the leader and damning the enemy, its mass organizations." It also had its controlled elections, its secret police, a constitution almost as superbly written as that of the North whose guarantees of civil liberties and political freedom were just as disregarded. As in the North, opposition against the government was not tolerated, no matter how genuinely anti-Communist its inspiration. Opponents were imprisoned and, as a rule, held without trial. Many were tortured. The elected legislature was a tool in the hands of the government, and the press was gradually reduced to the base function of praising the leader and blindly supporting his actions.

* * *

The evils of this system were not confined to those which excessive centralization and the absence of democracy in local government necessarily produce. They were compounded by the manner in which all administrative personnel was chosen from above, by the absolute dependence of all appointed officials on the central government, and by the officials' unlimited authority over a totally disenfranchised and subjugated population.

* * *

Under such a totalitarian system lacking devoted cadres and facing mass hostility, the process of selecting the agents whom the government needed to guide and control the population could produce only highly questionable results. This would have been the case even without two aggravating circumstances peculiar to South Vietnam: the first a heritage of ancient mandarinal and recent colonial Vietnam; the second, closely connected, the disdainful and ruthless treatment by the President's ruling family of those whom they considered their inferiors, meaning, in fact, everybody else.

The typical mandarin of the precolonial regime, although not living in caste-like separation from the people, nevertheless considered himself a being apart from the peasant, above him not only because of function but even more because of education. The mandarins' role as ruthless tax collectors, policemen, and

judges earned them the hatred of the people, who were naturally disinclined to respect knowledge and a cultivated mind in the service of exploitation and suppression. The mandarins came to take this as evidence of the common people's boorishness and animality, hardly admitting any human bond between themselves and the peasants. This notion was more conducive to the execution of their harsh duties than respect for the masses, and it marked the mandarins' attitude toward the people. Its corollary was an exalted notion of their own worth.

The colonial regime did not put an end to this deeply rooted attitude, not even among the mandarins who fought the French and appealed to the people for support. Of those who made peace with the French, it might be said that although they lost much of their old power, they tried to compensate for their loss by setting themselves even higher above the common herd. Mandarinal insolence and corruption increased considerably under the colonial regime. Even those privileged enough to receive a higher education in French schools, whether they obtained positions in the administration or entered professions, clung firmly to the traditional conceit of the mandarinal class. Among the leaders of the anticolonial movement, only the Communists insisted on a complete change in the traditional attitude of the elite toward the people.

It underlines the limitations of Diem's national revolution that under him the government and civil service largely perpetuated the tradition of oppression, venality, and intellectual conceit of their mandarinal predecessors.

* * *

Neither General Taylor nor any other American who proposed reforms realized in 1961 why their demands were never acted upon by the man who lived on American aid but refused to accept American advice. If Diem had ever seriously tried to raise the level of performance of his officials, he would soon have found that this was impossible. Opposed by the intellectuals, despised by the educated middle class, rejected by businessmen, hated by the youth and by all nationalists with political ambitions, and totally lacking in mass support, the Diem Government had to rely for its survival on an apparatus of coercion. It needed administrators willing to side with the government against practically the entire people. Its officials were the ones obliged to apply directly the means required to maintain the regime — primarily force. They could not be the servants of the people; they had to be watchdogs over them. This function, in the long run, could not be exercised by decent and honest men. Diem, at the beginning of his rule, attracted some men devoted to him as well as to the people, but as time went on such officials became exceedingly rare.

*　*　*

In justifying the harsh measures taken against its enemies, the regime constantly made reference to the dangers that threatened the republic if opposition to Diem was not stamped out, implying that all criticism was Communist or Communist-inspired, or at least effective aid to the Communists. The regime always denied that there was any significant opposition outside the Vietminh, claiming that the inmates of its concentration camps and prisons were without exception criminals and Communists.

*　*　*

Diem and Washington were always in basic agreement on the main purpose of American aid — its use as a means of securing the country's survival, by directing the bulk of all aid toward building up the regime's military strength, and in the clashes over secondary issues, Washington, not Diem, usually demanded, albeit in vain, that a greater share of the available funds be devoted to social and economic projects. If 78 per cent of the total U.S. aid was absorbed by the regime's military establishments, and no more than 1.25 per cent spent on industrial development and mining, this was because both the United States and Diem thought of maintaining security and the conditions of survival primarily in military terms, neglecting, despite frequent assurance to the contrary, the social, economic, and political requirements for making security measures effective. It is precisely this joint policy of neglecting economic development that explains why, as Milton C. Taylor put it in 1961, "after six years of large-scale American aid, Vietnam is becoming a permanent mendicant."

*　*　*

If the enemies of Diem had been made up only of the divided and unorganized anti-Communist nationalists at home and abroad, the regime's lack of economic progress, neglect of urgent reforms, and denial of basic freedoms would hardly have threatened its existence. The world is full of examples of the survival of such regimes. South Vietnam might have been just one more country in which the sullen masses become resigned to their fate and in which clandestine activities of small groups aspiring to overthrow the regime are successfully handled by the police.

Unfortunately for Diem, however, South Vietnam also had a Communist opposition, and this opposition was a well-organized, exceptionally strong movement. The Vietnamese Communists, after 1954, enjoyed greater popular support and were closer to victory than any other Communist movement in the world. Indeed, what might be called the uniqueness of Vietnam and what after 1960 turned the country into the principal battleground between East and West was precisely the strength of Vietnamese Communism — a heritage of the colonial regime and of the misguided French attempt to suppress the Vietnamese national revolution. The fate of the Diem regime therefore depended chiefly on the success or failure of the measures to reduce, and eventually put an end to, the deadly power of the country's native Communist movement.

During the war against the French, the Vietminh in the South, although less strong than in the North, had built up an efficient and almost indestructible network of underground organizations, and also enjoyed broad popular support. After the military units of the Vietminh were withdrawn from the South, as stipulated in the Geneva cease-fire agreement, Vietminh control of the countryside was hardly less effective than before. In part of the country it grew even stronger, since in many regions the French withdrew before Diem's army and administration were ready to establish control. Probably only a fraction of the best-trained cadres and guerrillas were sent North, joined by insignificant numbers of the people that had sympathized with and supported the Vietminh during the war. Vietminh control therefore long remained unchallenged in vast regions of the South. . . . The substantial quantity of arms left behind by the troops who had gone North were buried; Vietminh power, for the time being, was to be based on organization, open and secret, and on the influence the movement had

gained over the people. Some Communist cadres in the South found it hard to accept the Party's orders from Hanoi to limit their struggle against the Diem regime to organization and propaganda, but the majority was content to wait and lie low, particularly in regions under government control. Nothing was farther from the minds of the Communists and their close allies than the thought of organizing armed insurrection against the Diem regime. They were convinced that in the South, too, victory was already theirs, even if its consummation had to await the elections of July, 1956, through which the country would be united under Ho Chi Minh.

This was the situation Diem faced in regard to his chief enemy, Communism, during the first two years of his reign. It would seem that any leader of even moderate political intelligence should have been able to determine at the time what strategy would be most likely to defeat the Communist threat to the South. Such a strategy would have had to have two aims, neither of which could have been pursued successfully as long as anti-Communism was tied up with colonialism. One of the objectives should have been to separate from the Communist core of the Vietminh the various forces attached to it only because of their determination to oust the French. Diem, after his assumption of power, was supremely qualified for this task by reason of his anticolonial past and by his struggle to liquidate all remnants of French power. But his mind, blighted by dogmatism and filled with the pathological notion that he alone had been called upon to save the country, was unable to conceive of the measures that might have turned allies of the Communists into friends of his regime: the right to organize, to voice their grievances and demands freely, and

eventually also to share in the government. Only the granting of a minimum
of political freedom could have induced
these people to break away from the
Communist-led Vietminh. The loss of
these allies would have greatly diminished the ability of the Communist
cadres to keep their hold on the masses
of the Vietnamese people.

But it would have been even more important for Diem to set his course on the
second aim of a sound anti-Communist
strategy: depriving the Communist
cadres of the true source of their strength
— popular support. What this required
was known to everybody in Vietnam, including the spokesmen of the regime:
the reforms that would have added up to
the "social revolution" and the "genuine
democracy" about which Diem talked so
much but which his actions negated. . . .

Diem's method of fighting Communism
was to concentrate on destroying their
cadres, if necessary physically, instead of
making them politically impotent by depriving them of mass support. He had
not learned the lesson of the Indochina
War — i.e., that a political movement
cannot be destroyed by killing its exponents.

*   *   *

According to the official figures, 20,000–
30,000 former Vietminh cadres were put
into concentration camps (most observers believe the number to be considerably higher); but P. J. Honey, whose anti-
Communist record was well known, had
occasion to visit these camps. He reported that "the majority of the detainees
are neither Communist nor pro-Communist." This was probably true also of the
many who had been killed, and who,
together with their outraged families,
might very well have closed their ears to
Communist propaganda if the regime

had brought them social justice and economic progress instead of unfreedom,
misery, and death. The true result of the
regime's attempt to destroy the Vietminh, says Bernard Fall, was that "the
countryside largely went Communist in
1958–60." The Diem Government itself
created the conditions that pushed the
population to the brink of open rebellion,
and this convinced the Communist leadership that the South could be conquered
by force.

*   *   *

In both East and West, propaganda
has given the world a highly distorted
version of the beginning of the fighting
in South Vietnam that was to lead to the
second Indochina War. The Communist
story, put together in Hanoi and spread
abroad by Peking and Moscow, claims
that there was a spontaneous uprising of
almost the entire people, and the Communists could not help but join. The fact
is that the uprising, as a concerted effort
to overthrow the Diem regime and its
successor by force, was organized by the
Communists, and while it would have
made little headway without wide popular support, neither would it have had
its amazing success without guidance
and assistance from the North.

But the Saigon-Washington version of
these events, which has been reduced to
the flat assertion that "the Vietnam war
is the result of external aggression," strays
even farther from historical truth. Neither the strenuous efforts of Saigon nor
those of Washington have produced evidence that anti-Diem terror and guerrilla
warfare started as a result of the infiltration of combatants and weapons from the
North. No significant infiltration occurred
before 1960, and very little during the
next three years. The Saigon-Washington
version, which tries to deny that the war

started as a civil war in the South, "omits the embarrassing fact that anti-Diem guerrillas were active long before infiltrated North Vietnamese elements joined the fray." In 1961, years before any large-scale infiltration such as was claimed to have taken place after 1963, "the Communists had in fact extended their influence, in varying degrees, to about 80 per cent of the Vietnamese countryside."

There is another distortion in the version Washington and Saigon persisted in propagating as the truth about the origin of the Vietnamese war. While it is likely that the Communists, deprived of the chance of winning the South through elections, would sooner or later have resorted to terror and guerrilla warfare, the historical fact is that force in the struggle for the South was first used by the Diem regime, not by the Communists. Diem's terror against former Vietminh fighters, against known Communist cadres, and against villages and entire regions suspected of sympathizing with the Vietminh started long before the Communists slowly began their own campaign of terror. The military and police actions of 1956 against the Vietminh were not undertaken in reply to Communist acts of terror, which even by the admission of Saigon propaganda did not begin until 1957.

In contrast to government terror, which resulted even then in the indiscriminate killing and imprisonment not only of real enemies but also of mere suspects and innocent people, Communist terror was selective, and although in many instances also directed against the innocent, it was always guided by clearly defined political considerations. The aim of Communist terror was to paralyze the Diem administration by killing or kidnaping its officials and by interrupting all contact between the administration of the countryside and Saigon. The means of communication and economic resources were destroyed only in regions where the Communists failed to set up their own administration, and Saigon-appointed village officials, if willing to work under Communist control, were left at their posts.

In killing officials, the Communists concentrated largely on the brutal and corrupt, since this was likely to gain them the sympathy of the people. But honest and able administrators of strong anti-Communist convictions were also killed or kidnaped, the latter fate being reserved chiefly for medical officers and teachers, whom the Communists hoped to convert and use in zones "liberated" from Saigon control. . . .

By 1960, the movement that had begun with isolated acts of terror in 1957 had developed into full-fledged insurrection. It enjoyed broad support not only of the Vietnamese peasants in the Mekong Delta and the coastal provinces northeast of Saigon, but also of the ethnic minority tribes in the highlands of central Vietnam, among whom the propagandistic and organizational efforts directed from Hanoi were particularly effective. Insurrection took the form of guerrilla action against villages still under government control; it usually led to the surrender or the wiping-out of the local self-defense units and Civil Guards charged with ousting the guerrillas. Organized, indoctrinated, and led by Communist cadres, the Vietcong, as these guerrillas were henceforth called, soon controlled almost the entire countryside by night and about two-thirds of it in daytime. The Vietcong set up their own administration, imposed their own taxes, conscripted the local youth into military service, provided education and medical care, collected food supplies for their fighting units, dug bomb shelters, built

defense works along the regions they controlled, and continuously trained new
men for stepped-up military operations.
For years, they increased the number of
their fighting men (if not their cadres)
entirely through local recruiting, and
their arms supply more through the capture of arms from government units than
through infiltration from the North. "The
misery of the people was their ally, and
they played on it." From 1960 on, they
began to operate in ever-larger groups,
and to attack and overrun government
outposts held by the army, as well as to
ambush and destroy army units sent to
relieve outposts under attack. . . .

American military and civilian observers in the field had no trouble at all in
finding out why the armed forces of the
Diem regime failed so conspicuously in
fighting the Vietcong guerrillas. It needed
no military expert to see that the army
had been trained for the wrong kind of
war. Organized under American direction on a division basis instead of in small
mobile units, and equipped for the task
of holding off an invasion from the North,
the army was technically unprepared to
counter insurgency. When, after 1960, it
dawned upon some of the military lead-

ers that guerrillas have to be fought on
their own terms, everyone talked about
the need for organizing counterinsurgency units, but the little that was done
had no effect on the senseless and futile
way the war was being conducted.

But the main reason for the failure of
the regime's armed forces to contain the
Vietcong was political: Political conditions prevented the reforms needed to
make the army effective, and still more
important, they prevented the armed
forces from ever becoming determined
about fighting the Vietcong. There is
overwhelming evidence that neither men
nor officers wished to pursue the war
seriously. This came as a surprise only
to people who refused to believe that the
Diem regime, even before 1960, was
hated by the majority of the men expected to fight for it, as well as by the
majority of the civilian population. There
could be no more authoritative confirmation of the army's unwillingness to fight
for Diem than a statement made by
Prime Minister Nguyen Cao Ky in February, 1966: "We were dying for a cause,
but we saw little evidence that the cause
was worth laying down our lives for."

Arthur M. Schlesinger, Jr.: WHAT WE DID THERE

Mr. Schlesinger served as Special Assistant to President John F. Kennedy, and here offers a brief account of three important years, 1961–1963, during which the growth of a new perspective on the relationship between foreign policy and military power came to have far-ranging implications for the American role in Vietnam.

IN JANUARY 1961 the Vietnam mess fell to a new American president. Kennedy, who had long believed that the main communist reliance in the coming period would be on neither nuclear nor conventional but guerrilla war, saw the answer to the Viet Cong insurgency in counter-insurgency. For Kennedy counter-insurgency meant a good deal more than teaching soldiers to black their faces and strangle enemies in the night. Guerrilla warfare, he well understood, was essentially political warfare. Effective counter-insurgency, for example, depended on swift and accurate intelligence from the countryside. The Viet Cong could never be defeated unless the Saigon regime could enlist the support of the peasants. Magsaysay's campaign against the Hukbalahaps in the Philippines suggested the model: tough military action against the enemy, generous provisions for amnesty, real and sweeping social reform.

The first effort of the Kennedy years was to persuade the Diem regime to move along these lines. Success in this effort would have been unlikely in any case, given Diem's conviction that the Americans were impatient, naive and childlike, to be humored but never to be heeded. And it became all the more unlikely when the senior American diplomatic and military officials in Saigon decided that Diem was the key to stability and that the only policy was to win Diem's confidence by assuring him of Washington's unconditional support. Once he believed that Washington was with him, they thought, it might be possible to steer him gently and gradually toward reform, but attempts to bring pressure on Diem, in the view of Ambassador Nolting and General Harkins, would be self-defeating. American newspapermen in Saigon, less moved by the South Vietnamese leader, called this the policy of "sink or swim with Ngo Dinh Diem." Diem and Nhu no doubt swam, but the hope of effective reform sank.

The next question was whether Washington should increase its military assistance. Vice President Lyndon B. Johnson, who visited Saigon in May 1961, reported to Kennedy: "The basic decision in Southeast Asia is here. We must decide whether to help these countries to the best of our ability or throw in the towel and pull back our defenses to San Francisco. . . . More important, we would say to the world in this case that we don't live up to our treaties and don't stand by

Arthur M. Schlesinger, Jr., *The Bitter Heritage: Vietnam and American Democracy, 1941–1966* (Boston, 1967), pp. 20–28. Reprinted by permission of Houghton Mifflin Company and of Andre Deutsch Limited. Copyright 1966 by Houghton Mifflin Company. Copyright 1967 by Arthur M. Schlesinger, Jr.

our friends. This is not my concept. I recommend that we move forward promptly with a major effort to help these countries defend themselves." However, American aid to enable a country to defend itself was — in Johnson's mind in 1961 — very different from direct American defense of the country. "American combat troop involvement," he said, "is not only not required, it is not desirable." He went on: "Possibly Americans fail to appreciate fully the subtlety that recently colonial peoples would not look with favor upon governments which invited or accept the return this soon of Western troops. To the extent that fear of ground-troop involvement dominates our political responses to Asia in Congress or elsewhere, it seems most desirable to me to allay those paralyzing fears."

The situation in South Vietnam grew worse over the summer; and in October 1961 Kennedy sent General Maxwell Taylor and Walt W. Rostow, then (and in 1966 again) a White House aide, on a mission to Saigon. The Taylor-Rostow report recommended an enlargement of the American role, essentially through the penetration of the South Vietnamese army and government by American 'advisers,' attached to Vietnamese military units or government offices and designed to improve the level of local performance. Taylor and Rostow also recommended that an American military task force — perhaps 10,000 men — go to Vietnam, commissioned to conduct combat operations for self-defense and perimeter security and, if the Vietnamese army were hard pressed, to act as an emergency reserve. The report concluded by saying that this program would work only if infiltration from the north were stopped and that therefore, should this infiltration continue, the United States should consider a contingency policy of retaliation against the north, graduated to match the intensity of Hanoi's aid to the Viet Cong.

Kennedy rejected both the northern strategy and the use of combat soldiers. "They want a force of American troops," he remarked privately. "They say it's necessary in order to restore confidence and maintain morale. But it will be just like Berlin. The troops will march in; the bands will play; the crowds will cheer; and in four days everyone will have forgotten. Then we will be told we have to send in more troops. It's like taking a drink. The effect wears off, and you have to take another."

Yet he felt obliged to offer a small drink himself, and he increased the number of military advisers. More drinks were still to come. At the end of 1961, there were 1364 American military personnel in South Vietnam; at the end of 1962, 9865; at the time of Kennedy's death in November 1963, about 15,500. This was the policy of "one more step"— each new step always promising the success which the previous last step had also promised but had unaccountably failed to deliver. Once, early in the Kennedy administration, the then Chairman of the Joint Chiefs of Staff outlined to the National Security Council the processes by which each American action in Southeast Asia, if it provoked a communist counteraction, could in turn provoke an even more drastic American response. He concluded, "If we are given the right to use nuclear weapons, we can guarantee victory." Kennedy sat glumly rubbing his upper molar, saying nothing. After a moment someone spoke up: "Mr. President, perhaps you would have the General explain to us what he means by victory." Kennedy grunted and dismissed the meeting. Later he said, "Since he couldn't think of any further escalation, he would have to promise us victory."

With the Taylor-Rostow mission, the Vietnam problem passed in effect from the Department of State to the Department of Defense, and, in spite of Kennedy's early insight into the political character of the problem in Vietnam, the projected American solution in 1961–1963 was increasingly framed in military terms. Why did Kennedy permit this to happen? One reason was that Vietnam was still in these years a low-level crisis. It was far less urgent than Cuba, or Berlin, or Latin America, or nuclear testing, or preserving the European alliance, or fighting for civil rights in the United States; far less urgent than the neighboring Asian crisis in Laos. Another reason was that the strategy of unconditional support of Diem combined with the military adviser system seemed to be working — or so at least the senior American officials in Saigon assured the President. Their dispatches conveyed the picture of a regime led by a doubtless difficult but unquestionably statesmanlike and, in any case, irreplaceable figure making steady progress in winning over the peasants, pacifying the countryside and restoring the stability of government. If there was no surge of social reform, at least the "strategic hamlet" program — the relocation of peasants into fortified villages, surrounded by barbed wire fences and ditches filled with bamboo spikes — was giving the countryside protection and a new sense of security and cutting off the Viet Cong from their primary sources of food, intelligence and recruits. Ngo Dinh Nhu made the strategic hamlet program his personal project and published glowing reports of spectacular success. One might have wondered whether Nhu was just the man to mobilize the idealism of the villages; but Ambassador Nolting and General Harkins listened uncritically to his claims and passed them back to

Washington as facts, where they were read with elation.

Washington officials on hasty visits confirmed the picture. "Every quantitative measurement we have," Secretary of Defense McNamara said on his first trip to Vietnam in 1962, "shows we're winning this war." General Taylor, when he returned for a fresh look a year after his first mission, detected "a great national movement" rising to destroy the Viet Cong. It was hard to doubt a widespread and substantial improvement in the military situation. The President, who had other matters on his mind, accepted the cheerful reports from men in whom he had great confidence. His 1963 State of the Union message summed up the mood at the turn of the year: "The spearpoint of aggression has been blunted in South Vietnam."

The optimism continued well into 1963. In March the Secretary of State said that the war was "turning an important corner. . . . Government forces clearly have the initiative in most areas of the country." A month later he discerned a "steady movement toward a constitutional system resting upon popular consent," declared that "the 'strategic hamlet' program is producing excellent results," added that "morale in the countryside has begun to rise," assured his listeners that "to the Vietnamese peasant" the Viet Cong "look less and less like winners" and concluded, "The Vietnamese are on their way to success" (meaning presumably the South Vietnamese). In May the Defense Department announced, "The corner has definitely been turned toward victory in Vietnam." General Harkins predicted that the war would be won "within a year." "South Vietnam," said Ambassador Nolting in June, "is on its way to victory over communist guerrillas." "I can safely say," General Harkins unsafely said in October, "the end of the war is in sight."

There was another view of the situation — a view transmitted not in top secret cables but in dispatches to American newspapers and magazines. The American reporters in Vietnam saw Diem not as a selfless national leader but as an oriental despot, hypnotized by his own endless monologues and contemptuous of democracy and the west. They detested the Nhus. They considered the strategic hamlet program a fake and a failure; and their visits to dismal stockades where peasants had been herded, sometimes at bayonet point, to engage in forced labor confirmed their worst misgivings. They stopped believing Diem's communiqués; and, when Harkins and Nolting kept insisting they were true, they stopped believing Harkins and Nolting. Their picture of South Vietnam differed from the official reports by about 180 degrees.

In response, the officials assailed the journalists. Admiral Felt, the commander of the Pacific fleet, reproached the man from the Associated Press: "Why don't you get on the team?" In reports to Washington the officials even gave the astonishing impression that there would be no trouble in Vietnam if only the newspaper fellows would follow the line. "The U.S. Embassy," wrote David Halberstam of the New York Times, who later won a Pulitzer Prize for his work in Vietnam, "turned into the adjunct of a dictatorship. In trying to protect Diem from criticism, the Ambassador became Diem's agent." One experience after another made the newspapermen more certain that the Embassy was lying to them. They did not recognize the deeper pathos, which was that the officials really believed their own reports. They were deceiving not only the American government and people but themselves.

Then in May 1963 Diem forbade the Buddhists to display their flags on Buddha's 2587th birthday, Diem's troops fired into a crowd of Buddhists in Hue, and the situation suddenly fell apart. The Buddhist trouble was as much social as religious in its impulse. It was at bottom an uprising, wholly unforeseen by American diplomats, of the new generation of nationalists, drawn largely from the middle and lower classes, speaking Vietnamese rather than French, professing Buddhism rather than Catholicism, xenophobic and hysterical, in revolt against traditional Vietnamese society. Diem and the Nhus retaliated with equal hysteria. The result was to expose the optimism that had been flowing so long and so imperturbably out of American officials in Saigon and to strengthen those few officials in Washington — notably Averell Harriman, Under Secretary of State, and Roger Hilsman, Assistant Secretary for Far Eastern Affairs, who for some time had been questioning the orthodox picture. The appointment of Henry Cabot Lodge as Ambassador to Saigon reinforced the skeptics.

The Buddhist troubles finally made Vietnam a matter of top priority, even in the months of Bull Connor and his police dogs in Birmingham, of the American University speech and the test ban treaty, of the fight for tax reduction and the civil rights bill. "In my opinion," Kennedy said, "for us to withdraw from that effort would mean a collapse not only of South Vietnam but Southeast Asia. So we are going to stay there." But he could not forget the French experience of a decade earlier; if the war were ever converted into a white man's war, the Americans would lose as the French had lost. "In the final analysis," he said on September 3, "it is their war. They are the ones who have to win it or lose it. We can help them, we can give them equipment, we can send our men out there as advisers, but they have to win it, the people of Vietnam."

Finally the South Vietnamese army brought off its coup, killed Diem and Nhu, and the war entered a new phase. Three weeks later Kennedy too was dead, and a new President inherited the trouble.

Roger Hilsman: IF KENNEDY HAD LIVED?

Director of Intelligence in the State Department and then Assistant Secretary of State for Far Eastern Affairs in the last months of the Kennedy administration and the first months of President Johnson's tenure, Mr. Hilsman describes a key conflict within the American policy-making community and summarizes, at the end, his perception of the important differences in style and action between the two presidents that led him to resign his State Department post. The "stormy events" mentioned in the opening sentence refer to the period of political and military confusion in South Vietnam following the collapse of the regime of President Diem in November 1963.

IN THE State Department, we were acutely conscious that all these stormy events meant only that there was one more chance to carry out an effective counterguerrilla program. And we fully agreed . . . that Vietnam was a political problem of winning the allegiance of the people rather than a military problem of killing Viet Cong. But the rest of Washington also had to be convinced if the United States was to be effective in persuading Saigon. "The problem of Vietnam," we wrote in a memorandum which we circulated widely within the government, "is no different from what it was two years ago. The Viet Cong capability for action is based largely on their access to recruits, supplies, and intelligence from the villages of South Vietnam. Cadres, technical personnel, and special-

ized equipment are infiltrated from North Vietnam, but we have thus far no reason to believe that the Viet Cong have more than a limited need for outside resources. Our main effort must therefore be directed at cutting the links between the Viet Cong and the South Vietnamese villagers. The strategic concept for an effective counterguerrilla program must be based on certain fundamental principles . . .

The problem presented by the Viet Cong is by no means just a military problem. It is more accurately described as a problem in effectively coordinating military action with political and economic and social measures. The first essential is to provide the villager with physical security, so that he has a choice of refusing to cooperate with the Viet Cong. . . . The second essential is

Roger Hilsman, *To Move a Nation* (Garden City, 1967), pp. 525–537. Reprinted with the permission of Doubleday & Company, Inc. and of Robert Lantz Literary Agency. Copyright 1964, 1967 by Roger Hilsman.

to set up a system of government services and assistance that will break up the villager's isolation, tie him into the governmental structure, and earn his political support. To achieve these purposes a well-coordinated program must be conducted that combines military "clear-and-hold" operations with a strategic hamlet program, no matter what its name is. To be effective, it must be based on a national plan that establishes priorities for operations beginning in the more secure areas and extending outward to the less secure.

Operating within this national plan, regular forces should concentrate not on pursuing guerrillas and killing them, but on clearing them from the priority areas and holding those areas until strategic hamlets can be established. Provisions for the physical defense of the hamlet, the training of village defenders, and so on, should be combined with an adequate police program, identity cards and curfew hours to control the movement of goods and people . . . All this should enable the villagers themselves to deal with individual Viet Cong and with small Viet Cong units. Roving civil guard patrols, especially trained in counter-guerrilla warfare and night action should reduce or prevent the concentration of sizeable Viet Cong bands in the neighborhood of established villages. If a large group does slip through, each hamlet must have rapid means of communication, and the regular forces and civil guards must be able to respond immediately both day and night.

With the establishment of a reasonable degree of security, economic and social projects at the village level must be pushed vigorously and rapidly . . . to win the allegiance and support of the people. . . .

The infiltration problem is special. . . . While infiltration has played a relatively minor role in supporting Viet Cong activity, action to control and disrupt it has long been recognized as necessary. In such terrain, bombing would not be effective . . . [Because of this, we] recommended to the Diem government in 1961 the assignment of ranger units to patrol duties in the jungles

and mountains along the borders of Laos and Cambodia, themselves using the tactics of the guerrilla to fight the guerrilla. This recommendation was never put into effect . . . we should press the new government to proceed rapidly . . .

But getting a consensus among the agencies in Washington on the recommendations we should make to the new government in Saigon was proving to be a formidable task. The Joint Chiefs of Staff, smarting under the revelations coming out of Saigon, which destroyed the basis for past American optimism, began to talk again of the infiltration routes and of "striking at the source of the aggression."

After President Kennedy's death, the pressure was renewed. General Curtis L. LeMay, Chief of Staff of the Air Force, was particularly vigorous in advocating the bombardment of North Vietnam. "We are swatting flies," LeMay said, "when we should be going after the manure pile." General Thomas S. Power said that with conventional bombs alone the Strategic Air Command, which he headed, and its B-52s could "pulverize North Vietnam," and he made a special trip to Washington to plead the case for bombing not only North Vietnam but the Viet Cong and their bases *in South Vietnam.*

In the State Department, Walt Rostow presented to the new President, a well-reasoned case for a gradual escalation, and soon thereafter a proposal was put forward by the Pentagon and the CIA for a program of low-level reconnaissance over Laos and for a program of increased military pressures of various sorts on the north. . . .

Bombing the infiltration routes seemed promising at first sight, but the more we thought about it the more our doubts increased. The North Vietnamese, of course, had used the routes through Laos in violation of the Geneva agreements, and both reconnaissance and bombing should be justified on these grounds. But the Communists had kept their use of the trails at a very low level. At least 5000 men a month could be infiltrated over the Ho Chi Minh trails — over 60,000 a year. Yet from 1960 on, the monthly average had been only 650 and the yearly average only 7850. More important, the personnel coming over the routes were not North Vietnamese, but still only the pro-Communist southerners who had gone north in 1954 and were returning to serve in the Viet Cong as cadre. And as for supplies, so far the only equipment that had come over the infiltration routes was radios, codes, medicines, and a very limited amount of specialized equipment such as recoilless rifles. Even though this infiltration of men and supplies was small, it still constituted aggression and some sort of case could be made to justify bombing the north. But it was in the United States' interest, it seemed to us, to continue what amounted to a tacit agreement that we would refrain from bombing and the North Vietnamese would observe their self-imposed limitation not to infiltrate large numbers of northerners or North Vietnamese regular troops. Bombing could not "cut off" infiltration routes that consisted only of jungle trails, and the amount of men and equipment coming over them could be vastly increased in the teeth of the heaviest kind of pounding by bombers. If we openly violated the Geneva agreements, it would be politically easier for the Communists to violate them even more openly, actually increasing their infiltration through Laos.

. . . If we raised the ante by bombing, the North Vietnamese would respond by increasing the use of the infiltration routes to include northerners. We would be no better off than before and perhaps worse, and we would be paying the international political cost for nothing.

The way to deal with the infiltration routes, in our judgment, was on the ground, by using ranger companies as counterguerrilla guerrillas, ambushing along the trails. Since over half of the distance of the Ho Chi Minh trails from North Vietnam to the delta was inside South Vietnam, these could be chewed up with no violation of the Geneva agreements at all. To help protect the more northern portions of South Vietnam, it might be necessary to do the ambushing in Laos. But there was a world of international political difference between a black-clad company of South Vietnamese rangers ambusing a black-clad unit of Viet Cong infiltrators on a jungle trail in Laos and *American* jets dropping bombs in Laos. Militarily, ambushing was more effective than bombing and politically it was less costly.

. . . Our objections to the proposals for a large-scale bombing program inside South Vietnam were even more basic. A bombing program conducted solely by Americans against targets in South Vietnam violated the most fundamental principle of a strategic concept that was based on the idea of winning the allegiance of the people. In the first place, if Americans did the bombing it would give powerful support to the Viet Cong charges that the United States' purpose in Vietnam was a new form of colonialist-imperialism, and help them enlist the forces of nationalism on their side. In the second place, bombing would greatly increase the difficulty of a program to win the people. Air power and artillery are essential for close-in support for a unit locked in combat with a Viet Cong unit. In very special circumstances, when the intelligence was beyond question, artillery and bombers might also be used to good effect against Viet Cong jungle hideouts and base areas. But what was bound to be bad was preparatory bombing prior to helicopter landings or "interdiction" bombing of "suspected" Viet Cong areas. To repeat, more Viet Cong would be recruited than would be killed.

If bombing the south were accepted as just another routine weapon in the arsenal — no matter how stringent the "rules of engagement" — civilian casualties would be bound to occur in numbers that would be politically excessive. Two years later, in fact, after President Johnson decided to bomb South Vietnam, Clement J. Zablocki, Chairman of the House Foreign Affairs Subcommittee on the Far East, returned from a trip to Vietnam to announce that, although complete statistics were not available, he estimated that a "ratio of two civilians [killed] to one Viet Cong is likely" and that on some "search-and-destroy" operations the ratio was six civilians to one Viet Cong.

The argument over whether or not to launch a large-scale bombing program in South Vietnam was really a symbol of the basic disagreement over the nature of guerrilla warfare. Was revolutionary warfare on the guerrilla model no different from orthodox, regular war in its fundamentals or was it something new, a political struggle with terroristic and military aspects? "Interdiction" bombing — hitting communications routes and "suspected" enemy installations — is an ordinary tool of regular warfare, for example. Yet interdiction bombing is inevitably indiscriminate, bringing death and destruction to the population living in the theater of war. So is artillery fire, except for close support in areas removed from the population. So are large-scale military operations, when battalions and regiments of ground forces sweep a countryside. And so are all the other means of large-scale, regular warfare. These costs will be cheerfully borne by a population if the enemy army is a hated invader. It is a cost that can be tolerated by one side if the opposing army and the population in the theater of war are one and the same united enemy. But it is a cost that may not be tolerable if the allegiance of the population is the true objective. For the means of regular warfare tend to create a hostile population if one did not exist in the beginning.

Bombing North Vietnam itself also raised thorny problems. North Vietnam had only thirty-five or so industrial plants and power installations, which they had acquired through much sacrifice, and it was probably the risk of losing these that had deterred Hanoi from infiltrating their 250,000 regular North Vietnamese troops into South Vietnam. Once these factories and power plants were destroyed, they would have nothing left to lose. And the closer American power got to the border of China, the greater was the possibility of a massive intervention by "Chinese People's Army Volunteers," as had happened in Korea.

A more limited bombing program, attacking only military installations and communications routes in North Vietnam, ran much less risk of causing Chinese Communist intervention. Both the Soviets and the Chinese could be expected to step up their aid and might even bring in volunteers to man antiaircraft units and to pilot fighter planes, but probably not much more. The full strength of the North Vietnamese armies would probably not be infiltrated to the south in response to limited bombing. But as a way of matching the escalation initiated by the United States and in retaliation for it, they might begin to introduce battalions of North Vietnamese regulars into the south.

There were also political drawbacks to bombing North Vietnam. Any bombing of the north would be an escalation at American initiative and a violation of the Geneva accords at a time when prudence demanded that the United States should hold to a posture of restraint. Any other course would be bad international politics, raising questions about America's sense of responsibility among both neutrals and our allies. A posture of restraint was also essential in order to preserve as much of the 1954 Geneva accords as possible. For the 1954 Geneva accords would become, as they had in Laos, the basis for any negotiated settlement — and a negotiated settlement was probably the most likely outcome even if the effort in Vietnam were successful.

Another predictable result, it seemed to us, was that there would be formidable pressure from our allies and from a significant segment of domestic opinion pushing us toward offering to negotiate *prematurely*. If negotiations took place before there had been progress in winning the allegiance of the peasants, especially in the delta, the result would be the neutralization of Vietnam, which in those circumstances would be tantamount to the Viet Cong taking over completely.

Bombing the north would also put an obstacle in the way of furthering the *détente* with the Soviet Union, and make it difficult for the Soviets to follow their own national interest regarding Southeast Asia, which was to press Hanoi to keep the struggle damped down. And bombing the north would add force to the Chinese argument for more belligerent Communist policies, and strengthen their hand in the Sino-Soviet dispute.

But above and beyond all these unwelcome consequences, bombing the north would be a mistake for the fundamental reason that it probably would not work. The advocates of bombing believed that it would force North Vietnam to quit or that it would cut the flow of supplies to the south and make it impossible for the Viet Cong to continue. All-out bombing of the cities of North Vietnam might force Hanoi to quit, but that kind of massive bombing would also run too great a risk of massive Chinese intervention. Limited, measured bombing, on the other hand, could not hurt the North Vietnamese economy enough to matter. Nor could any bombing, no matter how heavy, "cut" the flow of supplies. Most of the supplies for the Viet Cong, like the recruits, came from the villages of the *South* — the Viet Cong required only five or six tons of supplies a day from the outside world. This was an amount that could be carried by three or four trucks or one large sampan or 150 coolies. Of course bombing the supply routes would hurt the Communists. They would have to travel at night. They would have to spend time and energy filling in craters in the roads, putting their supply dumps in camouflaged underground warehouses, and repairing bridges. But bombing does not "destroy" an underdeveloped economy, in which trade is often conducted by barter. Nor does bombing "destroy" communications lines that are really dirt roads and jungle trails with timber bridges that are usually sited where there was an old ford anyway. In a country like North Vietnam, bombing communications routes would do little more than make the enemy put more effort into maintaining the flow of supplies, an effort mainly requiring manpower. And manpower was the one thing that the North Vietnamese and their Chinese allies had plenty of.

There was a real question, in sum, whether the results of bombing would be substantial enough to justify the loss of the expensive American airplanes that would inevitably be shot down and the lives of the pilots that would be lost along with them. It seemed more likely that it would not be American air power alone that would deter the Communists from escalating the struggle by infiltrating regular North Vietnamese units and more supplies, but the totality of American power, including especially American ground power.

The fact of the matter was that Asians tended to interpret the use of air power *alone* as a weak response, even though they feared air power. The United States had so often flirted with the idea of "immaculate" war in Asia, war fought in the air above the muck and blood of jungle fighting, that Asians thought of air power alone as a bluff. In the circumstances, the only thing we could really be sure would impress either Communist or non-Communist Asians was ground forces.

But again, the purpose would be not to use American ground forces to take over the war effort, for that would be politically self-defeating. The purpose in using American ground forces would not be for the United States to escalate the level of fighting but to deter the Communists from escalating it. We suspected that the claims of vastly increased use of the infiltration routes was nothing more than a repetition of the "built-in excuse for failure" that President Kennedy had predicted. (It turned out, in fact, that fewer infiltrators had come over the trails in 1963 than in 1962.) But if the information when it came in did indeed show that the North Vietnamese had stepped up their use of the infiltration routes, our proposal was to put a division of American ground forces into Thailand as a warning and couple it with communications to North Vietnamese representatives in the various Communist and neutral capitals. If the warning was not heeded, that division could be moved right up to the Laos border, and a second division introduced into Thailand. If that set of warnings was also ignored, a division could be introduced into Vietnam, and so on — not to fight the Viet Cong, which should remain the task of the South Vietnamese, but to deter the north from escalating. . . .

The style of Roosevelt and Kennedy was to build into the situation around them conflicting advice, to have men around who had opinions of their own, and to encourage them to articulate their positions vigorously. In this freewheeling environment, they hoped to have all aspects of a question fully explored and to preserve for themselves the whole range of choices. The tasks of the presidency, however, are burdensome, and each new president must find his own way of coping with them. President Johnson seemed to prefer a more hierarchical way of handling the job, and from both the people he turned to for advice on Vietnam and his own approach to the problem it seemed clear that his natural instinct was toward attempting a military solution to the question of Vietnam, although hedging it with political qualifications. I was sure that the United States under his direction would not leap irresponsibly into a policy of military escalation, but it was obviously going to take the military path — even though it climbed the ladder of escalation slowly and deliberately.

On the other hand, I was deeply convinced that the political approach was the wiser course. The human costs of a military approach to Vietnam, both for Americans and Vietnamese, would be much greater, in my judgment, and success less likely — especially in the permanent sense of achieving a politically viable outcome. A military course of action in Vietnam would impede also the slow but significant movement toward a *détente* with the Soviet Union that President Kennedy had set in motion with the test ban treaty following the Cuban missile crisis. And a military approach would put enormous obstacles in the way of working toward a more realistic, "open door" policy toward Communist China, as we had planned. . . .

No one, of course, can know for sure what President Kennedy would have done in the future — had he lived. But his policy had been to keep the fighting as limited as possible, to urge the new government to pursue an effective counterguerrilla program designed to protect the people and win their allegiance. He preferred to treat the problem of Vietnam as something other than war and to avoid getting American prestige so involved that the United States could not accept a negotiated settlement along the lines of the Geneva accords on Laos — when and if the Vietnamese desired it. When President Kennedy died, there were just over sixteen thousand American advisers in Vietnam. When the Geneva accords on Laos were signed, there were 666 American advisers there — about the same proportion relative to the size of the country. In any event, President

Kennedy made it abundantly clear to me on more than one occasion that what he most wanted to avoid was turning Vietnam into an American war. He was skeptical of a policy of escalation and of the effectiveness of an air attack on North Vietnam. If the North Vietnamese had vastly increased their use of the infiltration routes, so as to include large numbers of North Vietnamese soldiers and regular North Vietnamese units, he might well have introduced United States ground forces into South Vietnam — although I believe he would not have ordered them to take over the war effort from the Vietnamese but would have limited their mission to that of occupying ports, airfields, and military bases to demonstrate to the North Vietnamese that *they* could not win the struggle by a policy of escalation either. President Kennedy's policy, in sum, was to meet the guerrilla aggression within a counterguerrilla framework, with the implied corollary that if the Viet Cong could not be defeated within a counterguerrilla framework and the allegiance of the people of Vietnam could not be won, then the United States would accept the resulting situation and would be free to enter negotiations without fatal consequences to our position in the rest of Asia. But President Kennedy did not live, and no one can say with absolute certainty what he would or would not have done.

Philip Geyelin: THE ORPHAN WAR

It was in the second year of the administration of Lyndon B. Johnson that the word "escalation" acquired common currency. In this essay, a distinguished Washington journalist offers his interpretation of how a government committed in 1964 to no wider involvement in Vietnam went to war there in 1965.

PUBLIC ATTENTION was caught by every reported Communist "peace feeler," by every hint that Hanoi might wish to negotiate. But the attention of policy-makers centered on coldly practical questions: what sort of settlement could conceivably be negotiated, given the existing balance of forces in South Vietnam, even assuming a willingness on the part of the Communists to talk? And what would be the most propitious time? When those questions were answered, the answers were remarkably uniform in their downgrading of prospects for constructive bargaining. In March, 1964, Senator Fulbright thought the war was going so badly that an equitable settlement safeguarding U.S. interests was probably impossible. In mid-campaign, the war was going even worse. And the tragedy of the electoral time table was that it allowed the military and political situation in South Vietnam to deteriorate still further.

*　*　*

How Kennedy might have moved to resolve the conflict is impossible to say, but almost certainly there would have been significant changes in policy. According to the account of Arthur Schlesinger, Jr., in *A Thousand Days*, Kennedy "no doubt . . . realized that Vietnam was his great failure in foreign policy, and that he had never really given it his full atten-

tion." So it was still an orphan when it was passed along to Johnson, and the options open to a new President, whose every move was examined microscopically for the slightest sign of slackening resolve or intention to alter course, were not the same options that would have been open to Kennedy. Further U.S. disengagement — perhaps through early negotiations with Hanoi — might have been possible for Kennedy. He might have made an effort to disconnect the dominoes by de-emphasizing the potential impact on other neighboring Asians of a losing U.S. effort to shore up a nation apparently incapable of helping to save itself. This was known as the "good doctor, sick patient" theory and it had strong adherents in the policy-making machinery. Or Kennedy might has seen U.S. prestige inextricably engaged and moved to bring U.S. power to bear more forcefully in 1964. Instead, transition made the timing out of joint. While Hanoi followed its own inexorable momentum, U.S. momentum was abruptly interrupted by the sanctification of "continuity," by the special electoral pressures on Johnson beyond those that an established President would have faced, by the bizarre foreign-policy issue that was to dominate the Johnson-Goldwater campaign. For another long year, Vietnam was fated to be an orphan war.

Philip Geyelin, *Lyndon B. Johnson and the World* (New York: Frederick A. Praeger, 1966), pp. 186–198, 204, 209–210, 212–216, 218–223. Reprinted with the permission of Frederick A. Praeger, Inc. Copyright 1966 by Frederick A. Praeger, Inc.

THE HOLDING OPERATION

With Vietnam, for most of 1964, Lyndon Johnson was in the awkward role of contortionist; he was propping up the tottery Saigon Government — or governments — with one hand, jabbing threateningly with the other in an effort to deter Hanoi, all the while faced around toward the American electorate, shouting reassurances. The result was a confusing cacophony of hawklike cries and dovelike coos. In a warm letter of encouragement to General Duong Van Minh, the military chieftain then in command in Saigon, Johnson, on December 31, 1963, pledged "on behalf of the American Government and people a renewed partnership with your government and people in your brave struggle for freedom." He said: "The United States will continue to furnish you and your people with the fullest measure of support in this bitter fight," and he promised "Big Minh" that the United States would have no part of any scheme to "neutralize" South Vietnam. Not even obliquely was there mention of what South Vietnam might do to help its own cause, by political or other reform.

In a February, 1964, address at the University of California, Johnson did stress that the conflict in South Vietnam was "first and foremost a contest to be won by the government and the people of that country for themselves." But in that same speech, he first introduced the threat of wider war, though in a curiously circumlocutory way. "Those engaged in external direction and supply would do well to be reminded and to remember that this type of aggression is a deeply dangerous game," he declared. . . . The "signal," of course, had been intended for Hanoi; but the flaw in the semaphore system of diplomacy was always that when the signaling is done publicly, everybody can listen in. The domestic backlash was such that Dean Rusk was obliged to summon a news conference for the purpose of playing down any speculation that the United States might "go North." From the White House came the curious news that the President himself could not imagine how such an extreme interpretation of his words could have gotten around.

So it went through the spring and early summer of 1964. One moment, McNamara was in Saigon, cavorting with the local government leaders like a politician running for office, and Dean Rusk was saying that if the Vietnam Government "could continue now, as we think it will, to finish up its pacification program, there is a country that can plan an important, strong active role among the free nations of Southeast Asia." As for thought of negotiations, Rusk, in a joint news conference with the President in April, said flatly: "There is no known question, at least no question that I know about, on which negotiations would appear to be successful." The next moment, both men were warning darkly that continued intervention by Hanoi could bring "the initiation of military actions . . . against North Vietnam" and a widening war.

Ironically, it was left to Senator Fulbright to state the harsh realities in terms which were remarkably prophetic, though not entirely consistent with the opposition role he was increasingly to take later on. On one point, he agreed with Rusk. "The hard fact of the matter," he said in March, "is that our bargaining position is at present a weak one; and until the equation of advantage between the two sides has been substantially altered in our favor, there can be little prospect of a negotiated settlement."

His remedy, however, placed him a full year ahead of official, acknowledged

Johnson Administration thinking. "It seems clear," Fulbright declared, "that only two realistic options are open to us in Vietnam in the immediate future: the expansion of the conflict in one way or another; or a renewed effort to bolster the capacity of the South Vietnamese to prosecute the war successfully on its present scale." The Johnson Administration remained anchored to unsuccessful execution of option number two for a year; when it finally elected option number one almost a year later, it found itself increasingly at odds with Senate Foreign Relations Committee Chairman Fulbright. . . .

Lyndon Johnson not only did not want controversial new initiatives; he did not really have time for careful consideration of the Vietnam war at all. "The word was to keep the tough decisions away from the White House," one of the State Department proponents of urgent action said at the time, "and this would have taken a major effort by the President."

. . . The center of gravity in Vietnam policy-making shifted to those who, for one reason or another, could think of little else at the time than to stand pat. The military had its own built-in paralysis against expanding the war. Dean Rusk was doggedly against losing it, firm in his determination that Hanoi "must leave its neighbors alone," convinced that Vietnam was a major test of U.S. will and the effectiveness of Communist wars of liberation — with implications for the validity of U.S. commitments and for national prestige around the globe. But he was not for pushing new courses of action at a time when the President was in an unreceptive frame of mind; at the White House, Mac Bundy apparently shared this view. It is difficult to detect the degree of Johnson influence in any of this. But the absence of decision-making,

as Dean Rusk was to say in quite another context (in defense of U.S. intervention in the Dominican Republic), can amount to a decision in itself. And the decision was more of the same, and not much more, in Vietnam.

There was less and less safety, however, in standing completely pat. First there was the Laotian flare-up, which the President was able to damp down more or less surreptitiously. Then in August, there came a quixotic attack by North Vietnamese torpedo boats on the "U.S.S. Maddox," a destroyer operating in the Gulf of Tonkin, and the President felt compelled to invoke the Lyndon Law "Don't tread on me." In the process, he also demonstrated vividly his capacity for extracting from almost anything — even an apparently adverse development — a political gain. At the first torpedo-boat assault, the United States merely protested to Hanoi and warned of reprisals if it happened again. For reasons still puzzling to most onlookers the North Vietnamese response was a second attack two days later against the "Maddox" and the "C. Turner Joy." To most of the President's advisers, it seemed a direct affront that could not be allowed to go unanswered lest grave miscalculations of U.S. resolve develop among the Communist war-managers in Hanoi and Peking.

Politically, there were limits as to just how prudent Lyndon Johnson could afford to be. He wished to appear more prudent than Goldwater. But he did not wish to appear to be a pushover. So there was little argument about launching retaliatory air strikes against the torpedo-boat facilities on a one-shot, tit-for-tat basis, and only brief debate over the details. . . .

The Tonkin incident was a brief flare-up, but it lasted just long enough to provide an opportunity for Johnson to arm himself with an overwhelming mandate from Congress to do just about anything he felt was necessary in Vietnam. On August 5, the day after the second torpedo-boat raid and the retaliatory American air strikes, the President sent a message to Congress stating that the shooting itself would have made a Congressional resolution essential "in any event" but that there was an additional argument because of the fact that the United States faced three months of political campaigning. "Hostile nations must understand that in such a period the United States will continue to protect its national interests, and that in these matters there is no division among us."

Congress had no real choice, even though nobody could make much sense out of the torpedo attacks and what they might portend. Two days later, by a unanimous vote in the House and with only two Senators dissenting, Congress wrote Lyndon Johnson a blank check for Vietnam, authorizing the President to take all necessary measures to repel any armed attack against the forces of the United States and to prevent further aggression." Johnson did not find a need to draw on this account for six months, but he was still drawing on it, to the increasing chagrin of his Congressional critics, in 1966, when U.S. forces were deeply committed to warfare in Vietnam, debate over the war was intensifying, and many lawmakers were asking who gave the President authority for such drastic measures. You did, the President was pleased to be able to reply.

It was not, strictly speaking, a completely convincing answer, as even Administration officials would concede. On paper, it looked convincing, and with the public at large, it doubtless served Johnson's purposes well. But Congressional acts have "legislative histories" which

must also be taken into account in weighing their real intent, and the legislative history of the Tonkin resolution is interesting, for an effort was made by Senator Gaylord Nelson to amend it precisely for the purpose of preventing its use as justification for a major change in the U.S. mission in South Vietnam. Nelson would have put Congress on record against "extension of the present conflict" and in favor of a continuing advisory military role. He was talked out of pushing the amendment by reassurances he received from Fulbright, who as Chairman of the Foreign Relations Committee was responsible for interpreting what the Administration had in mind. And he gave it as his opinion that the Nelson amendment was "an accurate reflection of what I believe is the President's policy," and, therefore, superfluous.

"I am concerned about the Congress appearing to tell the Executive Branch and the public that we would endorse a complete change in our mission," Nelson declared, and Fulbright responded: "I do not interpret the joint resolution in that way at all. It strikes me, as I understand it, that the joint resolution is quite consistent with our existing mission and our understanding of what we have been doing in South Vietnam for the last ten years."

In early 1966, Fulbright was publicly blaming himself for a "mistake" in not accepting Nelson's amendment. But by that time, of course, the U.S. mission in South Vietnam had already undergone fundamental change — at least in the way it was being carried out. And Johnson had been in a position all along the way to argue that, on the face of it, he had acted well within the law. Meantime, the Tonkin resolution had served a useful purpose in the pre-election period, even though at that point Johnson distinctly did not wish to widen the conflict. Further North Vietnamese attacks might still have forced his hand — forced him to take the very same sort of aggressive, dangerous steps he was accusing Goldwater of advocating. Had that happened, he would have at least had advance Congressional approval for whatever steps he had to take.

What developed was a deadly race against time; increasingly the question agonizing the war-planners in Washington and Saigon was whether South Vietnam could be kept from crumbling without a much more vigorous U.S. effort before November 3. If this developing challenge was evident to the President in mid-1964, however, there was little evidence of his concern. Indeed, the line offered publicly, and privately, in response to Republican arguments that the Communists should be denied a safe sanctuary in North Vietnam from which to subvert the South, was that the insurrection in the South was largely a home-grown affair. Maxwell Taylor made the argument privately, just before embarking for Saigon as Ambassador; bombing the North or otherwise moving to choke off infiltration, he contended, would still leave an indigenous, hostile force of 60,-000 or so insurgents capable of foraging off the countryside, capturing needed arms and ammunition, and carrying on the war.

The State Department's Director of Intelligence, Thomas Hughes, speaking in Panama on June 8, declared that "by far the greater part of the Vietcong forces in South Vietnam are South Vietnamese, the preponderance of Vietcong weapons come not from Communist countries but from capture, purchase, and local manufacture." In other words, there was no real need to expand the war beyond the South, leaving aside the question of risk.

"WE ARE NOT GOING NORTH"

Any political campaign would have had a distracting impact on the conduct of the U.S. effort in Vietnam — or any other place. But the 1964 Johnson-Goldwater contest was not just any campaign, and its impact was therefore a good deal more serious. The trouble started, some would argue, back in October, 1963, while John F. Kennedy was still President, and it started because Barry Goldwater never did seem to know what he was trying to say. What he said in Hartford, Conn., in the course of his campaign for the Republican nomination, was that NATO "commanders" ought to have authority to use tactical nuclear weapons without explicit authority from the President. Almost as soon as he said it, he and his advisers started saying that he didn't really mean it. Every awkward effort he made to explain just what he did mean only served to strengthen the impression of a man hell-bent for total victory over Communism at whatever risk of nuclear war. . . .

For Lyndon Johnson, this situation was like an exposed jugular, and the instinct to go for it was irresistible. Add to this Johnson's country-style campaigning, and the result could only be to sow seeds of confusion in the Communist power centers of the world. . . .

What he was saying, emphatically and repeatedly, was that he did not intend to lead the United States into a wider war in Vietnam. And while he was sometimes careful to qualify his pledge with such phrases as "at this time" or "if possible," just a few random samples of Johnson oratory in October of 1964 make his message unmistakable: it was not his commitment to Vietnam, it was Dwight Eisenhower's; while he intended to honor it, he also intended to avoid a deeper U.S. involvement in the fighting.

"There are those that say I ought to go north and drop bombs, to try to wipe out the supply lines, and they think that would escalate the war," he said in a speech on September 25. "But we don't want to get involved in a nation with seven hundred million people and get tied down in a land war in Asia."

What was his answer? Certainly not to "go south," to "get out and come home . . . [because] we don't like to break our treaties and we don't like to walk off and leave people who are searching for freedom," he explained in the same speech. "We're hoping that some way, somehow, these people that are invading them and trying to envelop them and trying to take their freedom from them will some day decide that it's not worth the price, and they will leave their neighbors alone, and we can have peace in the world. But we are not about to start another war, and we're not going to run away from where we are."

The image of Goldwater as the Democrats had gleefully helped paint it, and as the American public was rapidly coming to accept it, the image of the reckless international adventurer who would impose U.S. will and U.S. might upon the world at the risk of holocaust — this was always Johnson's backdrop. A good many of his close advisers who knew what he was saying in closed-door discussion of foreign policy considered a largely impromptu campaign speech in Manchester, N.H., on September 28, as perhaps the best public expression of his real beliefs. The adversities that had crowded in upon him in his first year in office were tempering his view of the U.S. role in the world. He began, as he usually began, with a brisk rundown of U.S. military potential, ticking off the billions that had been spent and would be spent for weaponry, cataloging the bombers and

ballistic missiles. But once having offered assurance that the United States had power enough to protect itself, he dwelt at far greater length on the limitations of that power to order world events to American liking. He spoke of the "illusion that the United States can demand resolution of all the world's problems and mash a button and get the job done." He said his country had "willingly accepted the responsibilities of world leadership, and when our own vital interests are challenged we act. But we are not the sole captain of the ship."

Another illusion he was pleased to attribute to his Republican opponent was that "force, or the threat of force can solve all problems." A third illusion was that "we could, if only we tried hard enough, put an end to all difficulty and danger and then retire from the world." In a moving passage, he declared that

the sound of gunfire in Asia echoes in the homes of Manchester. The speeches of a leader in Moscow or Peking helps shape the life of a subway rider in New York. An angry cry for freedom in Africa requires an understanding act in Washington. And as long as this nation endures we are going to be engaged in the affairs of the world. I welcome this involvement. I believe the American people welcome it. It may bring danger but it brings an added dimension to the prospects of freedom. In this world, as in life itself, there is really no escape from problems. You can't run away from them. [There is] no escape from peril.

But again he repeated: "We are not going north and we are not going south." Again he declared,

I didn't get you into Vietnam. You have been in Vietnam ten years. President Eisenhower wrote President Diem a letter in 1954 when the French pulled out of Vietnam, and he said, "We want to help you to help your people keep from going Communist, and we will furnish you advice, we will furnish you assistance, and we will furnish you equipment if you will furnish the men, and if you want to fight for your freedom we will try to help you."

And in Manchester, as at other way stations along the campaign trail, he repeated the familiar refrain on escalation:

As far as I am concerned, I want to be very cautious and careful, and use it only as a last resort, when I start dropping bombs around that are likely to involve American boys in a war in Asia with seven hundred million Chinese. So just for the moment, I have not thought that we were ready for American boys to do the fighting for Asian boys. . . .

Meanwhile, there were clear signs of growing anxiety, if not at the highest official level, at least at the lower working levels of the government; the experts could read the signs in the increased political shambles in Saigon, in the increased rate of infiltration, in a tide of war that was running unmistakably against the South Vietnamese. "It is going to be close," said one of the State Department's most reliable authorities as the U.S. election day approached.

By September, a new and, to some, more compelling argument for not moving quickly to expand the U.S. effort was beginning to take precedence above all others; this was the argument that the government in Saigon, roiled by continuous fighting and struggling for power among the generals, could not stand up under the strain of a systematic expansion of the war to North Vietnam and the risk it would bring of a wave of terrorism and subversion by the Communists in reprisal, or even, conceivably, of North Vietnamese air strikes to the south. Over and over, the President was repeating, in private as well as in public, his assurances that the United States would not "pull out and go home." But he shared the view of a number of his advisers, including, at this stage, Maxwell Taylor, that a political structure as rickety as the one in Saigon was in no shape to carry the war to the north.

* * *

[T]he key question in . . . any . . . approach to the prospect of negotiation was always the same: just what sort of settlement did the United States have in mind? By 1966, this too was beginning to be a subject for serious public debate. But any examination of how the United States got into the Vietnam war in such a big way has to begin with acceptance of the fact that this question wasn't being debated much by the men from whom Johnson could logically have sought counsel in the last months of 1964 and the first few weeks in 1965.

For at that point, the United States was bent on expunging South Vietnam of any lingering Communist threat. The infiltrators from the North were to be driven out, or obliged, under settlement terms, to withdraw. Vietnam was to be delivered "free and clear" of Communism. Hanoi, in Dean Rusk's litany, was to be required to "leave her neighbors alone."

Since Hanoi, at about that time, held sway over more than half of her southern neighbor and could see the Saigon Government crumbling before her very eyes, it is scarcely surprising that the "signals" from Hanoi should not have encouraged optimism about the sort of settlement the United States had in mind. Nor was it surprising that the United States should have had little interest in negotiating, for it could see the same things in South Vietnam that Hanoi could see.

❋ ❋ ❋

"Military pressure" on North Vietnam, "collapse" of the government in South Vietnam should diplomatic solutions be so much as discussed, a lack of "equilibrium" in the balance of forces — these were the essential, underlying factors in the Johnson Administration's Vietnam thinking at the turn of the year. And they pointed directly toward urgent measures to tilt the balance of forces the other way. The path to peace was not open, because neither Lyndon Johnson nor the key men around him — McNamara, Rusk, McGeorge Bundy — could see it leading anywhere. Johnson saw the situation, characteristically, in terms of an analogy to domestic politics. "I don't have to negotiate with Goldwater," he declared in one meeting with his aides, by way of demonstrating why, in his view, the Communists could think of no good reason for wanting to negotiate anything but surrender with an enemy which seemed in the process of suffering disastrous defeat.

THE HIGHWAY TO WAR

Pleiku was the trigger. Or so it seemed, when the Vietcong attacked American installations at that central highlands provincial capital in South Vietnam on February 7, 1965. Retaliatory U.S. aerial bombardment in North Vietnam was followed three days later by a similar Vietcong assault on an American billet in the coastal city of Qui Nhon, which brought further air retaliation and finally systematic air strikes to the north, the landing of the first contingents of U.S. combat troops, on March 6, for "perimeter defense" of American bases; and, ultimately, full-fledged combat, freely conceded as such, with U.S. soldiers pouring ashore.

But Pleiku was the trigger only in a technical sense. For if there was arguable diplomatic, political, and military logic in Lyndon Johnson's decision to escalate the U.S. effort in South Vietnam to build a stronger bargaining position — if not win total victory — there was also a high degree of political craftsmanship, no end of stage-management, and a good measure of legerdemain. As one of the very few high officials who opposed it at almost every step was to say later:

It was almost imperceptible, the way we got in. There was no one move that you could call decisive, or irreversible, not even very many actions that you could argue against in isolation. Yet when you put it all together, there we were in a war on the Asian mainland, with nobody really putting up much of a squawk while we were doing it.

To the President's admirers, his handling of Vietnam in the early months of 1965 was more than just skillful — it was a triumph of international and domestic politics. For if one accepts the need to right the "equilibrium," then it cannot be denied that Lyndon Johnson moved to do so with a bare minimum of dissent at home and less foreign opposition than might have been expected. And he did it, at least for a good many months, without giving the Communist Chinese or the Russians provocation in such intolerable degree that they felt obliged to move in any drastic way to the defense of Hanoi.

He did it, in brief, by making it all look like a logical sequence of almost unavoidable steps, starting with a simple, one-shot retaliation for Pleiku. It would not, of course, be fair to say that Johnson knew all along how far he planned to escalate; his moves had been carefully "calibrated," to use the term much favored by the war-game players among the policy-planners, to meet the real or anticipated moves of the enemy. But there was a master plan, and large parts of it dated back to before election day. Urgent consideration of what to do about Vietnam had begun among the President's advisers well before the November vote. . . .

The arguments, however, were not running all one way, and the President took pains to hear out the advocates of restraint. He studied reports that the Tonkin retaliation had done less to boost sagging South Vietnamese morale than many had expected. There were also projections suggesting that the most effective bombing of the North would not seriously cripple the insurrection, barring substantial improvement in the capability of the South Vietnamese to prosecute the war. There were warnings of adverse world reaction, of the danger of escalation, of the risk of a clash with the Chinese. Maxwell Taylor was still on a cautious tack arguing that any new moves against North Vietnam would be to invite disaster unless the political and military base in the South could be made more secure. Among the Washington sages, the betting in November and on into December was still running against major U.S. escalation of its effort in the war. The military argument was still going in circles; the army still didn't want to take on that orphan war without air power, and widespread use of air power to pound communications lines in the North was still thought liable to provoke reprisals which the Saigon Government would be unable to withstand.

Then, abruptly, the argument turned around; in December, the shambles in Saigon began to reach such a critical condition that officials feared total collapse might well be imminent. The generals were undercutting one another and quarreling with Ambassador Taylor as

well. Suddenly, it began to be said that doing nothing was coming to be more dangerous than doing something — almost anything — to keep the Saigon Government from going down the drain. This became the principal argument for expanding the war to the North, taking precedence over the arguments that air strikes would inhibit infiltration, or at least introduce a new element on the U.S. side of the scales in any future bargaining.

* * *

In the course of this happening, the whole Administration argument had been turned around and headed in a direction that would later prove dangerous for the President. During the election campaign, the case had regularly been made that the most important content of the insurgency was home-grown and self-supporting; now the argument became that there really wouldn't be much difficulty cleaning up the South if the infiltrators from the North would just go home. From this came the conclusion that the proper aim of the expanded war effort must be to "win" — to pummel Hanoi into "leaving its neighbor alone." This argument was to grow in force as U.S. involvement grew, and would, by the end of 1965, create a growing problem for Lyndon Johnson. It was no problem, of course, as long as it was accepted that the insurrection could be crushed. And increasingly, U.S. public opinion was to veer toward the view that with an investment of so much blood and treasure, the insurrection *must* be crushed. . . .

[The President] seemed convinced that Hanoi wouldn't negotiate while winning, but he still put emphasis on negotiation and compromise. "There's a small percentage that want to bomb Hanoi and there's a small percentage that want to get out," he told visitors, not long after Pleiku. "But I'm the ringleader of a political settlement." He talked with feeling of his hopes to avoid committing U.S. ground forces in large numbers and in one conversation discounted the possibility of providing absolute protection for U.S. air bases on the grounds that this might take 100,000 troops; by 1966, he was to have more than twice that number in Vietnam. But in late February, 1965, he sounded as if he believed the balance could be improved with a minimum of added American leverage. His discussion of the first two retaliatory attacks, following Pleiku and Qui Nhon, was almost offhand. . . .

Many officials close to the President insist this mood was to last only briefly. But it is also widely agreed that it was not until March of 1965 that Lyndon Johnson really began to give Vietnam intense and continuous attention. "That was when he really got into it and made it his own problem as only Johnson can do, once he gets engaged," said one man close to him during this tense period.

But by that time, it can also be argued, the force of events, the momentum of contingency plans, and the lack of acceptable alternatives were already propelling the United States toward a steadily widening war.

Inevitably, the demands of base security to protect the growing American investment in air power impelled the Administration to furnish more men for perimeter defense; the South Vietnamese, it was argued, should more properly be employed in hunting and killing Vietcong. So it was that on March 6, two reinforced U.S. Marine battalions, numbering aproximately 3,500 men, were sent ashore on what was officially announced as "limited duty." These were the first combat units organized as such,

and both Rusk and McNamara were quick to reassure the nation that the role of these American combat units would be limited strictly to defensive operations. Said Rusk: the Marines' mission "is to provide local, close-in security. It is not their mission to engage in pacification operations." McNamara was equally categorical: he said the U.S. combat forces were "to patrol within narrow limits" of the fast-growing airbase at Da Nang "and thus they should not tangle with the Vietcong."

But "tangle" they did, and as their numbers grew and their combat role increased throughout the spring of 1965, the State Department took the initiative in a public-relations campaign designed to prepare American citizens for the certain prospect of increased casualties. . . . [The] argument for the introduction of combat forces in growing numbers began with the case that U.S. air bases ought properly to be guarded by U.S. forces, freeing South Vietnamese guards for combat; then it was argued in Washington councils that the U.S. combat mission would only be temporary, while the South Vietnamese built up their own combat forces through a stepped-up recruitment drive. Only gradually did it become inescapable that the enemy was responding with increased escalation on its side, and that the South Vietnamese weren't going to be able to handle a war that was rapidly moving out of the guerrilla class, with its squad-sized units or perhaps platoons, into the battalion or regimental league.

There were, unquestionably, persuasive arguments at every step of the way for not acknowledging any larger U.S. involvement or commitment than was necessary — in hopes that the worst wouldn't happen. For every acknowledgement, every warlike pose, only encouraged a comparable response from the other side. It was, therefore, probably a sound strategy for a war of semaphore — a contest in which "signals" and the appearance of things and the general attitude struck can matter as much as, or more than, the respective casualty rates. It was also a strategy peculiarly suited for Lyndon Johnson, with his profound preference for saying no more and doing no more than is absolutely necessary at any given time, in hopes that somehow the more unpleasant things won't have to be done at all. But if this is a sensible approach to politics, it also is a good deal better suited for the cozy confines of the Senate cloakroom than for application to a complex, many-faceted international crisis under merciless global observation. For it was, at heart, not an easy strategy to grasp, if one accepts that Johnson's main purpose from the start was to pursue settlement by improving his bargaining position. The aim, in short, then becomes quicker peace through fiercer war — an unappealing proposition to sell.

Indeed, the Administration was quickly and increasingly caught up in a cross-fire of criticism, from those who wanted more war, faster, and total victory; from those who wanted peace and never mind the terms; from those who found the basic tactic certain to boomerang into an even larger war. Yet, the escalation remained, for most of 1965, very nearly a political masterpiece. Only Senators Morse and Gruening consistently fought the President's policy up until the big outbreak of opposition in early 1966, and even at that stage, only a score or so of Senators, out of a hundred, could be counted consistently and openly opposed to the Presi-

dent's aims. It was fully a year after Pleiku before opinion polls began to detect signs of public disaffection with the U.S. course, and it was a confusing disaffection, compounded of antiwar sentiment and of advocacy of more war, quickly, to end it all. Meantime, over that year, more than 200,000 U.S. troops had been dispatched to Vietnam; the "never again" syndrome had been demolished in slow, insidious stages.

As for the enemy, whatever the Chinese might ultimately do, by early 1966 they had not done anything nearly as drastic as many feared they would in the course of this steady build-up of U.S. power on the Asian mainland.

Critics argued — and will doubtless continue to argue — that somewhere along the line the hand had been misplayed, that somehow the mix of increased military pressure and increased diplomatic efforts for settlement had not been right. Even when Johnson altered the mix in his celebrated April 7, 1965, address at Johns Hopkins, by offering to engage in "unconditional discussions" in search of a settlement and by throwing in proffers of nearly boundless bounty for Southeast Asian reconstruction and economic development (including bounty for North Vietnam), there were many who continued to argue that it was too little too late. Only a much longer perspective will tell. Only time would test the highly flexible, somewhat cumbersome, often awkward, and even more often inscrutable Johnson policy for Vietnam. But from early 1965 onward, there was, at least, a distinctively Johnson policy — however much Vietnam might remain an orphan war, adopted but unwanted.

II. THE OBJECTS OF CONTAINMENT

Douglas Pike: THE VIET CONG: GOALS AND MYSTIQUE

"Never before," wrote one analyst in mid-1966, "has the United States fought a foe about whom so little is known." Drawing largely from captured documents, monitored communist radio broadcasts, and interviews in Vietnam, Douglas Pike has written a full-scale study of the Viet Cong. The following excerpt from his book first summarizes the goals and then focuses on the organizational and doctrinal character of the National Liberation Front (NLF), the political arm of the South Vietnamese communist (Viet Cong) war effort.

STUDY OF NLF policy statements, inspection of its [relations with those beyond the borders of Vietnam], and measuring its actions against its words leave one with a subjective impression of the general design of NLF goals and the parameters of those goals. These appear to be the following:

1. To achieve operative political control of South Vietnam; a willingness, but reluctance, to settle for some political power rather than all if it were clearly demonstrated that the alternative to some political power was either stalemate or total defeat.

2. To seek a South Vietnamese governmental policy of nonalignment in foreign affairs (but under a definition that would classify the DRV as domestic rather than foreign), one that in operational terms would permit the reduction of American troops in exchange for the withdrawal of PAVN [North Vietnamese Army] forces from South Vietnam but with the proviso that this arrangement must be agreeable to the DRV.

3. To work for reunification of the two Vietnams through a step-by-step process, the time limits of which would be negotiable.

4. To forge a broad base of world support, one principally rooted in Communist-bloc nations and not tied too closely with any one foreign country. (Again, in NLF terms, relations with the DRV would be internal, not external.)

5. To vilify the United States, mobilize world opinion against it, and heighten its feelings of frustration and futility in its efforts in South Vietnam.

6. To exploit every American and GVN weakness abroad regardless of how insignificant or transient any instance might appear to be.

7. With respect to the Sino-Soviet split, to contribute what little it could to healing the breach but not be forced into a position where it had to choose sides.

8. With respect to the DRV, to prevent itself from being submerged by Hanoi and to retain a bargaining position. Undoubtedly a schism existed: The majority of the politically acute NLF supporters realized that Northern and Southern interests were not identical. The cadres and the PRP members within the NLF shared the DRV goals; they grew progressively stronger and virtually monopolized the hierarchy by 1965. The

Douglas Pike, *Viet Cong* (Cambridge: The M. I. T. Press, 1966), pp. 370–371, 373–383. Reprinted with the permission of The M. I. T. Press. Copyright 1966 by The Massachusetts Institute of Technology.

most divisive issue in this respect was reunification. The indigenous elements maintained that reunification meant annexation by the DRV and at any rate was opposed by too many forces within and outside of Vietnam ever to be possible; the loyalists maintained, as did the DRV, that reunification must remain the central long-range goal.

9. To strive for the withdrawal of American forces from South Vietnam, based on the calculation that the United States could be persuaded to accept a coalition neutral government if its position in South Vietnam became sufficiently untenable.

10. To avoid a "negotiated settlement" at an international conference on the ground that it would almost certainly amount to a sellout of the NLF. (But this did not preclude acceptance, as a tactic, of a coalition government.) In the event that a negotiated settlement might be required because complete victory was impossible or because outright defeat was a growing prospect, the conditions it hoped to achieve included (a) an authentic coalition government that would include elements of the NLF at the cabinet level; (b) an understanding that South Vietnam would pursue a non-aligned but China-leaning foreign policy on the model of Cambodia; (c) closer economic ties with the DRV; (d) amnesty for its followers, or opportunity for them to move to the DRV; and (e) withdrawal of most, but not necessarily all, American military forces.

*   *   *

THE ORGANIZATIONAL WEAPON

The basic characteristics of the NLF and its activities were the use of a united-front organization to establish a mass base of support; organization of the rural people, employing both rational appeals to self-interest and coercion, and then using the specially created social movements in antigovernmental activity; heavy use of various techniques for the communication of ideas to foment social strife; use of specialized military actions, selective in nature and psychological in intent; use of the Communist party *apparat,* and Communist doctrine among the leaders and full-time cadres, to establish orthodoxy and maintain discipline. The goal was control of the population and, through this control, organization of the people as a weapon against the government. But it was more than this. It was more than simply the inculcation of new beliefs or differing attitudes. The NLF's ultimate objective taken together with other activities was to create a new socialization pattern.

The NLF was concerned with the deepest social values. It sought to create a new system of formal and informal groupings by which the socialization was to be accomplished and behavior regulated. It manipulated economic activities, the base for all human activities, in such a way as to increase the degree of communalism or collectivization and thus to some degree alter the village means of production; it introduced a new political structure to keep internal order and to regulate contact within South Vietnam, particularly with respect to villagers hostile to the NLF; it manipulated educational and other intellectual activities within the village. It apparently attempted to substitute a disguised brand of Marxism for traditional religious beliefs, although in an oblique manner; and it introduced a new language terminology, social mythology, and folklore. In short, it attempted to work within the totality of village life and provide a new cultural focus.

Understanding sociopolitical developments in Vietnam involves cataloging the various social and political groups, organizations, cliques, and clans — some of them covert and almost all of them parochial or regional in nature — and then mapping the interrelationships among these various forces. Political infighting consists not so much of open confrontation with one's opponent (or even directly and forcibly destroying him) as it does of drowning, absorbing, splintering, fragmenting, discrediting, turning him aside, or, if necessary, joining him and working at his side to eliminate him. The immediate goal is usually status or prestige more than pure political power. The NLF was superior in this type of political struggle — especially in the rural areas — chiefly because success in this effort depends on good organizational ability and skilled management of social movements. Therefore the secret of NLF success in the early years — and they were many — was organization. Probably the NLF expended more time, money, and manpower on organizational activity than on all other activities combined. Further, this effort was concentrated in what was an organizational vacuum.

In those areas of the country where it had firm and continuous social control the NLF was in effect a society within a society, with its own social structure, values, and coercive instruments. The NLF cadres made a conscious and massive effort to extend political participation, even if it was manipulated, on the local level so as to involve the people in a self-contained, self-supporting revolution. The functional liberation associations at the village level attempted to serve each individual member in terms of his own personal interests while at the same time developing a deep revolutionary consciousness. Ironically, as the result of increased coercion on the part of the NLF, as its popular support dwindled, its actual authority increased. What

had been essentially a persuasive mechanism became basically a coercive one, not so much because of the failure of the original NLF social organization pattern as because of the arrival of Northern cadres who were unwilling to trust the original form because they felt in the long run that it would not serve the interests of the Party and indeed might become a threat to it. Once again, the not unfamiliar story of the revolution betrayed. But the organization at all times, whether persausive or coercive, remained the central NLF activity in the village.

That the leaders of this enterprise were professionals must be evident from the structure they created. It is difficult, however, to estimate the number of NLF leaders and cadres who were professional revolutionaries. Most of them were vastly experienced, some by choice, some by circumstance. The initial NLF leadership corps was made up of the ex-Viet Minh. Many of these, probably the majority, were professionals such as doctors, lawyers, and teachers. They were competent and enjoyed high status among their followers. Most of them had been in the movement, either Viet Minh or NLF, for most of their lives, although generally the guerrilla leaders had served longer than the civilians. Within the NLF these early leaders came to hold the main-line administrative posts or became the commanders of the Main Force units. They were inclined to be more nationalistic and less doctrinal than those who came after them, and they were far less pro-DRV. Those who rose in prominence after the launching of the NLF, that is, in the early 1960's, were more politically oriented, less apt to have a professional background, and therefore of somewhat lower status in the eyes of the rank and file. They were more doctrinal, more anti-GVN, pro-DRV, and pro-Communist. With the regularization came both cadres and top leaders from the North; their great social trauma had been the Viet Minh war. Most had been young cadres during the Viet Minh war and had climbed the status ladder in the North according to DRV standards, which meant they excelled in Communist virtues, technical competence, zeal, discipline, and unwavering faith in the cause. They had a vested interest in victory through following orders from Hanoi, for it was there that their homes were located, their families lived, and their careers were rooted. Their motivation was quite different; it was North Vietnamese whether or not they had originally come from the South. Above all, these Northern-trained leaders, and they were found chiefly in the NLF military apparatus, were professionals, less marked by the self-righteous puritanism that characterized the earliest NLF leadership group or the individual initiative and revolutionary consciousness that marked those who rose in the ranks during the early stages of the insurgency. They were less moved by the deep sense of frustration that drove the earlier leaders, and their devotion to the cause stemmed more from career building than from ideology or hatred.

One of the most persistent questions asked about the NLF follower was "Why did he join?" The implication in the question is that for one or more rational or emotional reasons the individual Vietnamese decided to enlist in the cause, did so, and thus entered as a believer . . . almost the reverse was the case. The Vietnamese youth was first surrounded by a social organization that he had no hand in creating but to which he somehow belonged. Through a process of insinuation the youth came to realize that he was part of the NLF, never quite sure of how this happened and never with any overt choice presented to him. The process of glacially slow recruitment came first, the mystique was developed later. Or, as it has been aptly put, conversion followed subversion. Therefore not motives but circumstances must be considered in understanding the recruitment pattern and its contribution to the NLF mystique.

The most common answer given by a *quy chanh* to questions concerning the circumstances under which he became part of the NLF indicated that he was initially drawn into the organization and later recruited. He might first be asked to act as a messenger, or to take part in a struggle movement, or to deliver leaflets to an agent in the provincial capital. Then he would be urged to join his friends in a study group that might also be a literacy class. Then he would be asked to commit some act of violence; at this point, whether he knew it or not, he was in the net. When handled skillfully, subtly, and gradually, a teen-aged youth did not realize that he was involved until he was already enmeshed. This technique succeeded, for the most part, not in areas where the GVN was exerting itself but in the remote villages where the NLF and the Viet Minh before it were the only visible "government" the youth had ever known. And so the *quy chanh* would say, "Everyone seemed to think it was the correct thing to do," often adding plaintively, "There didn't seem to be any danger. The Saigon government was so far away I didn't think they would ever know about me." Of course a small minority actually sought out and joined the NLF. These included draft dodgers, military deserters, those who hated the government for some personal reason, opportunists, the ambitious who were seeking status, the rejected, the adventurers, and all the others in Eric Hoffer's categories of the True Believer.

For the most part, however, the supporters were recruited under circumstances where there was no alternative. Most recruitment was from among social groups such as the religious sects, with grievances against the government, and less effort was placed on the recruitment of individuals at random. At the same time the NLF sought to create situations that would give rise to grievances among such groups so as to facilitate recruitment. Once the youth was recruited, the training and indoctrination work supplied the rationale for belonging.

Americans and others often assumed that the NLF army members were fanatics. Because they performed well in combat, it was argued, they were highly motivated, which meant dedication to an ideological cause. Thus the search was for the essence of this belief. It proved elusive, largely because it did not exist. The best of the military units — the Main Force units — were highly effective because they were composed of professionals. These were not green young Vietnamese farmers, only recently introduced to the rifle, but experienced guerrillas who had been fighting most of their adult lives. What impelled them was not ideology so much as professional competence, much like the United States Marine or the French Foreign Legionnaire. The men in the best of these units were very good; their discipline was superb; they knew how to use camouflage well, a requirement for survival; they were well skilled in small-unit tactics, especially the ambush in its many variations; they trained hard, rehearsed, and practiced attacks until letter perfect, and then they fought hard. Their mystique should be attributed chiefly to a unit *esprit de corps* that stemmed from the

consensus that each man in the unit was a superior and vastly experienced professional.

DOCTRINAL CEMENT

The strength of the NLF was the result of careful organization building, not the product of some unique spirit or élan. The mystique, to the degree that it existed and bound together the separate building blocks of the movement, resulted from indoctrinational efforts, shared social myths, and leader-led relations. The mystique's functions were, first, identity, stemming from the doctrinal course of the Revolution, the ideology of communism, and the recruitment pattern; and, second, unity, resulting from the nature of the leadership, the indoctrination itself, and individual self-motivating standards of behavior.

Course of the Revolution

The various pseudoscientific laws that the leadership regarded as governing the Revolution were at no time themselves challenged by the NLF followers, nor was the principle that such definitive laws existed. . . .

The leadership considered its chief doctrinal task to be the translation of abstract theory into the setting of a traditional society. It did this by placing prime value on loyalty, as perhaps all such groups must. The Revolution assumed a pragmatic, not greatly intellectual, cast, and it was characterized by an absence of agonizing. It lacked the depth of thought marked by, say, the Russian Revolution and far more resembled the Chinese revolution. To both the NLF and the PRP, determinants of success were twofold: revolutionary capability, including the proclivity for revolution by the Vietnamese people themselves, and PRP leadership, which is to say Commu-

nist leadership. The people's revolutionary capability was more asserted than
proven, and the Party's monopolistic
leadership imposed rather than prescribed. Both developed into articles of
faith, a mystic belief in the power and
loyalty of the people and a sense of trust
in the omniscience of the Party. What
was then required was to put the formula
to work: The people would support the
Revolution if only the cadres would show
them that their interests were identical
to the cause, would constantly agitate
them so as to prevent loss of ardor, and
would develop them into creatures of
initiative who would act and not merely
react.

No evidence was ever uncovered to
indicate that schisms existed in the early
years on the proper course of the Revolution. The quarrel that did develop . . .
lay in writing the final act of the revolutionary drama — whether it should
consist of the General Uprising, the Mao-
Giap third stage, or negotiated settlement. The dispute was resolved in favor
of the Mao-Giap thesis, not through discussion or by successfully decimating the
two other alternatives but because the
new supraleadership in Hanoi concluded
that it represented the correct course to
pursue and used its Northern-trained and
Northern-loyal cadres to force acceptance
of its decision.

However, even in the days when it was
the dominant doctrine, the leadership
consistently overestimated its progress
and several times erroneously believed
that the moment of the General Uprising
had arrived. . . . These failures undoubtedly contributed to the decision to "mili-
tarize" the struggle and pursue victory
by means of the Mao-Giap third stage.
But this triggered a new level of American response, which meant that from a
doctrinal standpoint it had failed as

much as had the General Uprising thesis.

In sum, from a standpoint of mystique
the General Uprising served the NLF
well through the golden days of the Revolution. It was not mere window dress-
ing but the justification and rationaliza-
tion for the insurgency, the cement that
held the effort together, and a powerful
tool for agit-prop team use in working
with villagers. In the end it failed because it was not sufficiently rooted in
reality, because it could work only if the
Communists' assessment of the social
milieu in the South was correct, which
it was not.

The NLF and the people it influenced
lived in a muzzy, myth-filled world of
blacks and whites, good and evil, a simplistic world quite out of character with
the one to which the Vietnamese was
accustomed. But it created a powerful
external image for the Vietnamese im-
mersed in the cause, restructuring his
reality, providing him with a new identity and a boundless sense of unity. The
elements of this mystique were fourfold.

First, it was characterized by great
moralism and was far more moral than
ideological. Virtue was the golden word.
The cause consisted of moral duties
based on moral absolutes, guided by
moral imperatives; duty itself, under a
virtuous leadership, was the highest
value. Preoccupation with law and legal-
ity was not simply an effort to establish
legitimacy but a justification of the moral
correctness of the cause. Because he was
virtuous, the NLF supporter was morally
superior to the enemy and hence politically and militarily superior. The moralism manifested itself in a spirit of sincerity; the NLF surrounded its words
and actions with an aura of sincerity.

Second, it was characterized by extreme romanticism. The NLF leaders,
like Mao Tse-tung and Ho Chi Minh be-

fore them, were romantic rebels who saw themselves as idealists. Idealistic appeals abounded: the promise of the good life in utopian terms; the opportunity to revolt against all the evil, injustice, and inequity of this world; the chance to be part of a great crusade. But behind these was the romantic lure of the struggle itself; the means not the ends counted. There was more glory along the road than at its end. The clandestine organization made up of multitudes of inner groups, cults, and secret arrangements played on the Vietnamese individual's romantic love of the devious, and like Kim along the Grand Trunk Road he played The Game. (A psychiatrist visiting in Vietnam said it was actually a latent homosexual fear of penetration.) Yet in general the NLF mystique was less a positive cause than a negation. But this too had lure to the romantic — the lure of anarchy, beyond which, if it failed, lay the lure of martyrdom. The NLF in creating its mystique was acutely senstive to the age-old Asian attitude of fatalism.

Third, its mystique was imitative and therefore militantly defensive, which probably should be counted as a weakness. The NLF leader was driven by a compulsive search for answers from elsewhere, anywhere. Examples were taken from other places and they were forced, and from other times and they were distorted. If the NLF was not slavishly copying Mao Tse-tung on the Long March, it was employing the Viet Minh's analysis of French Maginot Line thinking as it applied to the Americans, or calling on all cadres to repeat in a literal manner some victory scored a few months earlier in another part of Vietnam. The constant scanning of the horizon was part of a preoccupation with contemplation and self-analysis. Cadres, in a curious

form of intellectualism, would explain the Revolution over and over to their most disinterested students — the rural Vietnamese. Copied though it was, it provided the supporter with a worldview that might not be understood but was satisfactory. Through indoctrination and even socialization he received needed psychological support and release from cultural tensions. (The same psychiatrist said the NLF was a father image led by Ho Chi Minh.)

And finally there was a will to believe, perhaps a characteristic of any mystique. It grew from the sense of universality of a movement representing Vietnam, the world, excluding not even a full social class (the enemies in Saigon and Washington). It was based on an assessment of the world environment that the NLF believed made Revolution in Vietnam irresistible and doomed GVN and U.S. prowess to steady deterioration. It was based on faith in the Vietnamese people's revolutionary capability, faith in the doctrinal approach, faith in revolutionary guerrilla warfare consisting of the combined armed and political struggle, and the infallible wisdom of the Party's leaders, who from long experience could divine the laws of history.

The Role of Communism

Marxism-Leninism as filtered through first Chinese and then Vietnamese thought contributed much to the NLF mystique. . . .

A Communist condition had prevailed within the NLF from the start and was assumed as a matter of course by Vietnamese of all political shadings. With respect to the mystique the matter of communism's paramountcy became somewhat more complex. Partly it was a matter of definition.

If a Communist is one who believes

that man's future is shaped by his tools of production, that history is dominated by a class struggle for control of those means of production, that capitalism must grow increasingly evil, and that a brotherhood of workers and farmers swearing allegiance to an international ideal must unite to seize power and build its own society led by the vanguard, the proletariat, and in turn by the vanguard of the vanguard, the Communist party — if this is a Communist, then there were few Communists among the NLF. If, however, a Communist is one who swears blind allegiance to the world movement whose loci of power are Moscow and Peking, from which in this instance via Hanoi he draws through a political umbilical cord sustenance and strength that he cannot, and does not want to, supply himself, then most of the NLF's leaders, cadres, and true believers were communists.

It was the difference between philosophic communism and alliance communism. For, in the first instance, to be a Communist meant mastering Marxism-Leninism, which NLF Vietnamese found notoriously difficult to understand since it is distinctly un-Vietnamese in nature and at variance with their most deeply ingrained views of the universe. (For example, it must have been indeed a Herculean task for a cadre to convince a Vietnamese that matter and not God or Spirit is the ultimate reality, or that nothing is inherently unknowable.) The second instance meant simply establishing identity and achieving unity in which an NLF supporter had only to approve of the powerful foreign forces that stood behind him and his cause. Only among the higher-echelon cadres, and even here not with total acceptance, was communism regarded as a new body of wisdom to be learned, understood, and put to use.

Thus the NLF was Communist not because it incorporated Communist doctrine but because it linked itself to foreign states that did. This distinction, or weakness, meant that the strengths that hold Communists and Communist movements together during dark days elsewhere were largely absent in Vietnam.

FINAL WORD

There can be little doubt that the combination put together by the NLF was a potent one. However, the fundamental question it raised — to which we have no final answer — is whether victory, that is, seizure of complete political power, could be achieved by means of the social-political-military techniques devised or perfected by the NLF. In NLF terms, to go almost the whole route to victory, to go up to the actual portals of victory, and then see one's forces either recede or be pushed back could mean only that the whole venture was futile and a failure. As in sports, it is the final score that counts. Using the General Uprising thesis the NLF came perilously close to victory — it was standing at the gates in December of 1963 and again in the spring of 1965 — but both times victory somehow eluded it. The conclusion of the Northerners, who by 1965 dominated the NLF, was that the General Uprising thesis could carry the movement along the path toward victory but could not carry it the entire route. And so the order came to switch doctrines and pursue the effort in the pattern of the Viet Minh war. Some Southern NLF members believed this was a disastrous mistake, that only the General Uprising thesis could win — but we will never know whether they were right. The possibility of the NLF returning to the General Uprising thesis was regarded by Vietnamese as remote. Said one *quy chanh*, "to return to the *khoi nghia* would be to slow down a typhoon; there is no such thing as a slow typhoon, for when a typhoon slows down it breaks up."

In the final resolve perhaps the Northerners were right. The NLF's functional liberation associations were highly effective, yet its organizational efforts among important ethnic and religious groups were far less successful. The social changes brought to the liberated area were perhaps more apparent than real. The NLF administrative liberation association was more manipulated than participational, and such an arrangement usually carries with it the seeds of its own doom. The great emphasis on communication of ideas failed to achieve its principal goal: The rural Vietnamese, lacking informational background, often failed to understand in context the meaning of the message. The rural Vietnam-

ese knew little about the social forces loose in his country and even less about the outside world, and he greeted NLF efforts to remedy this deficiency with indifference — the condition of parochialism in which the next village is in the other world dies hard in Asia. Finally, the effort mounted by the NLF required a type of cadre — talented, skilled, dedicated, an almost superhuman person — that did not exist in sufficient numbers to ensure success.

Yet the principles involved remain intact. The deeper one plunged into the study of the NLF the stronger became the feeling of being on the edge of a future social morass, only dimly seen. Here, one felt, was tomorrow's society, the beginning of 1984, when peace is war, slavery is freedom, the nonorganization is the organization.

Melvin Gurtov: HANOI ON WAR AND PEACE

In this original essay by a member of the Social Science Department of The RAND Corporation, the North Vietnamese (DRV) perspective on the war is analyzed: Hanoi's view of the American and South Vietnamese (GVN) enemy, the balance of forces, the communist great powers, and the conduct of negotiations.

IN THE COURSE of a lengthy conversation in Hanoi, Harrison Salisbury of the *New York Times* was told by North Vietnamese Premier Pham Van Dong that the war in Vietnam is a *"guerre sacrée"* — a "sacred war" embodying the spirit of national resistance that sustains North Vietnam's will to fight. The fact that Hanoi, confronted for over two years

with the systematic devastation of resources that took a decade to amass and build, has stubbornly pursued its war aims argues strongly against summarily dismissing Dong's remark as mere propaganda. The willingness to sacrifice hard-won achievements for the sake of a larger, though uncertain, future goal — here, the reunification of Vietnam — has

This paper was originally reproduced by The RAND Corporation, and is printed here with the permission of its author. Any views expressed in it are those of the author. They should not be interpreted as reflecting the views of The RAND Corporation or the official opinion or policy of any of its governmental or private research sponsors.

many precedents in wartime; like the constant calls Hanoi makes to its people to accept long-term hardship, this fierce resolution on the part of the DRV (Democratic Republic of Vietnam) leadership brings to mind similar reactions from besieged governments in the past. Thus, the rationale behind Pham Van Dong's talk of a *guerre sacrée* warrants close analysis, for the term implies a perception of the Vietnam conflict fundamentally different from our own in content as well as image.

This essay, then, while not pretending to be an "inside" glimpse into the deepest thoughts of Hanoi's decision-makers, does seek to offer some suggestive remarks about how and why they view the war the way they do. As with most analyses of a wartime opponent, this one relies on what is considered relevant of his past policies and practices, what he directly and indirectly tells the rest of the world as well as his own people, and what seems to be his major and secondary criteria for making assessments. Four areas have been selected for inquiry: Hanoi's primary assumptions regarding the United States and the Government of Vietnam (GVN); its assessment of the balance of forces in more recent years; its maneuvering within the Sino-Soviet rift, and particularly its relations with Communist China; and its standpoint on negotiations and their aftermath. These areas, while not exhaustive, seem to provide sufficient breadth for attempting to view the war through a different set of lenses — those of the North Vietnamese. Like any other state, North Vietnam has an independent orientation toward the war deriving from its own value system, sense of history, and national purpose. Whatever may be the true reality of the war — if, indeed, there is one — the DRV clearly

has its own version. Whether or not we share it is scarcely as important as acting in accordance with out understanding of it.

THE NATURE OF HANOI'S ENEMY

How the North Vietnamese leadership perceives the United States and the Government of Vietnam is obviously central to its attitude on war and peace. Whatever the "objective reality" of American willpower and U.S.–GVN capability, it is North Vietnam's perception of those characteristics which ultimately dictates its choice of strategy.

To Hanoi, the fundamental principle of the Vietnam conflict is that the United States is the invader and the Liberation Armed Forces (LAF, i.e., the Viet Cong and North Vietnamese Armies) the defenders of the nation. The United States, the world's leading imperialist power, is said to be carrying out what Lenin termed an "unjust" war, one in which the predatory nature of expansionism arouses the patriotic motivations of the oppressed nation. The root cause of conflict is therefore the offensive thrust of imperialism, which can only be deflected by the defensive efforts of socialism in a "just" war of liberation. Like the Soviet Red Army in its resistance against the Wehrmacht, the LAF find their greatest strength in being on the defensive against the imperialist invaders, in the same manner as other Vietnamese armies have withstood foreign incursions in the past.

North Vietnam's perpetual optimism is not only based on the imperialistic aims it attaches to the American presence in Vietnam; it also centers on the conviction that the great material power of the United States, which Hanoi does not deny, cannot overcome the tendency, common to all imperialist armies, to decay as the result of inherent weaknesses that build up over time. This way of looking at things borrows liberally from the Maoist prescription: once it is perceived that the American presence creates more difficulties for the United States than it resolves and that those difficulties are "antagonistic contradictions" (a Chinese Communist term) inevitable in relations between socialist and imperialist nations, then by capitalizing on those contradictions, a correct overall policy will emerge.

The kinds of contradictions (see the table on page 55) which the North Vietnamese see besetting the allies in South Vietnam are: contradictions in the imperialist camp as a whole; contradictions implicit in the American involvement in Vietnam; contradictions in American society; contradictions in GVN–U.S. relations; and contradictions between the Americans and the GVN on the one hand, and the Vietnamese people on the other. These are dealt with below.

1. Contradictions in the Imperialist Camp

In the imperialist camp, the American position is believed by the North Vietnamese to have weakened considerably over the years. They cite the lack of coordination and unanimity in such "aggressive blocs" as SEATO, CENTO, and NATO; and they declare that while the imperialist camp has weakened, the Communist camp has become stronger. These developments are, of course, favorable to North Vietnam's efforts for national reunification.

2. Contradictions of the U.S. Involvement

As already observed, the basic contradiction of the American "intervention" in Vietnam is the "unjust" war which the U.S.–GVN forces wage against the "just"

cause of the LAF, which struggle beside and for "the people." The contradictions are therefore between imperialist and civil war, between neocolonialist and national liberation war, between the exploiters and the oppressed — in short, between a policy of aggressive war and a policy of peace.

At a second level, the U.S. involvement is also perceived from Hanoi as having produced insuperable obstacles for the Americans even as it has forced the war into a new stage of greater destruction and wider boundaries. American technological supremacy, say the North Vietnamese, is contradicted by tactical inferiority: for all its advanced war machinery and firepower, the United States remains unable to match LAF maneuverability and knowledge of the terrain. In the air war against North Vietnam, moreover, U.S. escalation has only short-term significance. In the longer run, the bombing of the North tends to increase cohesion in the socialist bloc and, being a desperation measure, proves how much the United States is bogged down in South Vietnam.

3. Contradictions in American Society

While the contradiction between real and artificial power is apparent to Hanoi in the U.S. effort in Vietnam, there are equally, if not more, harmful contradictions within American society. President Johnson believes there is general pro-war sentiment in the United States; in fact, say the DRV leaders, the American people want peace. General Tran Do, for instance, has commented that the President's polls taken after U.S. attacks on Hanoi were incorrectly interpreted by the White House as showing increased popular support for Administration policy. Actually, the American people were expressing their desire for peace, for they "think that by bombing, the war can be rapidly ended and peace can be quickly restored."

(Major General Tran Do is one of eight North Vietnamese generals known to be commanding Viet Cong forces. He is Deputy Commander of the Viet Cong and an alternate member of the Central Committee of the Lao Dong (Worker's) Party of North Vietnam. Quotations by General Do are from a taped speech to the North Vietnamese Seventh Division in South Vietnam during August 1966. Parts of the recording were captured in January 1967 and made public by the U.S. Embassy, Saigon.)

America's weakness on the home front is also demonstrable, the North Vietnamese believe, in the psychological aversion of capitalist societies to protracted war. Not being used to hardships, Americans cannot for long endure a struggle that seems endless. As Tran Do has phrased it:

In fact it is a very arduous task for the Americans to fight a protracted war although they are a well-to-do people. We can endure the hardships of a lengthy war, but they are unable to endure the hardships of such a war because they are well-to-do people. A poor man can subsist by spending one piaster a day, but a man who is accustomed to living in comfort is uncomfortable even though he spends 10 piasters a day . . .

As war costs mount, the North Vietnamese expect that U.S. capitalist society, despite its vast riches, will not be able to sustain the financial burden.

4. Contradictions in GVN–U.S. Relations

Although the American effort is supposedly to assist the "puppet" Saigon regime, the inherent contradictions between the United States and the GVN will eventually produce the opposite effect. For all the assistance which the United States provides, the GVN will never attain stability. American aid has produced crime, economic disruption, usurpation of property, and incredible corruption, all of which will lead to the GVN's downfall. Furthermore, because American advice has turned into control, Vietnamese have come to understand that the Thieu-Ky regime, like its predecessors, has sold the country to foreigners. Thus, so-called U.S.–GVN cooperation is bound to be short-circuited by the disastrous side effects of total U.S. involvement.

5. Contradictions Between the U.S.– GVN and the People

The deeper American involvement, the more obvious is American control of the war, of the Saigon government, of the Vietnamese economy, and of Vietnamese society. Far from "liberating" the Vietnamese people, further American commitments to South Vietnam will certainly increase the antagonism which the people already feel for U.S. forces and their "lackeys."

Hanoi's perception of a wide range of contradictions affecting the American position in Vietnam by no means denigrates the immediacy of the U.S. threat. Contradictions are by nature long-term, requiring resolution over an extended period through military and political "struggle." In the course of resolving contradictions, a clear and present danger exists that the enemy, because he does not recognize the futility of his position, will continue to pursue reckless policies harmful to the liberation movement. Thus the United States, instead of becoming reconciled to defeat, has become more deeply involved in the war. Believing, like Mao, that the "logic" of imperialists is to "fail, fail again . . . until their doom," Hanoi has warned Communist troops in South Vietnam that American stubbornness has a staying power of its own. As put by General Do, the Americans "will not let themselves be brought to their knees like the French, who only wanted to do away with the fighting once and for all no matter how . . . They [the Americans] may be able to go on for *a short period of time* because of their stubborn nature. If they intend to continue for *five or ten years,* they will learn that we are a terribly difficult lot to deal with." (Emphasis added.) Thus, Hanoi finds it is the nature of the enemy to react negatively (by escalation) to defeat even though riven with unsolvable contradictions. In the just war, only protracted conflict can take advantage of those contradictions, mitigate the effects of imperialist recklessness, and reap the fruits of patience and endurance.

THE NORTH VIETNAMESE PERCEPTION OF CONTRADICTIONS IN THE "ENEMY" CAMP

Type of Contradiction	Substance of Contradiction	Result of Contradiction
1. Imperialist Camp	Distintegration of aggressive blocs and disagreement among imperialist powers *vs.* cohesion in socialist world over Vietnam.	Weakening of imperialist camp, strengthening of socialist camp.
2. U.S. Involvement in Vietnam	Imperialist *vs.* civil war; neocolonialist *vs.* national liberation war; exploiters *vs.* oppressed people. Technological supremacy *vs.* tactical inferiority.	"Just" struggle must succeed, "unjust" struggle must fail. People's war can prevail over technically superior foe; escalation founded on defeat.
3. U.S. Society	U.S. Government fights a war not supported by American people. American wealth *vs.* psychological incapacity to withstand long-term war.	American people will force Government to end the war. American people will react against costs of the war.
4. U.S.–GVN Relations	U.S. assistance *vs.* debilitating effects of that assistance in GVN economy, society, administration.	GVN will be recognized as having sold the country to foreigners.
5. U.S.–GVN and Vietnamese People	U.S. involvement *vs.* U.S. control of the war, the government, and society.	The people's antagonism toward the Americans increases.

THE BALANCE OF FORCES

For all their unwillingness to credit Chinese military theory, the North Vietnamese do abide by it. In their overall tactical assessment, the guideline is the familiar maxim of Sun Tzu: know the enemy and know oneself. Thus, Hanoi no less than Peking holds that only when the full array of enemy strengths and weaknesses is matched against "friendly" strengths and weaknesses can the equations of individual battles, large-scale campaigns, and the war itself be solved. It appears that the DRV leadership considers this balance of forces not to have been basically affected by the admittedly changed war picture since 1965. While recognizing their own failings, the North

Vietnamese continue to believe these are correctable, whereas those in the enemy camp will increase over time without being resolved.

Changing Assessments, 1965–1966

There is little doubt that the introduction of a large number of U.S. troops into South Vietnam during 1965, to the point where the year-end total of nearly 200,000 represented a quadrupling of American combat troops involved at the year's beginning, had a major impact on North Vietnamese war planning. Prior to the increase, North Vietnamese and Viet Cong assessments confidently concluded that the long-awaited "general uprising and general offensive" could take place during 1965 and bring about final victory in a short time span. After the increase, and probably because of it, the Lao Dong [North Vietnamese Communist] Party Central Committee convened its 12th plenum (December) to determine, among other things, whether in fact protracted war remained a viable strategic alternative.

The basic decisions of the Party Central Committee have become known to us as the result of the capture during 1967 of a "top secret" resolution issued by the Central Office for South Vietnam (COSVN), which is not only the leading politico-military organ of the Viet Cong, but is also the coordinator of directives from the Lao Dong Party to its "Southern branch," the People's Revolutionary Party (PRP). (This document was released to the press by the U.S. Embassy, Saigon, August 18, 1967.) The COSVN resolution, drafted during its 4th Congress in March 1966, was clearly the product of the Central Committee session of the previous December. Consequently, we now know that the North Vietnamese decided that the overall military strategy would be to gain "a decisive victory in a relatively short period of time," but within the framework of protracted struggle. The strategy required that as many American and "puppet" (GVN) forces as possible had to be put out of action; the goal set was between 30,000 and 40,000 U.S. soldiers, plus about 200,000 "puppet" troops. To achieve these ambitious aims, all three types of forces — guerrillas, regional units, and regular units — would be required as before; but guerrilla warfare was said to have the greatest potentiality "in both causing the attrition of and the destruction of the American and puppet forces . . ." In contrast to Chinese advice (to judge from their newspaper commentaries on the war), the North Vietnamese found it perfectly feasible to shift back and forth between so-called phase two (guerrilla) and phase three (conventional) warfare: "All the armed forces, from the regular forces to the regional forces, shall be responsible for participating in, assisting, and emphasizing guerrilla warfare."

This tactical shift evidently did not change North Vietnam's overall strategic outlook. Protracted war, as already noted, was still considered the proper approach, especially as the United States was seen to have moved from a stage of "special war," where reliance was on the advisory effort, to "limited war," where U.S. troops would undertake a major share of the fighting. What *did* change in North Vietnamese thinking was the time thought necessary to win the protracted war. In sharp contrast to early 1965, the resolution now considered that the LAF were merely to be "in preparation for a general attack and uprising which will take place when the opportunity avails itself and the situation ripens." The quick victory which, quite legitimately, was foreseen in early 1965 could no longer be anticipated.

Despite these apparent reassessments, Hanoi's optimism has not sharply diminished. And this optimism seems to rest, as much now as before, largely on the differing nature of difficulties believed facing the U.S.–"puppet" alliance on one side and the LAF on the other. As stated by Tran Do, the enemy's problems are so enormous and so complex that they can never be resolved. "Such difficulties as conflicting strategic matters, and low morale that becomes progressively worse, cannot be overcome." The problems facing the LAF, on the other hand, are those common to a movement that is growing and victorious. Thus, Tran Do has urged the NVA:

You must adopt a revolutionary spirit, you must look at things in a revolutionary and materialistic way, only then can you see that the difficulties and the weaknesses of the enemy are fundamental while yours are only temporary in nature. Our difficulties can be overcome, because they are inherent in the growing-up process.

What, precisely, is believed to undermine America's surface appearance of strength? According to various North Vietnamese commentaries, the principal U.S.–GVN weaknesses relate to problems of planning, manpower, technology, and morale — all of which, in combination with the internal contradictions already mentioned, erode enemy capabilities. Thus, strategically, the U.S. must face the fact that massive manpower increments in the South will only "gain some temporary advantages." The American command knows full well that 100,000 additional troops will be insufficient, especially since GVN forces are incapable of undertaking important military assignments. Hence, the Americans' real

problem is how and whether they "can bring in more men, say 500,000 or 600,000 or even 750,000," as General Do has put it. Second, and closely related to manpower planning, the United States must give serious thought to calling up the reserves. New recruits cannot be trained fast enough to be important to the war effort. Third, once-impressive U.S. military technology (e.g., the B-52's) has lost its frightening aspect; the LAF are now used to new weapons by experience. Finally, with his elite units beaten back, the enemy is faced with a serious morale problem. The LAF have been able to repulse attacks by the enemy's best units, causing his confidence to wane.

Against these American weaknesses, the LAF are said to possess considerable strength. In terms of manpower, the LAF have an "inexhaustible source" in North Vietnam, which is already sending "five or six thousand [men] each month" (Tran Do). Further, U.S. Air Force attacks on the DRV have not only resulted in high aircraft losses, but have also bolstered the morale of the Vietnamese people, as evidenced (according to Tran Do) in the "bitter reply" given U.S. attacks by Ho Chi Minh's call for a partial mobilization. Hanoi's very determination is a spur to the LAF. Finally, and perhaps most importantly, there is the Communists' staying power. The United States may state publicly that it can support the war for many years; "but as a matter of fact," Tran Do has remarked, the Americans "are actually apprehensive because the Vietnamese have fought continuously for ten years. There is no doubt about their concern." The persistent emphasis in NLF and Hanoi propaganda over the past two years on Vietnam's historic liberation struggles, of which the present conflict is the latest phase, lends credence to the view that prolonged fighting is regarded from Hanoi as one of the LAF's greatest assets. Even an enemy as intransigent as the United States cannot outlast Vietnamese who have been defending their country against foreign incursions for centuries.

Precisely because the North Vietnamese regard their tenacity as a major impediment to a U.S.–GVN success, the strategic imperative must be protracted struggle. The fact that the Americans are different from the French does not make the Americans any less vulnerable to prolonged conflict. Indeed, the longer the war, the more certain it is that the enemy's internal contradictions will multiply and intensify; already, Tran Do has said, the United States faces a "new strategic deadlock" because of its uncertainty over how many more troops it will require. Yet protracted war should not mean endless exchanges of blows with the enemy. As was true in 1965, protracted war must be coupled with "a decisive victory in a relatively short time." These two concepts are not contradictory; rather, they are mutually reinforcing, and stem from North Vietnam's definition of "victory."

Hanoi on "Victory": Its Nature and Timing

As used by Hanoi, "victory" does not refer to the final seizure of power from the Saigon government. Rather the term has two different and separate meanings: first, one or more decisive battlefield triumphs that will bring about a turning point in the war; second, partial annihilation of U.S. forces and near-total disintegration of Saigon forces, leading inescapably to an American withdrawal.

If these interpretations are accurate, the distinction in North Vietnamese statements between "a decisive victory in a relatively short time" and continued pro-

traction of the war is significant. The infliction of a single major defeat (Dienbienphu is the obvious precedent) or several defeats on the enemy will not end the war, but will so undermine his effort that he will be forced to reassess his total politico-military position. Thus, Tran Do stressed the importance of a dry season "victory" during 1966, by which he meant not a consummate success forcing the United States immediately to withdraw, but rather one or more triumphs of such proportions as to trigger a chain reaction of LAF successes that will further increase the tendency in Saigon toward disintegration and the strategic "deadlock" within the U.S. command over troop reinforcements. Tran Do hence characterized the dry season as "the key to change the face of the war and to change the balance of forces to *bring us nearer to bigger victories*, to push them [U.S.–GVN forces] to bigger defeats, to make them more willful and reckless." (Emphasis added). Significantly, Tran Do's comrades were advised to avoid the slogan current before the U.S. buildup — "the decisive victory is near" — and to employ instead the "more significant" phrase, "go forward to gain continuous and greater successes." Clearly, a "decisive victory" must take place, as Hanoi sees it, *within the context of* protracted struggle.

"Victory" defined as major short-term successes with long-term impact may also mean, for Hanoi, the attainment of a particular level of destruction against enemy forces. The North Vietnamese apparently believe it is neither possible nor necessary to destroy the Americans' entire military structure in South Vietnam. What can be of equal value, they seem to think, is the *psychological* impact on the U.S. command and on U.S. domestic opinion of mounting casualties, which will eventually so demoralize American official and public circles that pressure for withdrawal will prove irresistible. Here, however, Hanoi seems also to distinguish between American and other forces. Toward the South Vietnamese army, LAF strategy apparently entails the more ambitious aim of actually reducing it to the level of ineffectiveness. With the GVN armed forces no longer capable of even playing a supporting role, and with U.S. troops being forced to take heavy losses in order to keep South Vietnam from crumbling, the DRV sees every prospect that short-term "decisive victories" will evolve into long-term "victory."

Protracted war, then, does not appear to have a set timetable for the North Vietnamese leadership. To the contrary, as General Do has revealed, the Lao Dong Central Committee decided in December 1965 "to fight better and not to set up a time schedule for our fighting." A timetable was criticized as "rather too mechanical . . . , besides the fact that you have inadvertently imposed limitation on your facilities." In short, the Party has evidently decided that adherence to a rigid time frame is directly contrary to the open-ended nature of protracted war such as now must be fought until the Americans decide to leave Vietnam.

NORTH VIETNAM AND THE COMMUNIST BLOC

North Vietnam's ability to exact whatever material assistance its socialist bloc allies are comparatively advantaged to provide, and at the same time to avoid compromising its independence in policy-making, remains the signal achievement of the wartime Hanoi regime. While some analysts still choose to label Hanoi's leaders "pro-Soviet," "pro-Chinese," and "neutral," and then to assess DRV foreign policy in terms of the relative weight of Soviet and Chinese "influence," the reality of the situation seems closer to the opposite. Since 1954, the North Vietnamese have more often *adapted* the policies of other states (sometimes, as in the case of land reform, with disastrous results) than merely taken foreign orders or slavishly emulated non-Vietnamese programs. This experimentation has been particularly apparent, and thus far eminently successful, in foreign policy. At times to the chagrin of the Chinese and Soviets, Hanoi, by mastering the art of tightrope walking, has been able to avoid making a full-fledged ideological or political commitment to either power, yet has kept both at bay with piecemeal gestures of approbation. Moscow and Peking, trapped by the peculiar logic of their relationship and the demands of international politics, have probably concluded that they can only turn their backs on Hanoi to the detriment of larger policy interests. The DRV thus has reason to be proud of the way it has maneuvered between (and, one might even add, manipulated) its allies; but it is undoubtedly well aware that its vacillating position can be as much a liability tomorrow as it is an asset today.

Somewhat paradoxically, the escalating Vietnam conflict has increased both Hanoi's war burden and its maneuverability. Subjected to attack by the leading "imperialist" power, North Vietnam commands the attention and support of the entire socialist world. In the past, Hanoi felt disposed to accommodate to Moscow and Peking on foreign policy issues, although in differing proportion; but now that the war has spread to the North, the DRV, while still seeking to satisfy both allies, has not, so far as we are aware, conceded them either ultimate control of their aid or any of the prerogatives of decision-making. Far from having been forced to adjust its foreign policy to the demands of its bene-factors, the DRV has politely acknowl-edged Russian and Chinese munificence and then proceeded to frame decisions in accordance with Vietnamese interests.

The vagaries of North Vietnam's rela-tions with China illuminate this point. The Peking- Hanoi alliance has evolved, in large part because of the war, into a partnership of equals undoubtedly dis-tasteful in many ways to the Chinese. By the beginning of intense bombings of North Vietnam in the spring of 1965, Hanoi had apparently come to consider the Chinese more reliable allies than the Soviets in its fight for survival in the North and "liberation" of the South. Prior to that time, the Soviet Union had failed to respond to North Vietnamese gestures of ideological support, such as Party First Secretary Le Duan's speech of March 13, 1963 approving the notion of peaceful transition to power during revolutionary struggles. When Liu Shao-ch'i visited Hanoi in May 1963, therefore, the DRV took a number of steps in China's direction by backing Peking's position on the conflict with In-dia, the "liberation" of Taiwan, a China seat in the United Nations, and the inde-pendence and equality of Communist states in policy-making. Moscow's sub-sequent signing of the test-ban treaty led the DRV to state, like Peking, that the agreement would undercut Commu-nist bloc unity and should be rejected. Moreover, on the important issue of nu-clear weapons and global strategy, Le Duan, in December 1963, stressed the importance of not falling into a "defen-sive strategy"; the socialist world, he declared in support of China's stand-point, was already sufficiently stronger than the capitalist world to justify revo-lutionary struggle without fear of pro-voking a world war. Finally, proper obeisance was paid the brilliance and creativity of Mao Tse-tung. Mao was said by Le Duan . . . to have originated the theory of peasant-led revolution in agri-culturally based countries, and to have devised tactics which were "exemplary . . . for many Communists in Asia, Africa, and Latin America."

If these deviations from the Soviet line were in any way intended to provoke Moscow into greater commitments to the growing insurgency in South Vietnam, they apparently failed. Promises of sub-stantial aid for the Viet Cong were not made, it appears, when Le Duan led a North Vietnamese mission to Moscow in early 1964. This situation, coupled with China's positive response to the first U.S. air attacks on North Vietnam (August 1964) — with the equation "aggression against the DRV is aggression against China" — almost certainly led Hanoi to conclude then that Peking was the best hope for staunch support of liberation war.

Perhaps with considerable reluctance, the Soviet Union did come forth with important assistance to Hanoi once the bombing became a daily occurrence in March 1965. The U.S. attacks had transformed the Vietnam conflict, after all, from a limited "national liberation war" into a direct challenge to the ex-istence of a fellow socialist state. Fur-thermore, Vietnam had become a burn-ing issue in Chinese charges of Soviet "cowardice" before the U.S. threat; Pe-king termed the war the "focal point" of the world revolutionary struggle. The challenge, consequently, was as much to the Soviet Union as to Hanoi, and the resultant limited Soviet involvement in the war no doubt provided the leverage

Hanoi needed to stop short of acquiesing completely in China's foreign policy line.

In the past two years, Hanoi's half-way agreement with Peking has revealed itself in a number of ways. On the one hand, DRV spokesmen have frequently praised China's aid (mostly foodstuffs, construction materials, and personnel, resources for the development of light industry, and light arms) and spirit of sacrifice, and applauded China's consideration that the two countries remain as close as "lips to teeth"; lauded Chinese technological achievements, particularly with atomic and hydrogen devices; supported and remained close to the rabidly anti-Soviet Albanian Worker's Party; scathingly attacked Yugoslav (but not Soviet) "modern revisionism"; and rejected intimations of Chinese interference or tampering with Soviet aid shipped to North Vietnam via China.

But the DRV has not toed the line on other matters probably equally important to Peking. Overturning its previous views, Hanoi now refuses to acknowledge that the war in South Vietnam evidences the correctness or brilliance of *Mao's* doctrine of people's war; instead, North Vietnamese military authorities hold, in what Peking must deem a heresy, that it is *the Lao Dong Party* which, on the basis of past Vietnamese experience against foreign invaders, has creatively developed the people's war in the South. North Vietnam's struggle for national unity, it is claimed, is unique in the history of liberation movements; were this not the case, outside assistance alone would not account for the DRV's success against the Americans.

Hanoi boasts of being an ideological no less than a military innovator. Le Duan, for instance, no longer repeats his 1963 comment on peasant revolution. In a major theoretical statement of December 1966 which, significantly, was not published until the following May, he asserted that Vietnam's revolutionary struggle was never and could never be led by the peasant class. The working class, although numerically inferior, is always the core element, the implication being that the Party has consistently guided the revolution along lines quite different from those pursued in Maoist China.

Also at sharp variance with Peking has been Hanoi's thinly veiled criticism of the "great cultural revolution" on the mainland. Official DRV organs have pointedly failed to rejoice in or even directly refer to that major event, yet have indirectly attacked it by chiding those national leaders (such as Mao) who, unlike Ho Chi Minh, have been deified to the detriment of close Party relations with the masses.

In the international context, the North Vietnamese have maintained a certain flexibility on the question of negotiations to end the war. They have refused to consider the Geneva accords "scrapped" (as Peking has long insisted), and have apparently decided that the "four points" can be subjects for discussion rather than (as China would prefer) the absolute preconditions for peace talks. Finally, whereas Chinese leaders have castigated those nations that refuse to take a firm position on the Sino-Soviet dispute, the North Vietnamese have maintained their neutrality and consistently called for the very "united action" on the war which the Chinese vigorously assail.

Hanoi's evident tenacity on foreign policy issues that potentially may compromise its independence probably stems from its boundless faith, anchored in Vietnamese history, that the expulsion of invaders such as the Americans can be accomplished primarily through its own efforts. Yet the DRV has admitted that international aid is vital to the war effort; its continuing calls for unity in the socialist bloc apparently reflect the view that victory would come sooner were Moscow and Peking acting in concert. The dilemma facing the North Vietnamese may therefore be that while victory is achievable through long-term patience and endurance, the allies whose assistance can guarantee success show no sign of readiness to set aside their differences for North Vietnam's sake; their aid, however valuable, falls short of the optimal level their unity could provide and, should their relations worsen, the danger exists that Hanoi might be called upon either to choose between them or, barring that, to make important concessions on their independence in policy-making.

NEGOTIATIONS AND AFTER

As we have already observed, North Vietnam's position on negotiations by no means coincides with China's. That position drew direct fire from Peking when it reduced, in January 1967, to the single precondition of U.S. cessation of the bombing of the North; the Chinese may well be concerned that while Hanoi today is not at the bargaining table, its public posture leaves open the chance that tomorrow it may accept a date for talks to begin. Leaving aside the question of a possible agenda, which for Hanoi apparently means the four points originally proposed by Pham Van Dong on April 8, 1965, recent North Vietnamese documents illuminate Hanoi's policy on the timing of, participants in, and future of Vietnam after negotiations. As with other matters, the DRV's determination to retain a free hand is indisputable.

A brief glance at recent history seems worthwhile to provide the setting for the DRV's attitude toward a war settlement.

Hanoi's present approach, it seems, parallels that adopted in the months prior to and during the Geneva Conference of 1954. It will be recalled that, by late 1953, the Viet Minh were preparing for the "general counteroffensive" that would end the war — the same position taken and subsequently retracted by COSVN in early 1965. While the French, with full American support, were busily implementing the much touted Navarre Plan for the defense of Dienbienphu, the Viet Minh enjoyed considerable territorial advantage in northeastern Laos, the Tonkin Delta, and parts of central and southern Vietnam. From Ho Chi Minh's viewpoint, however, the military situation in late 1953 was not sufficiently favorable to justify negotiations. His peace feelers in November and December were intended more to influence French political and public opinion than to manifest an interest in negotiating for an equitable settlement.

When the Big Four (the United States, Great Britain, France, and the Soviet Union) concluded a conference on Germany and Austria in February 1954 with the announcement that an international roundtable would be convened to discuss Indochina in late April, the Viet Minh could not have been pleased. Negotiations in the absence of a decisive military victory, Viet Minh broadcasts of the time implied, were premature. But Viet Minh interests were evidently less important than Soviet and Chinese interests; for separate reasons, Moscow and Peking favored gathering at Geneva to discuss the Indochina question.

With significant Chinese assistance, the Viet Minh still attained their decisive victory at Dienbienphu the day before the first Geneva session on Indochina (May 8, 1954). But as was the case in Soviet agreement to bring the Indochina war to the conference table, potential

Viet Minh bargaining advantages based on predominant territorial control were erased by higher priorities in other Communist capitals. The Viet Minh's basic position at the Conference was that a military solution, i.e., a cease-fire, had to await a prior political solution, i.e., the establishment of conditions for an all-Vietnamese settlement certain to produce a Vietnam united under Ho Chi Minh. From the conference record, it is abundantly clear that the chief Soviet and Chinese delegates, Molotov and Chou En-Lai, worked independently of their Vietnamese allies, initiated many of the vital concessions for a settlement, and consequently sharply undercut the Viet Minh position. The Viet Minh were left with little alternative but to accept terms different at almost every point both from their original demands and their compromise proposals. Political and military solutions occurred simultaneously at considerable sacrifice of Viet Minh-held territory. The very real Viet Minh capacity to continue military action in the event of an unsatisfactory political settlement was overridden by their self-appointed leaders.

Hanoi's position today can only be understood against the background of the events of 1954. Now an independent member of the socialist camp — a point the DRV consistently brings home — Hanoi is evidently determined that the Geneva experience not be repeated. The line of 1954, namely, that negotiations be undertaken only when the military phase of the war assures success, remains virtually unaltered. This much is clear from the COSVN 12th Resolution referred to earlier: ". . . we are determined," this document states, "not to entertain any illusions concerning a negotiated settlement of the problem of Vietnam . . . Only when the American imperialists' aggressive will is crushed and the objectives of independence, peace, democracy, and

neutrality of the South are guaranteed can we negotiate a settlement of the Vietnam problem." Apparently anxious to avoid the fatal error of 1954 by not exploiting military gains for diplomatic leverage, the same document urges that political and military "struggle" proceed hand in hand so that, "*At a certain time, we can apply the strategy of fighting and negotiating at the same time*, in order to support the armed struggle, and thus accelerate the disintegration of the puppet army and regime, and create more conditions favorable for our people to win a decisive victory." (Emphasis supplied.) When negotiations occur, military "struggle" clearly will not cease.

Confirmation of COSVN's instructions on negotiations comes from General Do. From the context of his remarks, it would seem that Do, although a ranking party figure, was wearing his army hat when he spoke to the 7th NVA Division. Perhaps more concerned than his Party comrades about the timing of negotiations, Do argued forcefully that peace talks should not be permitted to interfere with successful culmination of the military struggle:

Our basic intention is to win militarily. We use military victories as decisive factors to end the present conflict. *We want to end the war through military victories and not peace negotiations.* Negotiations are a form of diplomatic struggle. *We are military men* and we must concern ourselves with military struggles and not consider diplomatic struggles . . . we must gain military victories *before even thinking* diplomatic struggles. And even when we are fighting diplomatically, we must go on with our war efforts, we must multiply our military victories if we want to succeed diplomatically. (Emphasis added.)

For Tran Do, then, the military struggle takes priority over the political struggle;

one cannot even "think" about negotiating in the absence of military victories.

We cannot say that Tran Do was at the time of his talk concerned about a danger he perceived to the army's position, although he did criticize "some of our comrades" for not being as "determined" as the Americans. What is unequivocal is his conviction that the army's duty is to carry on armed struggle in order to assure that a negotiatory solution confirms Hanoi's complete victory. He told the troops, for instance, that the Party can carry on its diplomatic contest with "one hundred men or less," while "we belong to the hundreds of thousands who have to fight with weapons, and all we have to do is to fight, there is nothing else for us to do." He admonished the men not to be disturbed by "stories" suggesting that "the [U.S.-] proposed negotiation can end the present conflict . . ." The army not only fights *for* peace, but also to "seize" it. "We must remain until the final victory," he concluded. Tran Do, in sum, seems to have stated the army's "hard line" for not stopping the fight until the hard-won achievements of the past are secured in total victory.

While Tran Do's comments may indicate the NVA's sensitivity to Party control over the precise moment for shifting from military to political struggle, he did not challenge the view that the decision to negotiate rests with the Politburo of the Lao Dong Party Central Committee. "Negotiation or diplomatic struggle is the work of the Central Headquarters and the Politburo; we [in the army] do not have to worry about [those matters]," the General stated. His assertion of the Lao Dong's primacy in the military and political spheres, coupled with the previously-cited comment of the COSVN resolution that the People's Revolutionary Party is merely a "vanguard element" of the Lao Dong, raises the question of the National Liberation Front's involvement in the process of restoring peace to Vietnam. Comparing the once-secret Do speech and COSVN resolution with Hanoi's public posture on the NLF, it seems that Hanoi intends to relegate the Front to an at best minor role in the peace talks but, on the attainment of a settlement, is prepared to have the NLF conduct the reorganization of the South prior to national reunification. It will be recalled in this connection that Hanoi's four points include two relevant to the NLF's role: first, that South Vietnam's "internal affairs . . . must be settled by the South Vietnamese people themselves in accordance with the program of the NLFSV without any foreign interference"; second, that the Vietnamese people, north and south, must alone determine the country's ultimate reunification. If only to avoid arousing foreign hostility and the threat of renewed external intervention, Hanoi might very well wish to keep Vietnam divided for a reasonable time after a negotiated settlement satisfactory to it.

Both North Vietnam and the NLF have, in fact, elaborated on the post-settlement environment. To set the stage, the DRV has sought to portray the Front as the only true representative of the South Vietnamese people, as not simply a revolutionary movement but an organization "actually *performing the function of* a national and democratic state," and hence as a separate entity which, upon the re-establishment of peace, can negotiate with Hanoi on reunification. In December 1966, Nguyen Van Tien was appointed permanent delegate of the NLF to Hanoi, a move designed to underline the Front's autonomy without, however, giving it the diplomatic status of a government, provisional or *de facto*.

In stopping short of treating the NLF as a completely independent authority, Hanoi has probably recognized that to do so would challenge its consistent contention that Vietnam is and always has been a single nation.

The Front's post-"liberation" program, epitomized in the slogan "independence, democracy, peace, and neutrality," derives from the governmental authority it claims in "four-fifths" of South Vietnam. Both North and South Vietnamese Communist leaders have averred that the socioeconomic and foreign policies of the two zones are quite different; some time would therefore be required before reunification would be feasible. Thus, Nguyen Van Tien told a Japanese correspondent in May 1967 that there were fundamental differences between North and South Vietnam: in the post-settlement period, the South would be neutral and unaligned in its foreign affairs, and probably would not seek diplomatic recognition from other countries; economically and politically, the two zones are also unique (he did not specify in what way). Moreover, the South would seek to form a broad coalition government which, as the Front's president (Nguyen Huu Tho) said in August 1966, would comprise "representatives of all social classes, all religious communities, and all patriotic groups," but evidently not key figures in the post-Diem governments of Saigon.

Insofar as reunification is concerned, the Vietnamese Communists of both zones have made clear that the process would be lengthy and have to be carried out by stages. To date, there has been no indication just how reunification would be accomplished, whether by national elections or direct negotiations, whether to create a single national administration or to devise some federal formula. In any event, as Pham Van Dong has put it, "we will not be in haste" to achieve peaceful reunification.

To summarize, Hanoi, undoubtedly bearing in mind the impingements upon its freedom of action in the past, is seemingly determined not to accept again the dictation of its political decisions. Premature negotiations, it evidently believes, can only lead to partial political success. If negotiations are ever to be undertaken again, they must be preceded by clear-cut military gains that will guarantee complete victory at the bargaining table. Beyond that, the negotiatory stage will itself be accompanied by continued fighting and, we may assume, recruitment and undercover political activities. The DRV does not intend to repeat the mistake of allowing the final political settlement to be determined by, and to occur coincident with, a cease-fire. The cease-fire must follow in the wake of successful negotiations; Communist forces cannot stop fighting merely because peace talks have begun. The North Vietnamese thus envision negotiations as a preliminary tactical stage which will lead to a settlement only when complete victory becomes a formality; and while we have quoted from 1966 materials, there is no reason to believe that position has measurably changed since then.

The Vietnamese Communists in the South have been informed that whatever settlement is formulated will be the handiwork of the Lao Dong Party. While this would seem to exclude the Viet Cong from determination of the timing and conditions of negotiations, the DRV has publicly declared its preparedness to postpone reunification long enough to allow the Northern and Southern societies to adjust to peacetime conditions and resolve the problem of disunity between themselves. The consistent thread running through the DRV's public and private comments on the period of the restoration of peace remains, however, that Hanoi will be the principal judge of when to negotiate, with whom, for what purposes, and with what goals.

CONCLUSIONS

In early 1965 the Viet Cong could legitimately expect that continuation of military and political pressure against the Government of South Vietnam and its American advisors would lead to complete victory within a relatively short time. Like the Viet Minh in late 1953, the Viet Cong were prepared to launch major new military thrusts, spearheaded by their main forces. While the bombing of North Vietnam intervened, it was principally the introduction of sizable American reinforcements which frustrated Viet Cong plans for a "general offensive" and forced the Viet Cong, in conjunction with Hanoi, to reassess their strategic requirements and redraft their timetable of victory. The 12th Conference of the Lao Dong Party Central Committee in December 1965, by which time U.S. troops in South Vietnam numbered nearly 200,000, provided the Viet Cong — now supplemented by North Vietnamese regulars — with their new instructions.

General Do's speech of August 1966, following in the wake of the COSVN meeting and resolution that March, may be viewed as a personal transmittal of decisions taken by the Party Central Committee. Interestingly, Do's speech and the numerous North Vietnamese public statements since then are remarkably consistent in their reasoning, perception, and conclusions despite being directed toward different audiences. That Do chose to be as uncompromising, optimistic, and determined as his compatriots speaking openly from Hanoi says

a great deal about the mood of the North Vietnamese leadership. While it may be perfectly true that the DRV's private and public comments on the war have been uniformly based on faulty, inflated reports from the front, on distortions of "enemy" strengths and weaknesses, and on exaggerated notions of Viet Cong resiliency in recent years, the apparent fact is that the overall situation which Hanoi reports to the LAF in South Vietnam and to the rest of the world basically represents "reality" to its leaders and the fighting men under them. Optimism, after all, expands far faster than it contracts, and is, moreover, a commodity on which Hanoi has no monopoly.

It seems accurate to conclude, then, that Hanoi anticipates very deleterious effects on American willpower from the cumulative impact of GVN defeats, antiwar U.S. domestic opinion, and mounting attrition in the ranks of U.S. forces. Seen through North Vietnam's telescope, the United States will gradually prove either unable or unwilling to sustain a high casualty rate, a situation that will interact with the Americans' loss of determination once inevitable internal contradictions begin to take effect. U.S. power has Hanoi's respect, it appears; but by the very nature of the Americans' military apparatus, their relationship with the GVN and the Vietnamese people, and their cruel, "unjust" intervention for imperialist ends, they cannot escape eventual defeat. The LAF, with superior staying power and morale, a firm rear to the North, successful experiences at waging people's war, and the full support of the socialist world, have every reason to expect victory regardless of changes in the complexion of the war.

Yet the DRV may also see the future as holding certain ominous signs. Its constant stress on the point that additional U.S. troops cannot alter the fundamentally favorable balance of power on the ground may reflect anxiety that time can work against the LAF in the long run. The consistent refusal of the American command to recognize the futility of fighting on might be interpreted in the LAF camp as evidence of U.S. determination never to withdraw short of complete military victory. This may in turn account for the reluctance of DRV leaders to speak in terms of a definite timetable of victory, and to stress instead the virtues of protracted struggle for the long run coupled with efforts to achieve "decisive victory" (or, as suggested, victories) in the meanwhile. How long local LAF commanders are willing to persevere may therefore be a major question mark.

The DRV is also evidently concerned about the ultimate import of further major U.S. troop increments. The COSVN resolution, for instance, mentioned the possibility of having to engage anywhere from 800,000 to 1 million Americans in the future. And General Vo Nguyen Giap, the hero of Dienbienphu, wrote in September 1967 that the United States might move from its present "local war" to a ground conflict throughout Vietnam. Nor can the North Vietnamese rule out direct American attacks against LAF troop concentrations and supply routes in Laos or Cambodia.

Finally, continued exacerbation of Sino-Soviet relations and the increasingly chaotic state of China's cultural revolution must also be unsettling to Hanoi. Its call for bloc unity has not been heeded. The possibility always remains that at some point the DRV will be forced to modify its middle position or face cutbacks in vital assistance. At the same time, North Vietnam's solid stance against a Maoist-style cultural revolution can also precipitate a Chinese reaction, although there is no evidence to demonstrate either that such has occurred or that the cultural revolution has affected the flow of goods across the Sino-Vietnamese border.

These negative signs, however, are apparently viewed from Hanoi as qualifiers of an otherwise favorable picture rather than as imminent dangers. Militarily, Hanoi seems to look to a tactical approach in South Vietnam that can accommodate to even larger numbers of U.S. troops. By gearing the LAF to rely primarily on local and guerrilla forces, to take the defensive against large-scale U.S. attacks while inflicting the maximum amount of casualties, to take offensive actions against U.S. units only when certain of resounding victory (as when boasting a decisive numerical advantage), and to concentrate main force actions against the GVN as a means of undercutting U.S. support (particularly in the pacification program presently manned by ARVN), Hanoi can hope to force a U.S. withdrawal from Vietnam without physically defeating the bulk of the American army. Time, Hanoi believes, is on its side, and American impatience for success, although dangerous (as evidenced by the bombing, the North Vietnamese say), eventually will push them in the direction of a face-saving withdrawal.

Politically, however much the Soviets and the Chinese may pressure North Vietnam toward policy changes, the DRV quite clearly remains insistent that matters of war and peace be decided in its own councils. The war seems to have assisted that determination by centering the so-called world anti-imperialist struggle on Vietnam, by placing the Vietnamese Communists at the battle's forward point, and by forcing Moscow and Peking, in the midst of their rift, to rally around Hanoi and pledge their moral and material support. In these critical times, the DRV can approach China and the Soviet Union as equals whose help is not only needed but can even be demanded; aid to Hanoi has become the mark of a Communist state's devotion to "proletarian solidarity."

Given independent North Vietnamese decision-making, it is obvious that peace will come to Vietnam only when Hanoi finds a settlement in its own best interests. Negotiations, as we have seen, are unlikely to be attempted until the LAF are militarily dominant. Hanoi considers negotiations merely an extension of the battlefield, "political struggle" which will precede, strengthen, and ultimately be decided by military struggle. As matters now stand, when Hanoi sits down to talk, the outcome will not be in doubt. While the Viet Cong would seem to be left out of this arrangement inasmuch as the Lao Dong Party will determine and control any peace talks, their interests need not be sacrificed. Hanoi's present attitude of fighting while talking, and talking seriously only when fighting from an unassailable vantage point, converges both with its aim of national liberation and the Viet Cong's goal of uncontested sectional control.

The changing military picture in Vietnam, in sum, has resulted in a revision of North Vietnamese-Viet Cong tactics, but apparently not in any fundamental alterations of strategy. In the broadest sense, Hanoi, like other capitals, Communist or otherwise, views the world through a set of lenses which, as was suggested at the outset, provide a unique vision of reality. The substantive is sharply differentiated from the intangible, the objective from the subjective, with the result that what others, including ourselves, might choose to regard as factors influencing Hanoi's war assessments may be relatively unimportant to the North Vietnamese in comparison to other factors we (but not they) choose to give secondary weight.

More specifically, Hanoi's perspective on the war seems to be based, first, on its firm sense of history and destiny. It sees itself, as General Giap has stated, leading a battle of worldwide significance that has attracted the admiration and support of numerous states great and small. While Russia's October Revolution and Communist China's revolution provide lessons for the Vietnam conflict, the most relevant experiences remain successful Vietnamese resistance against attempted domination by the Chinese, the Japanese, the French, and now the Americans. Hanoi's persistent claim that "the Vietnamese people can win" against any foe, including one with the power and resources of the United States, must be taken seriously, for it stems from a deep-seated nationalistic strain not readily susceptible to military pressure.

Secondly, in its distinction between substantive and intangible things, Hanoi apparently leans strongly on the latter. How can "inherent contradictions" be more real than military hardware, it might be asked? The North Vietnamese would probably answer that contradictions are in the nature of things, they are unchangeable, while hardware, awesome at first encounter, *can be adjusted to over time*. For Hanoi, the highest level of reality seems to consist of those unmeasurable assets which inevitably lead to victory as they interact over time: morale, nationalism, tenacity, "just struggle," and, above all, the moral no less than the material backing of "the people." When victory comes, as the North Vietnamese seem certain it will, it will be because the final contradiction, between "the enemy and us," has been successfully resolved.

Raymond L. McGovern: MOSCOW AND HANOI

The author, an American specialist in Sino-Soviet affairs, here considers the extent of and reasons for the Soviet Union's involvement in the Vietnam conflict.

OVER THE past two and a half years the Soviet Union has pursued a course in Vietnam determined first and foremost by the exigencies of its conflict with Communist China. Khrushchev's successors decided soon after his fall to invoke the USSR more deeply in the Vietnamese conflict, calculating that this course would enable them, more effectively than anything else, to counter and neutralize Peking's campaign to supplant Moscow as leader of the Communist movement and other "progressive" forces throughout the world. They judged that such action would not entail prohibitive risks of an armed confrontation with the United States.

Even though this initial decision was almost immediately overtaken by events which Moscow had not anticipated — *i.e.*, the massive US military buildup in South Vietnam and the inauguration of a sustained program of air strikes against the North — the Soviet leaders have managed to make the best of a potentially dangerous situation and have displayed a flexibility that has enabled them, by and large, to achieve their primary objective of frustrating the Chinese challenge. Hence the Chinese-inspired complaint that Moscow is doing its utmost "to exploit the Vietnam issue against China."

Any study of recent Soviet tactics in Vietnam must go back to the autumn of 1964 and the fall of Khrushchev. It is clear that the ex-leader's associates had become increasingly disenchanted and alienated by his erratic, impulsive behavior, which had had deleterious effects in various domestic and foreign areas. His successors soon indicated their feeling that the cardinal fault in his conduct of foreign affairs had been the way he handled the conflict with China. He had left the international Communist movement a shambles, and Moscow's claims to leadership in serious jeopardy.

The new leaders gave first priority to doing what they could to repair the damage to Moscow's international position. A careful reassessment of Khrushchev's anti-Chinese crusade led to the conclusion that, although his basic policy of unflinching opposition to the Chinese challenge was correct, his manner of conducting it was foolish and, in fact, played into the hands of Peking. In the Kremlin's judgment, a more subtle tactical line was demanded.

The Soviets clearly were not prepared to introduce any essential changes in the Khrushchevian policy of peaceful coexistence. Here too, however, they reasoned that the ousted leader had been unnecessarily and unwisely straightforward in the manner in which he had pressed for improved relations with the West, especially with the United States. Moscow had been stung more than once because of this unsophisticated approach, and Peking had been quick to exploit the propaganda windfall. A more adroit approach was drawn up to counter more effectively the challenge from China.

Raymond L. McGovern, "Moscow and Hanoi," *Problems of Communism* (May-June 1967), pp. 64–71. Reprinted with permission of *Problems of Communism*, which is published by the U. S. Information Agency.

Preoccupied with the Chinese problem, Khrushchev's successors decided to readjust the priorities given to the USSR's various foreign policy goals. While retaining the essence of their predecessor's policies toward both Peking and Washington, they proceeded to modify the trappings with which the world had become familiar while Khrushchev was in power. The resulting shift in emphasis was manifested in various ways, most obviously in the propaganda emitting from Soviet media. Less stress was given to the necessity for, and the benefits of, a global policy of peaceful coexistence, and Moscow's press and radio broadcasts played up the firmness of Soviet support for "national liberation movements" throughout the world.

But propaganda alone was insufficient. The Soviet leadership was clearly in search of other relatively cheap — but more concrete and hopefully more convincing — ways of demonstrating its revolutionary élan. A Soviet reassessment of the situation in Vietnam made it increasingly apparent that the first and most effective step might be taken there. What better way to draw the sting out of Chinese accusations than for Moscow to launch, with appropriate fanfare, a dramatic campaign of political and material support for the Vietnamese Communists, who alone were engaged in an open military confrontation with the "arch-imperialist" United States?

A move of this kind could not, of course, be taken lightly. We can be sure that Brezhnev and Kosygin carefully weighed the risks against the anticipated benefits in the light of all the evidence available in late 1964 and early 1965 pertaining to American intentions in Vietnam and the military prospects of the Viet Cong. We can be just as sure that the vast preponderance of this evidence led

the Soviet leaders to feel relatively safe in concluding that the risk of a dangerous and open Soviet-US military confrontation would be minimal.

In order to comprehend fully the reasons for this conclusion, it is necessary to reconstruct — at least in outline — the situation as it must have appeared to the Russians in late 1964. The Soviet leaders, of course, paid close attention to the Johnson-Goldwater presidential election campaign and drew from President Johnson's overwhelming victory what they thought to be appropriate conclusions as to its implications for the Vietnam struggle.

Moreover, the Soviets may already have been somewhat predisposed toward the judgment that Washington would probably shun deeper involvement in Vietnam. Quite conceivably, they were influenced by their own assessment of what policy alternatives were feasible, even for such superpowers as the United States and the Soviet Union. As for themselves, the Russians had hitherto shown a determination to avoid becoming too heavily committed in an area such as Vietnam, geographically distant from the USSR and with relatively slight relevance to Russian national interests. They probably judged the situation to be analogous from the standpoint of US interests and consequently would have considered it highly unlikely that Washington would in two years time have committed close to half a million men to the struggle in Vietnam. Even now that this has happened, it apparently remains somewhat incomprehensible to Moscow.

Anticipating no significant change in the extent of the US commitment in South Vietnam, the Soviets also doubtless took a rosy view of the prospects for the Viet Cong war effort, which in late 1964 looked very good indeed. It is clear that — barring a drastic and speedy step-up in US involvement — the Vietnamese Communists expected at that time to be able, within a matter of months, to drive such South Vietnamese and US troops as were left into the sea. Moreover, it seems universally recognized now that these expectations were not mere wishful thinking.

Thus, convinced that Washington would not take the drastic steps necessary to prevent or even delay an otherwise inevitable Communist victory in South Vietnam, the Soviet leaders evidently judged it safe enough to become more deeply involved in Vietnam. They may indeed have reasoned that they could hardly afford not to. For here lay what appeared to be a ready-made opportunity to get in before the dénouement and claim a share of the credit for the imminent Viet Cong victory, thus bolstering Moscow's position in the cold war with China and preventing the latter from gaining most of the benefit. . . .

On January 31, 1965, *Pravda* published the announcement that Soviet Premier Kosygin would shortly lead a top-level delegation to Hanoi, and the inclusion of high-ranking military and economic officials in the delegation clearly indicated Moscow's intention to step up Soviet assistance to North Vietnam. The Chinese immediately saw in this a dangerous challenge to their influence in Hanoi and, as will be shown later, overreacted in such heavy-handed fashion as to play ultimately into Moscow's hands.

Kosygin's eye-catching visit to the North Vietnamese capital was overtaken, however, by unanticipated events. Even while he was there, US bombing of the North in retaliation for the Viet Cong attack on the US base at Pleiku added a new dimension to the conflict. Surprised and angered, the Soviet leaders

were forced to reassess their increased involvement in Vietnam.

After Premier Kosygin returned home, the Soviet leaders accordingly faced some hard decisions. Their approach to the North Vietnamese had been predicated on the need to give priority to challenging Chinese influence in Hanoi and in the Communist movement generally. At the same time, however, they had sought to employ tactics that would not entail excessive risks of a serious military confrontation with the United States, as this would not only run counter to the USSR's vital national interests but would also, to some degree, lend weight to Peking's thesis that peaceful coexistence between the Communist and capitalist powers is impossible. As a result of the new developments in Vietnam, the Soviet leaders could no longer feel quite so confident that the risks involved in increased Soviet involvement were as controllable as they had previously calculated. Nevertheless, in spite of the new uncertainties resulting from open US raids against North Vietnam, they evidently concluded that the risks were still manageable and worth taking in view of the anticipated advantages in the struggle with the Chinese.

To be sure, a larger Soviet role in Vietnam would necessarily lead to a worsening of the atmosphere in Soviet-US relations. Moscow's leaders, however, considered this disadvantage tolerable when weighed against potential Soviet gains in the conflict with China, and they thought that the deterioration could almost certainly be kept within safe bounds. These calculations have proven essentially correct. The Soviets have coupled their more active opposition to the United States in Vietnam with a "freeze" in such well-publicized areas of Soviet-US relations as cultural exchanges, but at the same time they have avoided other provocative moves they might have made — in Berlin, for example — and have displayed a consistent desire to keep the lines open to Washington. . . .

Apart from this generally reassuring review of the probable impact of Soviet support for Hanoi on relations with the United States, the Soviet leaders probably felt that they could not afford to back away from their decision in favor of increased involvement in Vietnam without serious prejudice to their position vis-à-vis China. Kosygin's visit to Hanoi obviously made it even more difficult for Moscow to extricate itself, and even if the Russians had not already committed themselves, they would almost certainly have felt compelled, in view of increased US military support of South Vietnam, to provide some aid for the defense of a "brother socialist state."

Moreover, on the positive side, Moscow had already derived tangible advantage from its more cooperative attitude toward the North Vietnamese, in the form of the virtual cessation of the rather obvious — albeit indirect — criticisms of Soviet "revisionism" which had been voiced by Hanoi during Khrushchev's tenure. With this as a beginning, the Soviet leaders naturally hoped that material aid to the North Vietnamese would elicit positive expressions of gratitude from Hanoi which would draw much of the sting out of Chinese allegations of Soviet perfidy.

While they thus appeared determined to proceed with their plans for more positive support of North Vietnam, the Soviet leaders were manifestly alarmed by the launching of sustained US air strikes against the North and set about mustering political pressure for an early cessation of the bombing and a damping down of hostilities. . . .

Moscow's interest in stemming the con-flict in Vietnam is readily understandable. Not only have the Russians from early on displayed an apparently genuine concern over the potential dangers of escalation of the war, but they have been acutely embarrassed by the fact that the US has been able to carry the war to North Vietnam, a brother Communist country, with relative impunity. This embarrassment has, of course, grown to the extent that the more sophisticated Soviet weaponry supplied to North Vietnam since early 1965 has proved ineffectual. Hence Moscow's recognition that its interests would be better served if it could persuade Hanoi to make a tactical move toward some kind of negotiations, if only to bring an end to US air raids on the North.

The Soviet leaders quickly learned, however, that they could do virtually nothing to move the expanding war to the negotiating table. This did not prevent them from trying, but it did compel them to employ the utmost discretion in their overtures so as not to leave themselves open to new accusations from Peking. Accordingly, the USSR — with as much tact as possible — kept exerting pressure on the North Vietnamese to adopt a more flexible diplomatic posture toward possible peace talks. . . .

Soviet experience over the past two years has thus indicated a clear inability to make Moscow's influence felt and its advice heeded with regard to the tactics to be pursued in the Vietnam conflict. In fact, it would probably not be an exaggeration to say that the USSR's advice counts for little in Hanoi; certainly this is very close to the truth when it comes to North Vietnam's conduct of the war.

In a sense, the North Vietnamese have no foreign policy; they have only a Vietnam policy, the struggle for the South being a domestic issue to their way of thinking. Their relations with other countries are almost exclusively determined by whether or not, and to what degree, a given country is prepared to support Hanoi's war effort. The willingness of Khrushchev's successors to render substantial military and economic aid as well as diplomatic support to Hanoi has, to be sure, won them the good will of the North Vietnamese, and it has brought a halt to the more obvious sort of criticism formerly voiced in the North Vietnamese press against Soviet "modern revisionism." It has indeed elicited open expressions of gratitude from the North Vietnamese leaders — no mean achievement for Moscow from the standpoint of the contest with Peking, the prime motivating factor behind Soviet involvement. These gains are, of course, important for Soviet political purposes, but they are relatively inconsequential in terms of their impact on the Vietnam war.

The North Vietnamese, for their part, realize only too well the limited nature of the Soviet commitment. They understand quite clearly that the Soviet Union remains determined to avoid any step that would entail real risk of a direct Soviet-US military confrontation, and that Soviet assistance to North Vietnam is motivated not so much by altruistic devotion to the principles of proletarian internationalism as by the desire to do what is necessary — and only what is necessary — to win the battle with Peking for leadership of the world Communist movement.

In attempting to gauge the extent of current Soviet influence in Hanoi, particularly with respect to the question of peace negotiations, it is also important to bear in mind that the North Vietnamese leaders are not likely to have forgotten the bitter lesson of the 1954 Geneva Conference and the role of the USSR

therein. It is hardly necessary to reconstruct the events that led up to the Geneva Conference, when the Ho Chi Minh regime, with complete military victory over the French well within sight, nevertheless came to the bargaining table and agreed, in effect, to postpone full realization of its goals for what it thought would be two years. Why did the Vietnamese Communists go to Geneva at all; and more important, why did they make important concessions when total victory was already all but assured? They were certainly motivated in part by a desire to avoid deeper US involvement in Vietnam, but there is good reason to believe that Soviet pressure also played a role in influencing Hanoi's decision. The Soviets, who historically have subordinated Southeast Asian policy to higher-priority national interests in Europe, were determined at that time to block Western plans for the European Defense Community (EDC), and France's attitude was, of course, crucial. It seems fairly clear in retrospect that the USSR, in the hope of inducing Paris not to ratify the EDC, made a strong effort to prevent the total humiliation of France at the Geneva Conference — at the expense of the North Vietnamese.

In the light of this past experience, it may safely be surmised that the North Vietnamese are somewhat suspicious of Soviet intentions now, and certainly not very confident that Moscow will not again be willing to sacrifice their interests in favor of more important Russian national interests in the West. Soviet attempts to bend Hanoi toward peace negotiations over the last two years can only have fed such suspicions and made the North Vietnamese more sensitive to Peking's allegations that Moscow is prepared in the final analysis to sell them out. Needless to say, this imposes severe limits on Moscow's capability to influence Hanoi's decisions relative to the war.

On the other hand, China's influence on Hanoi's policy is not decisive either. Many have been inclined to blame North Vietnam's intransigent stand on Chinese pressure (the Soviets themselves have not been reluctant to propagate this line), but this is misleading. The Vietnam conflict is not a Chinese war by proxy; it is being fought by the Vietnamese Communists for their own ends. Peking would, of course, seek to capitalize on a Communist victory; still, the North Vietnamese are their own agents and — while obviously aided and abetted by Peking — are capable of determining the policies they will follow quite independently of Chinese pressure. There is no good evidence to support the suggestion that Peking alone is responsible for preventing Hanoi from negotiating a peaceful settlement.

Nevertheless, Communist China's basic aims and tactics are a great deal closer to those of Hanoi than are Moscow's. The North Vietnamese have been inclined to look on China as their ace in the hole. Indeed, one of the most significant lessons taught by the experience of the last two years is that despite the traditional distrust of the Vietnamese towards China, and despite their evident reluctance to see a substantial increase in China's presence in Vietnam, the North Vietnamese leaders have been willing to invite in sizable numbers of Chinese specialists and give them a greater role in defense of the North rather than bow before increasing US military pressure.

Hanoi's leaders must consequently be extremely anxious over the uncertainties created by the current upheaval in Communist China. The North Vietnamese press has been noticeably reticent regarding China's so-called "great prole-tarian cultural revolution," but there have been signs that the extremism of Mao's supporters has repelled the North Vietnamese and caused a cooling of relations between Peking and Hanoi. The confused situation in China, moreover, introduces a very big question mark into the evolving conflict in Vietnam. Unlikely though this may seem at present, there is a possibility that at some point in the future the North Vietnamese leaders will want — or will be obliged — to write off China as a dependable and desirable supporter of Hanoi's goals in the South. They would then be obliged to reassess the war in the light of the new equation and might eventually decide that Hanoi's aims could best be served by the line of tactical concession and political maneuver long urged on them by the USSR. Any such turn, however, would have to be predicated upon a prior basic decisions by the Hanoi leadership that North Vietnam would have to settle for a good deal less than it has heretofore shown itself willing to accept.

Even though the Vietnamese Communists have suffered sharp reverses in recent months, their determination to carry on apparently has not yet been seriously shaken. Nor has Chinese support of North Vietnam yet shown real signs of faltering despite the bizarre goings-on in Peking. Consequently, even if the present military trend should continue and North Vietnam should come to feel really hard-pressed, Hanoi seems more likely, for the time being, to ask Peking for greater help and to press on with the fight, rather than heed Soviet advice to moderate its stand.

From North Vietnam's point of view, however, excessive dependence upon either the Russians or the Chinese holds serious disadvantages. The preponderance of available evidence suggests that

Hanoi will most probably try to avoid a definitive swing toward either Moscow or Peking, even if the military situation should force it to recognize that its goals in the South have become for a time unattainable. In such a case, the North Vietnamese would probably opt for a quiet and temporary tapering off of Communist military and guerrilla activity in the South.

For the immediate future, we can only expect more of the same, both in terms of Vietnamese Communist tactics and in terms of Moscow's policy toward the war. All things being equal, the USSR would almost certainly like to see the fighting brought to an end through some sort of compromise political settlement. But all things are never equal: Moscow simply does not now — and may never — have the influence to force a change in Hanoi's policy, and Soviet determination to exploit the Vienam issue against China precludes a resort to heavy-handed pressure tactics in North Vietnam, even if Moscow thought such moves might have better prospects of success. On the diplomatic front, the USSR clearly cannot afford any open divergence from Hanoi's position on the war.

Meanwhile, the Soviet leaders can derive comfort from the fact that the tactics they have pursued in Vietnam have yielded them appreciable gains in the crucial contest with China, their primary objective. It must be pointed out, however, that Peking's own heavy-handed reaction to the Soviet challenge for influence in Hanoi contributed immeasurably to the success of Moscow's maneuvers. The Chinese have indeed displayed an uncanny knack for blackening themselves.

When Kosygin passed through Peking in February 1965, Mao Tse-tung presumably made clear to him that the Chinese viewed his mission to Hanoi as a direct challenge to them in an area that they considered within their own exclusive sphere of influence. It was apparent that the Chinese were adamantly against any kind of cooperation in Vietnam with a Soviet regime which Peking held to be "revisionist" and "in collusion with imperialism." Consequently, Moscow decided to exploit Peking's vulnerability on this issue and launched a major campaign in favor of Communist "united action" and joint meetings to coordinate aid in defense of North Vietnam, knowing full well that Mao would continue to reject all such proposals.

The exceptional virulence of China's reaction to this maneuver actually brought the Russians dividends exceeding their own expectations. According to Soviet allegations, the Chinese even went so far as to obstruct Soviet aid shipments moving to North Vietnam via China. This "dog in the manger" attitude was just what the Russians needed to help them achieve their primary aim, which after all was not so much to aid North Vietnam as to counter Chinese allegations of Soviet "collusion with imperialism" and betrayal of Communist internationalism. The Soviets used all this to good effect in weaning important Communist parties, such as the North Korean and Japanese, away from their former almost total identification with Peking's policies and toward a position of neutrality in the Sino-Soviet dispute.

In November 1965, the Chinese came out with an open denunciation of all proposals for Communist-bloc "united action" in support of North Vietnam and demanded instead that "a clear line of demarcation" be drawn to separate China and its supporters from the Soviet Union and all other wrong-thinking "revisionists." This, of course, was tantamount to an open acknowledgment that China was out to split the Communist movement — a charge that Khrushchev had frequently hurled at Peking without ever succeeding in proving it conclusively.

The Soviet leaders have since gone so far as to lay virtually all the blame for the continuing Vietnamese conflict on Peking's shoulders. Premier Kosygin, for example, in a speech last October, contended that China was responsible for continued "US aggression" in Vietnam. He claimed that if China had only agreed to a joint rebuff of US actions there, "a quick end would have been put to US outrages." More recently, Kosygin added a new twist in alleging that US efforts earlier this year to "eliminate" any prospects for talks on Vietnam had "received support from Peking." Soviet President Podgorny took this line a step further in accusing the Chinese of opposing a "proposal" by North Vietnamese Foreign Minister Trinh that talks with the US "could" begin if attacks on North Vietnam were stopped unconditionally. Podgorny cited Peking's silence on the Trinh initiative as proof that China's policy "does not accord with the views of the North Vietnamese government.'

Such remarks and Moscow's general propaganda treatment of the war graphically illustrate Soviet determination to exploit the Vietnam issue primarily against China. The thrust of the Soviet message is this: "US aggression" is the sort of thing to expect from "imperialism" but there is no excuse for the behavior of the Chinese, who claim to be Communists.

Turning to the prospects ahead, it seems certain that the Russians will continue their attempts to exploit the Vietnam issue to discredit China. They will doubtless carry on their program to supply North Vietnam with weapons and equipment, while scrupulously maintaining a public position in support of Hanoi's terms for a settlement of the conflict. Moscow's policy for the foreseeable future will undoubtedly continue to eschew any strong diplomatic initiative for a resolution of the war not having North Vietnam's prior endorsement.

The USSR's posture will also require a continuing coolness in Soviet-US relations. However, the supposition that Moscow entered the fray in Vietnam with the intention of directly confronting the US is clearly a gross oversimplification. As this brief survey has attempted to show, recent Soviet policy on Vietnam strongly suggests that Moscow's tactics have been conceived and implemented primarily with a view to undercutting China's anti-Soviet offensive, and Khrushchev's successors can take some measure of satisfaction at the extent to which these tactics have achieved their aim.

William P. Bundy: THE UNITED STATES AND COMMUNIST CHINA

Assistant Secretary of State for Far Eastern Affairs, Mr. Bundy delivered the following address at Pomona College on February 12, 1966. It is a concise statement of the official U. S. view of China and its challenge to American interests, and places the Vietnam war in that context.

COMMUNIST CHINA is without doubt the most serious and perplexing problem that confronts our foreign policy today. Peking's foreign policy objectives, and the tactics it employs to achieve these objectives, sharply focus for us the issues of war and peace in Asia and the freedom and lives of millions of people, not only in Asia but throughout the world.

U. S. OBJECTIVES

The key questions we must ask at the outset are: What are our objectives, in Asia and in the world as a whole? What are Communist China's objectives? and, What kind of policy is best for the United States in the light of those basic assessments?

And, viewed in this light, the unfortunate fact is that the kind of world that we seek and the kind of world our Asian friends seek is totally antithetic to the kind of Asia and the kind of world that Communist China seeks. What we seek is a situation where small as well as large nations are able to develop as free and independent countries, secure from outside aggression or subversion. We look toward their economic, political, and social development and growth; we hope their development will be in the direction of increasingly democratic institutions, but we recognize that these nations must develop as they themselves see fit, in accordance with their own traditions and customs. Their rate of progress, we be-

lieve, will vary according to individual situations, but progress will inevitably take place and toward goals which are deeply rooted in individual aspirations.

In harsh conflict with these objectives is any situation in which a single nation or combination of nations sets out to control others in the region or to exercise political domination over other nations in the area or any major part of it.

Our objectives are consistent with the spirit of the Charter of the United Nations and, I believe, with the aspirations of the peoples and the governments of the area and of the nations in contiguous and other areas that share with us a concern for what happens in Asia in this and in the next generation. We believe, too, that our objectives accord with the whole tide of history at the present time. They are not abstract principles. They are the bedrock of our policy throughout the world. Governed by what the nations themselves wish to do and by practical factors, what we seek is to assist the nations that are trying to preserve their independence, trying to develop themselves, and, therefore, necessarily trying to resist forces working in the contrary direction.

CHINESE COMMUNIST OBJECTIVES

There is today in Communist China a government whose leadership is dedicated to the promotion of communism by violent revolution.

U. S. Policy with Respect to Mainland China, Hearings before the Committee on Foreign Relations, U. S. Senate, March 1966 (Washington: U. S. Government Printing Office, 1966), pp. 641–646, 648–649. Reprinted with the permission of William P. Bundy.

The present leaders in Peking also seek to restore China to its past position of grandeur and influence. Many of Peking's leaders today, now grown old, are proud and arrogant, convinced that they have been responsible for a resurgence of Chinese power. The China of old exercised a degree of control over Asia that waxed and waned according to the power of the ruling emperor. Under strong rulers this meant a type of overlordship, sometimes benign but frequently otherwise, over the countries around its borders. And the restoration of that image and controlling influence is certainly a part of Communist China's foreign policy today.

In the 1930's Mao Tse-tung called attention to areas controlled by China under the Manchu Empire but since removed from Chinese control: Korea, Taiwan, the Ryukyus, the Pescadores, Burma, Bhutan, Nepal, Annam, and Outer Mongolia. In more recent years, Chinese Communist leaders have added to that list parts of Soviet Central Asia and eastern Siberia. I think we can take this as valid evidence of Peking's Asian ambitions. As Prof. Oliver Edmund Clubb, in his "Twentieth Century China," says: "The urge to revolutionary empire is fortified by the feeling drilled into all Chinese since the beginning of the Republic that all territory ever included in the vast Manchu Empire rightfully belongs to China."

In addition to these historically rooted aspirations, the present leadership is inspired by a Communist ideology still in a highly militant and aggressive phase. This phase is ideologically akin to that in the Soviet Union in the 1920's or early 1930's. It coincides, however, with a situation in which the opportunities for expansion are, or appear to Peking, more akin to those available to the Soviet Union at a much later phase in its ideological development — in 1945 and the immediate postwar years. This Communist element includes the advocacy of change through revolution and violence throughout the world and particularly in China's neighboring areas — not revolution seeking the fruition of the national goals of the people of these areas, but revolution supplied or stimulated from outside and based on a preconceived pattern of historical development.

Their vision of this Communist mission extends to countries far from China — including, as we all clearly have seen, Africa and even Latin America. Peking's plans for carrying out its objectives have been delineated in a series of pronouncements issued by its leaders, one of the latest and most widely publicized having been that issued last September by Marshal Lin Piao, top military leader in Communist China, in which Lin Piao offered Chinese Communist experience in the war against Japan as a lesson to be emulated by the less developed countries in Asia, Africa, and Latin America in their pursuit of "revolution."

As you know, the Lin Piao article draws an elaborate analogy based upon the domestic experience of Mao and his cohorts in taking over China: The organization of the rural areas against the urban ones. It extends that analogy to the thesis that the less developed areas of the world are all in the rural category which will be mobilized in order to destroy "the cities"; that is to say, all the Western, more advanced centers — ourselves, of course, at the head.

I mention this article because it is a clear and comprehensive indication that there has not taken place any moderating, but if anything a solidifying at least at this stage, of this virulent revolutionary policy that is central to our discussion of Communist China. And, of course, we have seen it in action over and over again.

THE CHINESE THREAT IN ASIA

. . . It is sometimes argued that the ambitions of Communist China in the areas contiguous to it do not mean outright control; and it can certainly be argued that they are tactically cautious in pursuing these ambitions. They have not wished to seek a confrontation of military power with us, and in any situation that would be likely to lead to wider conflict they are tactically cautious. But in looking at the extent of their ambitions one cannot, I think, simply take the historical picture of tributary governments that would be tolerated as long as they did roughly what China wished. That indeed was the historic pattern in many periods when powerful governments ruled in the mainland of China. It is also, perhaps, the pattern one might draw abstractly from the desire any major power might feel not to have hostile military power based in areas adjacent to it. Those two logics, historic Chinese logic and "great power" logic, might appear to point to something less than total political domination as the Chinese Communist objective around their borders.

And yet we must recognize, I think, because of the Communist element in the thinking and practice of the leaders of Peking today, that there is another factor that raises strong doubts whether their ambitions are in fact this modest. We have seen, for example, in the contrast between what the Soviets have done in Eastern Europe and the behavior of predecessor Russian regimes, that there is a Communist logic that does insist on total control, that will not tolerate anything other than the imposition

of the full Communist totalitarian system. The experience of Soviet control in Eastern Europe suggests that this same kind of Communist logic does and would apply to the behavior of Communist China.

That it would is further strongly suggested by the way that the Communist Chinese regime has treated Tibet. The fact that Tibet was within the historic limits of Chinese suzerainty does not explain why Communist China has virtually obliterated the culture of Tibet in seizing control of it. One cannot rationalize this on grounds of history or of the need of a great power not to have hostile forces adjacent to it. So I suggest that we must give great weight to the probability that the ambitions of Communist China do extend, not necessarily to the degree of obliteration of the local culture that we have seen in Tibet, but at least to a fairly total form of domination and control in areas contiguous to it.

What, then, would be the consequences if Communist China were to achieve the kind of domination it seeks? Here again one is tempted to look for analogy to Eastern Europe, where there is a growing will to pursue national and independent policies and to adopt domestic policies that differ sharply from the original Communist model. Yet it has taken 20 years of virtual subjugation for the nations of Eastern Europe to move this far, and their nationalism, traditions of independence, and capabilities for independent development were in general far more highly developed than those of the smaller nations on China's borders. To accept mainland Chinese domination in Asia would be to look forward to conditions of external domination and probably totalitarian control, not merely for 20 years but quite possibly for generations.

Moreover, the spread of Chinese domination would inevitably create its own dynamic and in the end threaten even the most securely based and largest nations within the area of that threat, such as India and Japan. One does not need to subscribe to any pat "domino" formula to know from the history of the last generation, and indeed from all history, that the spread of domination feeds on itself, kindling its own fires within the dominant country and progressively weakening the will and capability of others to resist.

PAST MISTAKES AND THEIR RELEVANCE TO PRESENT

This is what we are dealing with. We can all think, as we look back at the history of China, of errors that we as a nation have made and that other nations of the West have made — errors in justice and conduct in our relationships with China. We should search our souls on these and set our objectives and our principles to avoid repeating them over again. In Asia, at last, the colonial era is for all significant purposes at an end.

But to say that the West itself bears a measure of historical responsibility for the strength of the feelings of Communist China does not deal with the present problem any more than discussion of the inequities of Versailles dealt with the ambitions of Hitlerite Germany. Whatever the historic blame may be, we have to deal with the present fact of a Chinese Communist Government whose attitudes are very deeply rooted in China's national history and ambitions to revive its past greatness, and in an extremely virulent Communist ideology.

In the words of a recent article by Professor (John K.) Fairbank:

We are up against a dynamic opponent whose strident anti-Americanism will not soon die away. It comes from China's long background of feeling superior to all outsiders and expecting a supreme position in the world, which we seem to thwart.

TACTICS AND STRATEGY

I would like to emphasize that up to this point I have been speaking of the basic objectives of Peking's policy. To describe these objectives as deeply expansionist is by no means to paint the picture of another Hitler, building a vast military machine with the aim of conquest by conventional warfare on a timetable backed at some point, in the Chinese case, by a nuclear capability.

This has not been the historical Chinese way, and there is every reason to believe that it is not their present preference. Chinese are patient and think in long historical terms. Military force is important and they would like to think that their nuclear capability may at some point be useful in backing the picture of and overwhelmingly strong China whose will must be accepted. But the doctrinal statements of Lin Piao and others speak rather in terms of what they call "people's war," which plainly means the instigation and support of movements that can be represented as local movements, designed to subvert and overthrow existing governments and replace them by regimes responsive to Peking's will.

This is what we are seeing today in Thailand in the form of a so-called Thai Patriotic Front established and supported from mainland China. This is the direct form of Communist Chinese role in support of the PKI (Communist Party of Indonesia) in Indonesia.

But equally important to Peking is its encouragement and support of the parallel efforts of the other Communist Asian regimes in North Korea and North Vietnam. What is now happening in Vietnam is basically the result of Hanoi's own ambitions and efforts. Peking might wish eventually to dominate North Vietnam or a unified Vietnam under Hanoi's initial control. But if this were resisted by the Vietnamese in the classic historical pattern of relations between the two areas Peking would still gain enormously from the success of Hanoi's effort, which would clear the way for Peking to expand and extend the kind of action it is undertaking on its own in Thailand. It takes no vivid imagination to visualize what Peking would do in Malaysia, Singapore, and Burma if Hanoi were to succeed in Vietnam and Peking itself succeed in Thailand.

This, then, is the preferred Communist Chinese tactic and strategy. Ideas are a part of it, although Communist China's image as a successful model of social and political organization is hardly as attractive today as it may have been before the disastrous mistakes of the "great leap forward" and the uneven progress of the years since. Few Asians today think of the Communist Chinese structure as a model, although individual ideas such as land reform and attacks on "feudal" social structures are a part of Peking's tactical efforts.

But essentially we are dealing here not with the power of ideas but with the power of subversive organization — perhaps the one field in which Communist China has shown real innovation and skill. In mainland southeast Asia, as today in South Vietnam, what we could expect to see as the spearhead of the subversive effort would be terrorism, selective assassination, guerrilla action, and finally, if it were required, conventional military forces largely recruited by the tactics of the earlier phases. . . .

OUR BASIC POLICIES

I repeat, we must look at things and deal with them as they are, if we are to hope for change. Our basic policy must include, as major elements, two interrelated efforts: to assist the free nations of the area, as they may desire, to preserve their security; and to help them, again in accordance with their own wishes, to improve their political, economic, and social conditions. The latter is an effort that I am sure we would be making even if there were no security threat.

These two fundamental elements of our policy have much in common with the policies that we and our NATO allies pursued so successfully in the areas threatened by the Soviet Union after the war. And surely there is, to a very high degree, a valid parallel between the situation we continue to face vis-a-vis Communist China and that we faced with the Soviet Union after the war. We have dealt with the Soviet Union fundamentally by assisting in the restoration of the power and strength of Europe so that Soviet ambitions were successfully checked. Since 1955, although Soviet ambitions remain, we have seen a trend toward moderation in Soviet policy and a turning inward by the Soviets to their domestic problems.

There are, of course, myriad differences between the situation in Asia and that in Europe in terms of sophistication of economic and political bases, the stability of the societies, and the unity of national cultures. But basic to our policy in respect to Communist China, as in the case of our policy toward the Soviet Union, must be our determination to meet with firmness the external pressure of the Communist Chinese. Again, in Professor Fairbank's words: "We have little alternative but to stand up to Peking's grandiose demands."

So the effort to assist in preserving security is fundamental to our policy. It is reflected in our treaty commitments — bilateral with Japan, Korea, the Republic of China, and the Philippines, multilateral (but individually binding) through the SEATO (Southeast Asia Treaty Organization) and ANZUS (Australia-New Zealand-United States Security Treaty) treaties, and extending to South Vietnam through a protocol to the SEATO Treaty.

Necessarily, our security effort and commitments have a major military element, for the threat of military action is direct in relation to Korea and the Republic of China and lurks in the background of the Communist Chinese threat to southeast Asia, as it does for India. The day may come when other nations in the area can join in assuming more of this burden, but the simple fact is that today there cannot be an effective deterrent military force, and thus a balance of power, around China's frontiers without major and direct military contributions by the United States.

But even in the security area the effort is far from merely a military one. Local military forces should wherever possible be adequate, so that an external attack would have to take on large proportions immediately identifiable as aggression. But at least as basic to the preservation of the independence of the nations of Asia is their capacity to insure law and order and to deal with subversion, and this in turn relates to the whole nature of their political structures and to their social and economic progress. So in the end what is done under the heading of "security" merges almost indistinguishably into what is done under the heading of "development."

And so, at one time or another, we have had assistance relationships with all of the non-Communist countries of Asia. Today three of these — Burma, Cambodia, and Indonesia — have chosen to follow paths that involve little or no assistance from us. And there are nations such as Japan, and more recently the Republic of China, which have made such economic progress that they no longer need our direct help. Malaysia and Singapore are other special cases, which look for historical and practical reasons to Britain and the Commonwealth.

So the pattern is varied. In a very few instances we supply major assistance to conventional military forces. In others, such as Thailand, the emphasis is as great or greater on nonmilitary measures to better the lot of the people and thus to strengthen the fabric of the nation. And throughout the area, even where we are no longer giving direct economic assistance, we have joined in supporting the increasing efforts of the World Bank and private lenders to pitch in on the economic side, and more recently the profoundly important regional economic developments represented by the formation of the Asian Development Bank and the growing, though still embryonic, effort to provide an effective framework, through the United Nations, for assistance in the Mekong Basin and on a regional basis to southeast Asia.

All of these efforts are linked together. They represent the kind of activity which, as I have said, we would be supporting in large part in any case irrespective of the threat of Communist China and the other Communist nations. What they should do, over time, is to help build in Asia nations which are standing on their own feet, responding to the needs of their peoples, and capable of standing up to the kind of tactics and strategy employed by Communist China, backed where necessary and in accordance with our treaty commitments by the assurance that, if external attack in any form should ever take place, the United States and others would come to their help.

This is the essence of what we are trying to do. Containment, yes, but containment carried out by actions that run clear across the board. And containment in the last analysis that depends upon the performance of the Asian nations themselves. As one looks back over the short historical span of the last 15 years, one can surely see throughout the area tremendous progress where security has been maintained. Even though present difficulties are formidable, the nations of Asia have great capacity, and there is much reason for encouragement at the long-term prospect.

* * *

CONCLUSION

. . . We are Peking's great enemy because our power is a crucial element in the total balance of power and in the resistance by Asian states to Chinese Communist expansionist designs in Asia. That is the really controlling fact, not sentiment, not whatever wrongs may have been done in the past, but that very simple fact and the very fundamental conflict between their aims and objectives and the kinds of aims that we have — above all, our support for the right of the nations of Asia to be free and independent and govern themselves according to their own wishes.

All of us must hope that this picture will change. Mainland China is, of course, a great power in the world historically.

How it will develop economically and in other respects remains to be seen. I myself think that they will have considerable problems that will tend over time to absorb them if their external ambitions and desires are checked. There are those who argue that mainland China's great size and population, its historical and cultural links with the areas around its borders, and its economic potential make inevitable the growth of a Chinese "sphere of influence" in Asia. Those who advance this fatalistic theory discount the aspirations of the peoples in the area, their ability, and the effectiveness of U.S. aid, and they ignore the historical trends of our time.

In sum, I repeat that the problem must be considered basically in the same way we did that of the Soviet Union. We must, on the one hand, seek to curtail Peking's ambitions and build up the free nations of Asia and of contiguous areas; on the other hand, while maintaining firm resistance to their expansionist ambitions, we can, over time, open the possibility of increased contacts with Communist China, weighing very carefully any steps we take in these general areas lest we impair the essential first aim of our policy, including our clear commitments.

It is unlikely that the present leaders, who have become doctrinaire and dogmatic, can be expected to change, but they in due course will be replaced with a new generation of leaders. It is our hope that these men will see with clearer eyes and better vision that China's best interest lies in pursuing a peaceful course.

David P. Mozingo: CONTAINMENT IN ASIA RECONSIDERED

David Mozingo is a member of the Department of Government at Cornell University whose research and writing have been focused on China's relations with Southeast Asia. In this essay the intentions of China's foreign policy are examined in the light of national rivalries among Asia's noncommunist states. The author concludes that "it is primarily the evolution of nationalism, not the foreign policies or ideology of the Peking government, which frustrates the United States in Asia."

SINCE the Korean War, United States policies in Asia have gradually developed along the lines of the "containment" doctrine so successfully applied in Europe after 1947. Washington has increasingly seen the problem of Chinese power in Asia in much the same light as that posed by Soviet power in Europe and has behaved as if both threats could be contained by basically the same kinds of responses. In both Asia and Europe, containment measures have reflected a perceived need for complementary interaction between military policies and aid programs in order to prevent aggression by Communist powers and to foster the internal stability of nations in the area. Although difficulties have arisen in seeking the best balance of these components of the containment policy in Europe, most of the essential American objectives in the West have been attained.

For some time, however, it has been apparent, particularly in Southeast Asia, that the application of containment measures in the Far East has not yielded results comparable to those achieved in Europe. While it is widely recognized that this disparity in results reflects special Asian problems not encountered in Europe, there has been a general reluctance to question whether the contain-

ment philosophy really addresses the basic sources of the instability in Asia that alarms the United States. It is time to analyze the relative failure of the containment doctrine in Asia by considering both the obvious special difficulties confronting the United States there and the inherent differences between the situation in Asia and that in Europe.

Had the sense of historical perspective exerted a more prominent influence on Asian policy formulation, it is likely that containment's central objective of establishing a hard political and military line between a U.S. and a Chinese sphere of influence would have seemed infeasible from the beginning. In Western Europe, the basis for effective U.S. containment measures was soundly conceived because these measures were applied in defense of communities long-established within the framework of a nation-state system. Moreover, special ties bound the United States to Great Britain and France. By applying the containment doctrine in the West, the United States, for the third time in this century, reaffirmed the strategic principle that had formerly governed Britain's policy toward Europe: No single continental power was to be permitted to conquer or dominate the European nation-state system. Further,

David P. Mozingo, "Containment in Asia Reconsidered," *World Politics*, Vol. XIX, No. 3 (April 1967), pp. 361–377. Reprinted with the permission of The RAND Corporation.

the U.S. measures to contain Russia in Europe were strengthened by the historic determination of the Western democracies to preserve their established order and values.

In Asia, the containment doctrine has been applied to an area where a nation-state system is only just beginning to emerge amid unpredictable upheavals of a kind that characterized Europe three centuries earlier. It is only since 1949 that the restoration of a strong, unified China, the withdrawal of the Western colonial powers, and the formation of new independent countries have created the beginnings of a modern nation-state system in Asia.

The question in Asia is not how a traditionally functioning system can be rehabilitated but how a very new system will evolve and mature. The kinds of American technical and economic power that helped to restore the historic vitality of the European system would seem to have, at best, only partial relevance to the Asian situation. It may be doubted whether the kinds of tools and power available to the United States can induce stability in an environment in which most countries are experiencing a profound and rapid transformation of their societies, values, and attitudes. Much of the American experience and structure of values has already shown itself to be not only inapplicable but also not even wanted. The results of the competition between the United States, Russia, and China in Asia thus far seem to indicate that attempts by external powers to shape the merging Asian system are unlikely to succeed. None of these powers has been able, whether by appeals to ideology or common national interests or by large-scale economic and military aid, to exert enough influence to draw the more important Asian powers into close

alignment. In the absence of firm ties and mutual interests of the kind that have bound the United States to Western Europe (and these did not emerge overnight), a policy of containment in Asia must rest on unstable foundations.

THE EFFECT OF NATIONAL RIVALRIES ON A CONTAINMENT STRATEGY IN ASIA

The Soviet threat to Europe has been regarded primarily as a military one. Even when the Western part of that continent was most weakened, immediately after World War II, Communist parties were unable to take power in any country by popular consent. Western Europe's economic recovery was rapid. National conflicts were not so severe as to prevent the formation of an alliance. Until very recent times, there was broad agreement among the Western powers about the nature of the Soviet threat and how to meet it. Consequently, it was possible to lay a firm political foundation for the NATO structure.

The political conditions that were indispensable to the creation of security arrangements in Europe are absent in Asia, where very few powers see their security interests in the same way. Except for Taiwan, all of the Asian powers have an enemy or enemies whom their leaders apparently regard as more threatening than China. . . .

In Southeast Asia, the menace to Thailand, Laos, and South Vietnam comes in the first instance not from China but from a very independent and highly nationalistic regime in Hanoi. North Vietnamese expansion into Southeast Asia also alarms Cambodia, but not as much as her fear of Thai and South Vietnamese aspirations to recover lost territories at Phnom Penh's expense. Prince Sihanouk believes these two historic enemies have aligned themselves with the United States, not so much to contain China or North Vietnam as to secure the arms and tacit backing of the United States for the pursuit of their irredentist claims on Cambodia — hence, his close ties with Peking and deference to Hanoi. . . .

Such strife among Asia's non-Communist powers, for which their own governments are responsible, has been far more beneficial to China's aspirations and interests as a great power in the Far East than have any actions she has initiated herself. It is therefore difficult to see how a containment policy directed primarily against China can be truly effective as long as the Far East seethes with conflict between jealously independent rival nationalist regimes whose policies are essentially their own. To a certain extent it would seem that previous U.S. attempts to back one or another potentially anti-Communist state and to promote the growth of its petty military power have not so much deterred or contained the dubious military threat from China as they have sharpened the very national conflicts, internal and external, that undermine local stability and hence frustrate the development of a broader basis for conciliation among the nations in this region. American objectives would perhaps have been better served by policies that emphasized the American role as a "conciliator" in Asia (for example, in the India-Pakistan, Indonesia-Malaysia, or Cambodia-Thailand-Vietnam disputes) than by so much emphasis on building anti-Communist "positions of strength" through military alliances aimed at China. Actually, the United States has the strongest kind of interest in promoting conciliation between all the states of Asia in this century of intense nationalism. . . .

The existence of intense rivalries among Asia's non-Communist powers, rivalries that result from their own conceptions of national interests and objectives, has produced a response in Asia to the fact of Chinese Communist power that is altogether different from Europe's reaction to the Soviet threat. At no time has there emerged anything like an Asian consensus about how to regard Chinese military or political intentions. It would be difficult to show that any Asian countries capable of independent action have accepted the United States' assessment of China. This judgment is supported by the fact that the United States has been unable to construct, even informally, an alliance structure in the Far East, directed against Peking, which includes the major Asian powers. It is well known that even some allies of the United States, given the balance of power that so heavily favors Russia and the United States, do not regard Peking as a serious military menace to themselves. At the same time, there can be scarcely a government in the Far East today that is not aware of how useful it is, in dealing with the United States, to invent or exaggerate fears of a Chinese bogeyman.

The United States, far removed from Asia and from direct threat by China, stands almost alone in emphasizing the urgent menace of Peking, while most of the countries in the region, who ought to be highly sensitive to any Chinese threat, have taken a more conservative view of their Chinese neighbor's intentions. Even India's bitter hostility to Peking has not produced anything like the devil-theory of China that has grown up in the United States. To sum up, the states of Asia have not agreed on the existence of a common external threat; but such an agreement seems to be an indispensable condition for the success of policies modeled on European-type containment.

APPRAISING CHINA'S INTENTIONS

It is not only the inherent differences between the political structure of non-Communist Asia and Western Europe that cast doubt on the validity of applying European-type containment doctrines to the Far East. The aims and direction of Chinese Communist policy — indeed, the nature of the Communist challenge in Asia itself — must be evaluated in terms that are largely irrelevant to European experience. Menacing Soviet actions in Europe presented such a clear and present danger to all concerned that they provoked the creation of the NATO alliance. Since the Russian forward pressure came after the Western powers had already acquiesced in considerable territorial and political concessions in Eastern Europe to meet alleged Soviet security interests, there was general agreement in Western Europe that Moscow's intentions were not defensive in nature. The American effort to equate China's intervention in the Korean conflict and her use of force in the Taiwan dispute, in Tibet, and on the Indian boundary with Soviet behavior in Eastern Europe has obviously failed to convince most Asian governments that China has aggressive intentions toward them. This failure suggests why the United States has been unable to crystallize opinion in these countries behind any genuine Asian regional security arrangements to curb a supposed threat of Chinese expansion.

In explaining Chinese action, Pakistan, Burma, Cambodia, Nepal, even Indonesia and our ally Japan, have tended to give more weight to traditional, nationalistic, and defensive motives than to purely "aggressive" Communist revolutionary impulses. This is not to say that these non-Communist Asian countries have been unconcerned about China's actions, her power, or her Communist system. But it is clear that most of these countries rely on their own perception of their Chinese neighbor, and their perception is such that the United States is unlikely to succeed in arousing a high level of Asian fear about China unless Peking behaves in a manner far more threatening to them, collectively and individually, than she has done to date. It is recognized in a number of Asian capitals that China's belligerence is largely a function of her special rivalry with the United States over Taiwan and other issues. Hence these countries have chosen to avoid alignments that would conflict with their own interest in stabilizing relations with Peking. Their aim has been, quite obviously, to avoid inflaming relations with China, and they do not wish to be drawn into the Sino-American quarrel. Asian reactions to the issues raised in Korea, Taiwan, Tibet, India, and Vietnam have been extremely varied and at no time has any of these conflicts produced an Asian front against China similar to that which the Soviet Union brought on herself by her actions in Europe. The disparity of views among the non-Communist Asian powers, and between them and the United States, about China's intentions robs the policy of containment of the basic consensus that was essential to its success in Europe.

China's foreign policy has also helped to undermine the appeal of the containment doctrine in Asia. The basic direction of her foreign policy in Asia since 1954 has been toward seeking an adjustment of contentious issues between herself and such of her neighbors as were not allied with or seemingly under the control of the United States. Thus, for more than a decade, China has worked to normalize relations with Afghanistan, Burma, Pakistan, Cambodia, Ceylon, Nepal, and Indonesia. Peking is outspokenly hostile to all members of the American anti-China bloc. She seeks in various ways, including the threat to support revolutionary elements, to convince their leaders that making common cause with the United States carries certain risks; that it is not possible for any of them to support the United States in opposing China and have friendly relations with Peking at the same time. Even in relation to countries in this category, however, China's actions — as distinguished from her verbal condemnations — have been cautious and restrained. To those Asian governments that decline alignment with the United States, Peking offers such explicit rewards as border settlements, aid, and China's nonsupport of insurrectionary tactics by local revolutionaries. This Chinese stance reflects not only the limitations on Peking's military capabilities for large-scale aggressive actions, but, vastly more important, her recognition that naked and unprovoked aggression against her neighbors would threaten the collapse of her entire diplomacy in Asia. Since the Bandung Conference, China has attempted to compose her relations with any genuinely nonaligned neighbors in order to identify and isolate the United States as the aggressive power and to find common ground with Asian nationalism for the purpose of organizing opposition to the policies of the United States.

Since the mid-1950's, China's diplomatic efforts to prevent her neighbors from being drawn into the American anti-China alignment have consistently enjoyed priority over Peking's commitment to support Communist revolutions. The Chinese position on revolution, which is central to an accurate understanding of her policies in Asia, should not be misunderstood or distorted. China encourages armed "revolutionary" action on the part of Communists or other dissidents in countries where special conditions exist — that is, where the so-called "imperialist" powers have interposed themselves, as in Taiwan, South Korea, Japan, Laos, South Vietnam, and most recently, Thailand (after U.S. military forces arrived in that country). Ostensibly nonaligned governments, as in India, have also to reckon with Peking's anger when they adopt "anti-China" policies. One listens in vain, however, for the strident Chinese call to "revolution" in any Asian country that is clearly independent of American tutelage and pursues a policy of accommodation with Peking.

Where supporting revolution conflicts with China's hope to wean non-Communist Asian governments away from the United States, revolution is pushed into the background. China has advised in her ideological pronouncements on revolution that local Communist parties, though they should learn from Chairman Mao, must in the final analysis find their own formulas for taking power. In those Asian countries that remain independent of the United States and friendly to China, Peking shuns calling upon the local parties to attempt "adventurist" revolutionary actions that conflict with her own diplomacy. Toward governments in this category, China's basic policy for more than a decade has been to concentrate wherever possible on currying favor with nationalist leaders (some of whom, from the Communist viewpoint, can scarcely be described as "progressive") and to encourage the local party to develop the art of skilled united-front tactics. Local Communists are expected to exploit the various "contradictions" in their own country so as to place themselves in a position to take power when the old incompetent order collapses. Peking encourages local parties to take power by the parliamentary or peaceful path if they can, but she points out that there is no instance in which the bourgeois classes have permitted a Communist party to win power "democratically." Hence, the Chinese argue, it is indispensable that a real Marxist-Leninist party organize for and be prepared to use armed revolutionary struggle. Otherwise the chances are very slim that a Communist party could come to power, much less be strong enough to carry out a dictatorship of the proletariat.

Peking's actual behavior and her ideological theses on revolution reveal that she is prepared to refrain from direct interference in the competition (whether peaceful or violent) between Communist parties and the "bourgeois" classes in Asian countries, so long as the United States also does not directly intervene in these countries' politics. This is the essence of the Chinese version of peaceful coexistence in Asia, formulated more than ten years ago at the Bandung Conference. . . . The dispute with Moscow on the meaning of peaceful coexistence has arisen over the issue of what the policy of the Communist powers should be in situations where the United States rushes in to prop up a non-Communist regime that is in danger of losing the competition with its local Communist opponent. China argues that the Communist bloc should try to deter, or by various means oppose, attempts by the United States to use her own power unilaterally to determine the outcome of the competition between the bourgeois elites and the Communist forces. The Chinese leaders' view of their own national interests requires this position, for they regard the United States as bent on organizing all Asia into a belt of client-states opposing Peking. These fears are less disturbing to the Soviet leaders, who have long betrayed noticeable ambivalence about the desirability of fully opposing the United States in Asia if to do so would benefit the interests of the Chinese state.

As her power increases, of course, it is possible that China may abandon her present compromise with independent Asian nationalist regimes and, under the protection of her own nuclear deterrent, energetically attempt to impose Communist regimes on her neighbors. That possibility cannot be dismissed lightly, but it is a course of action fraught with grave risks for Peking. While it is conceivable that China might attempt to invade small neighboring countries or to foment and support revolution in them, it is far less likely that she will feel confident enough to undertake such measures against large Asian powers such as India, Pakistan, Indonesia, and Japan. Some of these nations will be able to move in the nuclear direction at some future time; should Peking, without provocation, take an aggressive attitude toward these countries, she would run the risk of hastening the development of an anti-China nuclear club. Nothing would seem so well calculated to drive non-Communist Asia closer to the United States (or Russia) as an attempt by Peking to coerce her neighbors into unconditional surrender to Chinese demands.

Seen dispassionately, China's policies in Asia are more characteristic of a traditional great power than of a revolutionary renegade. The commitment to revolution plays a special part in Chinese policies, but in aspiring to great-power status, Peking emphasizes such traditional and conventional instruments as diplomacy, economic power, and the presence or threat of force. The demands of the Chinese regime for certain irredentas, spheres of influence, and concessions to its security interests are opposed by the United States and the Soviet Union, each of them much more powerful than China. Peking cannot hope to force concessions from either of these powers by provoking a direct test of strength. But it is quite evident that Communist China does not intend to accept passively a position and influence in the world, particularly in Asia, that she regards as being dictated either by the Soviet Union or by the United States. It is doubtful that any Chinese leadership born in this century would react differently. But the Chinese leaders are not the only ones in Asia and in other areas with aspirations that go beyond the position Russia or America would assign to them. China's call to "revolution" is directed primarily to existing and potential elites in Asia and elsewhere whom she regards as likely to share with her an interest in altering any status quo imposed by U.S. or Soviet policies.

The model she has offered to these potential Communist and nationalist allies, in the hope that their revolutionary efforts will shake U.S. and Soviet domination, is one derived from Chinese Communist revolutionary experience. The Chinese leaders believe that under favorable conditions, well-trained and indoctrinated Communist parties can integrate this model with their own concrete situations and can ultimately take power. The Chinese do not say that revolution can or should be launched everywhere; they actively support unrest only in certain carefully defined revolutionary situations: where "imperialism" (i.e., the United States) is present, and where the prescribed local conditions of success exist. Peking is the master, not the servant, of its revolutionary ideology.

The entire Chinese line on revolution has been fashioned to support the great-power policies Peking pursues in her contest with the United States and the Soviet Union. Where China's leaders have believed their interests in this fundamental struggle could be best served by supporting foreign Communist revolutionary movements, they have done so. But wherever they have believed they could advance in the contest with Moscow and Washington by supporting an odd assortment of friendly nationalist, militarist, or monarchial regimes, they have not hesitated to leave local Communist parties to their own fate. Had Peking's actions conformed to the devil-theory of China that has grown up in the United States, the appeal of the containment policy in Asia would no doubt be much greater than it is today.

OBSTACLES TO CHINESE PREEMINENCE IN ASIA

It is not surprising that a state with China's present power and long history should aspire to regional preeminence. But the task of transforming such ambitions in Asia into reality promises to be very difficult. Various forces in Asia, independent of American power, seem likely to curb Peking's influence.

The position of the Chinese state in Asia is not comparable to that of the United States in the Western hemisphere or to Russia's position in Eastern Europe. In addition to the United States, Peking confronts, in Russia, Japan, India-Pakistan, and Indonesia, large powers which, irrespective of their political order, have reason to oppose mainland China's hegemony in Asia. Russia's and Japan's interests are very different from China's, and the power complex developing in both these countries would act as a major curb on Chinese expansion in the most decisive theater, Northeast Asia, even in the unlikely event of a total with-drawal of American power. The depar-ture of the United States from Asia would no doubt gratify Peking, but it would not clear the path for Chinese hegemony. Rather, it would set the stage for a different kind of power struggle in the area.

Since the nineteenth century, both Japan and Russia have tried to be expan-sionist powers at China's expense. No Chinese government is likely to rid itself of the old fear that these two powers might again take the path of aggression against China or combine against her interests in Asia. If a disengagement were ever to occur between the United States and China, it seems very probable that China's attention would turn to the older problem of opposing Russian and Japanese penetration of the Asian main-land. In the twentieth century this old three-power rivalry might take a differ-ent form than it did in the past, but the steady rise of Russian and Japanese power would continue to be a basic ob-stacle to Chinese hegemony. The longer and much deeper history of China's fear of Russia and Japan may one day exert a powerful influence on future Chinese leaders' attitudes toward the United States, if a major conflict between the two powers does not come to pass.

The natural direction for Chinese ex-pansion, it is usually thought, is into Southeast Asia, where China has histori-cally exerted influence. China's nearness and the absence of strong indigenous military powers have led to the assump-tion that she is destined to dominate Southeast Asia unless resolutely deterred by the United States. This fits in neatly with theories about power vacuums. But the major Southeast Asian countries them-selves have strongly resisted the idea of being drawn into China's orbit (or any-one else's). All of the countries in this area, including Vietnam, share an antip-athy toward Chinese pretensions to supe-riority and dominance, whether on the part of local Chinese populations or of the Peking government. Nearly all the countries of Southeast Asia possess im-pressive geographic barriers against a major Chinese invasion. Moreover, they all are well aware that Soviet and Ameri-can power interests are also opposed to Chinese predominance, although not all agree with the United States about how to deal with China. Contrary to the expe-rience of past centuries, when her spread-ing culture was a powerful vehicle for claims to regional predominance, China's influence as a whole has been declining in Southeast Asia. Recently excluded from the area by the Western imperial powers, China now faces the intense nationalism that has captured the suc-cessor states since World War II.

The existence of fraternal Communist parties, the most successful of which have been every bit as nationalistic as the Chinese party, has not constituted an unmixed blessing as far as Peking's search for preeminence in the area is concerned. These parties have been useful and nec-essary allies, as in Vietnam and Laos, in opposing the American effort to turn the 1954 Geneva agreement on Indochina into an anti-Communist and anti-China front. On the other hand, some of these highly nationalistic and ambitious Com-munist parties, like the Indonesian one, often complicate China's diplomatic deal-ings with nationalist governments. The stronger Asian Communist movements have all shown an independent temper, and this has increased their freedom to take actions contrary to China's interests.

The Chinese leaders believe that the removal of Western influence from Asia, coupled with prolonged internal insta-bility, will eventually aid local Commu-nist movements in coming to power. But

China's leaders, no less than Russia's, are already discovering in their relations with North Vietnam and North Korea that ideological affinity and territorial proximity between Communist states do not result in the subordination of the smaller partners. Already it is evident that North Korea and North Vietnam will develop their own distinctive national personalities and forms: neither is now or is likely to become simply a small replica of "the thought of Mao Tse-tung." In the past, both regimes have shown a willingness to depart from the Chinese line on key issues. Should other Communist regimes emerge in Southeast Asia — in Vietnam, say, or possibly in Indonesia — Peking cannot assume on the basis of past experience that they will follow her lead. Actually, China must remain worried that such regimes may seek more freedom of action by currying favor with the Soviet Union — or, for that matter, with the West. Consequently, it is by no means clear at this point that China's leaders would prefer the development of stable, independent, diverse, and highly nationalistic Communist regimes in Southeast Asia in preference to the prolonged continuation of weak non-Communist regimes led by men willing to defer to China's interests in return for Peking's respect of the essential sovereignty of their countries.

None of the elites of the principal Asian nations — Japan, India, Pakistan, Indonesia — on whose political and military stance a great deal of China's ultimate position and influence in Asia depends, have shown themselves to be anybody's pawns — Russia's, China's, or America's. The United States and Russia have failed on the whole in their attempts to manipulate Asia nationalism so as to support their own state strategies in the cold war. By now it ought to be apparent that there is not going to be either an American or a Soviet solution to Asia's postcolonial problems. By its nature that goal was never really attainable, but it seemed to be a serious aspiration at one time because both Russia and America have been attracted, to a different degree and in very different ways, to the notion that they have special world ideological missions. Peking may believe China can succeed where two vastly richer and stronger superpowers failed, but the post-World War II history of Asian nationalism indicates very clearly that none of the great powers will be likely to succeed in this endeavor.

It should not be forgotten that between 1948 and 1951, during the heyday of Sino-Soviet cooperation, the Communist parties of Asia tried very hard to use armed insurrection as a means of discrediting and destroying such leaders as Nehru, Sukarno, U Nu, and others. In every instance where the non-Communist leadership could lay genuine claim to representing the force of nationalism, the Communist rebellions were crushed. So complete was the failure of these parties' assaults on nationalism that the Communist movement was forced to come to terms and to shift to policies of peaceful coexistence — a new line first championed by the Communist parties of China, India, and Indonesia, and only later by the Soviet Union. It should also be added that except for the special case of Malaya, the most politically significant defeats inflicted on Communist movements have come at the hands of nonaligned nationalist governments, and, as the recent suppression of the Indonesian Communist party again demonstrates, these defeats were brought about without the assistance of the United States.

The fear, expressed in the argument that neutralism or nonalignment is simply a temporary way station on the road to communism, that Peking and other Communists can push over popular nationalist regimes like "dominoes" once a Communist revolution succeeds somewhere else, is overwhelmingly contradicted by the proven vitality of Asian nationalism in the last twenty years. The Chinese Communists were the first to recognize, more than a decade ago, that genuine non-Communist nationalism was nobody's pushover and that efforts by local Communist parties to prove the contrary would bear bitter fruit. In Asia, it is only where an existing leadership has not earned, and therefore cannot claim, the mandate of nationalism that Communist parties have been able to make a serious challenge for power — a challenge based on their own attempt to seize power from those who either lost that mandate or never had it.

THE REAL AMERICAN PROBLEM IN ASIA

Much discussion about the threat of Chinese Communist expansion exaggerates what Peking is capable of doing both now and later and underplays the role of indigenous forces at work in neighboring countries affected by Chinese policies but clearly free from Chinese domination. This is a critical distinction to make, for the fact is that China is assigned far more responsibility than she deserves for the disturbances that lie at the roots of American anxiety about Asia. It is simply not true that Peking or any other Communist power can successfully "turn on" a Communist revolution wherever it chooses. Neither Peking's actions nor her ideological pronouncements have created the essential conditions that have energized the growth of the Communist movement in Asian countries. Local Communist parties have scored impressive gains, invariably, in

those countries where native non-Communist elites have, by their own actions, failed to gain or retain their people's recognition as popular, effective nationalists. Local non-Communist elites themselves, not Peking, created the basic sources of internal discord in Laos, Vietnam, and Indonesia, where the most successful Communist movements to date have developed. Communist strength in these countries would be far less today had the non-Communist political elements subordinated their private rivalries to the larger task of national consolidation. Where the competition among the non-Communist elites has not reached the point of destroying the national fabric — for example, in Japan, Thailand, Pakistan, Burma, Cambodia, Ceylon, India, Maylasia, and the Philippines — the Communists have been unable to make a serious bid for power.

The plain fact is that Asian communism's greatest asset is not, and never has been, Communist China's potential military threat or her support of revolution. It has been, and continues to be, primarily the existence of incompetence and corruption and the lack of a genuine, socially progressive, nation-building ethic within the non-Communist elite in every country where communism has made serious advances. Conversely, the most effective deterrent to Communist gains has proved to be the existence of a non-Communist elite dedicated to solving its country's problems and therefore capable of holding the loyalty of its own people. American military power and aid, in themselves, have not proved adequate to find, to build, or to replace a dedicated, hard-working, non-Communist elite.

In the absence of indigenously inspired civil strife, gross incompetence among the non-Communists, or a foreign colonial enemy, no Communist movement in any Asian country has come even close to taking power, through either revolutionary or conventional political strategies. The political, economic, and social upheaval indispensable for a successful "people's war" cannot be manufactured abroad, and it does not burst on the scene overnight. Fundamentally, the prospects for successful Communist movements in Asia depend far less on contriving armed insurrection than on the character and ability of the non-Communist elites. Asia's non-Communists, the Chinese believe, will do the basic job of disintegrating their own societies and reputations to the point at which Communist parties can effectively exploit the situation. If the Chinese are right, and the evidence suggests that in some countries they are, the Communist threat to Asia would not disappear if Communist China's presence vanished from the scene tomorrow.

There most certainly are both immediate and long-range prospects that the kind of future the United States would like to see develop in Asia will not come about. And the nature of the threat to idealized U.S. hopes is primarily the potential rise of authoritarian or totalitarian regimes in response to a broad pattern of grievances long felt and long uncorrected. But this danger comes not from the Left alone, in the shape of communism, but also from the Right, in the form of authoritarian, oligarchic regimes representing the military, the privileged social classes, and the commercial element. There are numerous examples — Laos, Indonesia, Vietnam, Kerala — to show that when the Communist parties are likely to take power, whether through elections or revolution, the rightist classes are likely to agree on a coercive political solution of their own invention, rather than to accept one formulated in Moscow and Peking.

For a long time, United States assumptions about political developments in Asia have contained the unwarranted expectation that somehow national communities based on some form of democratic consensus ought to, or are likely to, flourish in the area, provided an assumed Communist threat to their institutions is checked and economic development is encouraged. It is quite natural that the United States, in view of her values and traditions, should act to promote economically viable and politically responsible regimes wherever there is a *clear* indication of local purpose and desire. But successful policies for the long run — not based merely on the year-to-year fluctuation in Communist fortunes — must take account of the limitations on what the United States, great though her power is, can realistically expect to achieve in a vast and varied part of the world that has very different traditions from her own. History thus far would appear to show that overt Communist military aggression can be defeated and that artificially contrived "people's wars" do not succeed in countries whose leaders command the consent and loyalty of their own people. There is, however, serious reason to doubt that any foreign power, including the United States, can redeem the image of harsh and unpopular governments or can persuade or force unwilling governments to take those measures of reform that alone can win the support of their own populations or build a nationalist following where one does not exist.

Unfortunately, the painful truth is that Asia's strongest political tradition is the very authoritarianism that stands in the way of such reforms. The variations in this authoritarian tradition have been either despotic or benevolent but have remained authoritarian. The sharing of state power under the rule of law is an alien conception in many parts of Asia. Moreover, the desirability of political Westernization is not at once obvious to most Asians, as it is to Americans. Except where Western institutions have been imposed forcibly by Western powers, there has been little lasting, indigenously sustained commitment to socially progressive or politically democratic ideas in any Asian country. There is no "free Asia" counterpart to the Western democratic traditions on which to build except in our own imagination. The United States can have hope for and can act to sustain Japan's, India's, or any other country's adoption of consensus-type political communities, but there should be no illusions. The foundations of transplanted Western political and social ideas in Asia are weak. Institutions based on them have already been overturned in Burma, Korea, Pakistan, Laos, and Indonesia; they have hardly existed in other countries of the Far East. One may even fairly doubt that Western political forms would survive in India or Japan in the event of a serious crisis.

In Asia, however, the absence of quasi-democratic, pluralistic institutions has not proved to be an insuperable obstacle to maintaining stable political communities based on the tacit or expressed consent of the governed. Indeed, some Asian societies are likely to find what they regard as the appropriate balance between the conflicting demands of progress, justice, and order best achieved within a traditional-authoritarian political system that is in harmony with their historical development. What has proved to be the indispensable condition for maintaining a stable non-Communist political order is that the government and its leaders win and retain the confidence of their people as genuine exponents of nationalism. Where this common bond of nationalism

links leaders and citizens, no Communist movement in Asia has been able to sever it at the polls or on the battlefield.

All this is true even in an era when U.S. military power has been overwhelming and when vast sums have been made available for aid to any regimes that would hoist the anti-Communist banner. The United States has been at no disadvantage compared to the Communists in her resources for waging the contest in Asia. Quite the opposite is true. The real difficulties that beset the United States arise primarily from the nature of the task she has set out to achieve. That task has become, evidently, nothing less than to act as a vehicle shaping the basic forces of change in a vast part of the world that not only is entering the nation-building stage of development, but is also undergoing at the same time the profound experience of total cultural transformation. But the United States has virtually no ties linking it to the traditions that are bound to govern the evolution of most Asian countries. In the context of the profound upheaval now occurring in Asia independently of great-power action, it would be well to ponder whether even the United States can reasonably expect to exert a decisive molding influence on the form or spirit of new national communities that must ultimately reflect their own diversity, peculiarities, needs, traditions, and aspirations. It is leaning on a weak reed, in truth, to base long-range policies on assumptions that the United States, or any combination of Western technological expertise and aid, will somehow be able to channel and mold the vast revolution in human attitudes and behavior that is painfully under way not only in Asia but in three-quarters of the world. But if the United States is determined to substitute American power for the absence of indigenous, non-Communist nationalism and to attempt a basic transformation of the elites and the societies of the far-off countries of Asia, let *that* true purpose be defined for what it really is, not displaced onto the myth of a Chinese Communist bogeyman.

It is primarily the evolution of nationalism, not the foreign policies or ideology of the Peking government, which frustrates the United States in Asia. The power fundamentally to change the basic indigenous forces shaping the development and character of nationalism in Asian countries lies in neither Peking nor Washington. No internal or external Communist power has yet been able to force the submission of an independent Asian country, however poor and whatever its political system, whose non-Communist leaders can justifiably claim the mandate of nationalism. It is incredible to suppose that the United States can, by the exercise of her own power, claim that mandate for any non-Communist elite that has not earned it from its own people. And until the United States comprehends the full meaning of nationalism in Asia, Communist and non-Communist alike, the gap between America's expectations and the real world around her will remain frustratingly large.

Lucian W. Pye: CHINA IN CONTEXT

Lucian Pye is a political scientist who is well known for his many writings on the political development of emerging nations in Asia. The following article provides an analysis of American and Chinese attitudes that attempts to look beyond the Vietnam war to a "post-containment Asia."

FOR SOME MONTHS, 1966 promised to be a year of significant albeit gradual change in American policy toward Communist China. In a strange and paradoxical fashion, the emotional issues of the Viet Nam War opened the way for the most sober, responsible and even-handed public discussion of China since the Communists came to power. At Congressional hearings and in the mass media, scholars and leaders of opinion have dispassionately calculated the possibilities for change, and Administration leaders have in their customarily guarded language intimated that change was not impossible. Most significant of all, the American public demonstrated a gratifying degree of maturity by forgetting the old passions and asking for only facts and analyses about the new China. Our national mood was increasingly one of believing that with prudence and wisdom it would be possible to work toward gradually incorporating China into responsible world relationships.

All of this, of course, was before the Cultural Revolution and the startling appearance of the Red Guards shook the gradually emerging American consensus as to what China was likely to become. While it is still too early to forecast the full implications of the current upheav-

Reprinted by special permission from *Foreign Affairs*, January 1967, pp. 229–245. Copyright by the Council on Foreign Relations, Inc., New York.

als, we manifestly shall have to revise some of the estimates which informed that growing consensus. The Chinese are going to have more difficulties with the problems of succession than was generally believed a few years ago. Also, it now seems likely that more time than we had expected will have to pass before Chinese Communism will accept the realities of domestic economic and social life as inevitably limiting change. Although it is still appropriate for American policy to be guided by the certain fact that eventually Chinese Communism, like all underdeveloped but modernizing systems, will have to come to terms with both its own society and the world community, there is now more uncertainty as to how soon and in what form this will take place.

Once again we may be in the classic situation in which American hopes and sentiment are out of phase with Asian developments. It would indeed be tragic if the current American mood of exploration for new approaches should be frustrated by the current phase of Chinese domestic developments. Yet to humor this mood without regard to Asian realities could lead to an even greater tragedy, for it would surely produce bitterness toward those who were seen, however unjustifiably, as having given false forecasts about the Chinese response to our efforts at being reasonable. If we are to take advantage of the opportunities offered by current American attitudes, and to avoid the dangers of bitter backlashes if all does not go well, then it is important to reach a realistic judgment of the precise limits of our capacity to influence Chinese developments in particular and Asian events in general. What can we realistically expect of American policy? And what are the responsibilities we must try to meet?

When nearly thirty years ago A. Whitney Griswold sought to find the central theme in American policy in East Asia, he was most impressed with the rhythmic fluctuations of our involvement and withdrawal. This pattern suggested that we were indeed the masters of our policies, that we could choose at will to become more or less deeply committed. Today some Americans feel that the inevitable change in the tide has come and that we should be working gradually toward disengagement from the exasperating problems of Asia. Others are equally convinced that only a little more intensification and determination in our Asian involvements will bring a new era of security. Both points of view, however, share the assumption that the initiative lies primarily with the American government.

Today we see a more complex picture than that of rhythmic involvement and withdrawal. We can now appreciate that our involvement in Asia has been governed not only by our own inspiration but also by the instabilities of Asian politics. Indeed, it has become increasingly clear that the principal dynamic element has been shifts in the Asian balance of power itself. The profoundly destabilizing consequences of the modernization process in Asian societies have made these shifts sharper and more extreme than in Europe. The rhythm of change has been Asia's and it has dictated both the depth of American involvement and the possibilities of American withdrawal.

In coping with the situation, the United States has been prone to take as permanent what are separate and at times only limited phases in the history of modern Asia. Of equal importance, American policy has tried to increase predictability and purposeful change. Time and again we have followed the cycle of recognizing a disruptive situation early, proclaiming a principle in order to give support to the forces of order, and then stubbornly holding to a position so that others could adjust their behavior in response to the element of predictability we had introduced. The effort to interject a greater sense of stability into the area has at times made American policy appear to be a blend of opportunism and rigidity.

This combination of contradictions has been heightened by the fact that although we have been a constant actor on the Asian scene we have been only marginally absorbed with Asian affairs. Our typical policy approach has been to adopt unambiguous postures of a high order of generality which can easily be explained to the American public and which appear to provide a steadfast element in a changing Asia. We have not had to engage in the continual adjustment and manoeuvre characteristic of deeply involved participants in an intense political process. The risks and returns alike have generally been uncertain and remote enough so that we could afford to stress high principles. Whenever the stakes have risen and we have had to follow more subtle and ambiguous policies, large numbers of the American public have been easily confused, for this is not what they have expected of Asia.

These are some of the themes and realities that have to be appreciated as a part of the historic American approach to Asia. They were all present at the time we responded to the realities of an impotent Chinese empire by enunciating the Open Door. Much has been made of our propensity at that time for legalistic formulations and moralistic pronouncements, but the basic fact was that we were trying to offset Chinese weakness by strengthening the prospects for orderly development. Later American policy had to respond to the reality that

a modernizing and militaristic Japan was disrupting the Asian balance by its growing naval power. Again, behind the legalism of the Washington Naval Conference and the non-recognition of Manchukuo there was the reality of the American effort to bring stability and order to changes in the Asian power balance.

After World War II and the collapse of Japanese power, we were suddenly confronted with the unexpected phenomenon of a united China, apparently strong, and allied to the Soviet Union, leading to the theory that a Communist bloc would be forever bound together by ideology. Meantime, in Southern Asia the emergence of the former colonial countries, dramatized above all by India, produced the American stereotype, if not the doctrine, that Afro-Asian societies are typically devoted to rapid and planned economic development and neutralism in cold-war affairs. In seeking to stabilize a new Asian balance of power around the effort to contain China and vitalize a string of weak and disorganized new states, the United States has once again been led into being rigid and uncompromising. And since the Chinese threat has seemed more real than the prospects for rapid nation-building in the rest of Asia, the dogmatic element in the American position has had to be more negative than constructive.

As we have continued responding to erratic change in Asia, our position has inevitably become more complex. We have over the years developed a variety of commitments, a system of military bases for dealing with an assortment of contingency threats, and an array of techniques and programs for assisting Asians. These elements of policy have not been fitted together in an orderly or coherent fashion and in consequence provide only the bases for dealing pragmatically with new crises. Thus we now seem to be in the unique situation in Asia of having a greater potential for policy action but less coherence in policy than at any other time in our history.

II

The process of change in Asia and of response by America is still going on, and now American policy will have to respond to a new and complex set of changes. However, we have not as yet settled upon a new set of principles to guide us in dealing with an Asia with the following features: first, an emerging but isolated China absorbed with the domestic traumas of purge and succession; second, an India bitter toward China but ambivalent toward Communism and still groping for the key to both domestic development and greater international prestige; third, a vigorous Japan with more potential for power and influence than it is yet prepared to realize; fourth, a bankrupt Indonesia that has swung back from the brink of Communism to violent anti-Communism. And finally, of course, there is Viet Nam, not to mention the old problem of Laos and the possibilities of further crisis in Thailand.

The problem of finding an appropriate and coherent response to these novel developments is further complicated by the fact that American policy, at least since the Korean War, has been composed of two quite separate, but presumably complementary, dimensions. One has consisted of direct responses to the phenomenon of Communist China, in the form largely of security and general military measures, but involving also such troublesome diplomatic issues as recognition of the Peking régime and its admission to the United Nations. The other dimension has been our policies toward the countries of free Asia, including our concern to provide various forms of aid and assistance for economic and social development.

In the rather loose and general rhetoric in which grand policy pronouncements are made, it is possible to pretend that what our left hand and our right hand have been doing are all a part of a single great mission to contain Communist China and build up the rest of Asia. In practice, however, there has been a great gulf between those who have been centrally concerned with the problem posed by China and those who are professionally concerned with mainly economic but also other forms of development. The first have tended to feel that they are dealing with the basic problem of Asia and that all else is rather marginal. On the other hand, those absorbed with development problems have frequently been impatient with the logic of the cold war, bored with Chinese Communism and unconvinced that China is nearly as important as the China watchers claim it to be.

Each approach has had its distinctive rationale and each has called for different emphases and priorities. Yet for nearly a decade after the Korean War it has been possible for different Americans to react to their rather different Asias on the basis of a tolerable division of labor. At times one prong of the policy would compromise the other, as for example when the desire for security alliances and the apparent advantages of military aid challenged the logic of pure economic development strategies. In the main, however, the question of priorities could be put off, and there seemed to be little need to combine all our efforts into a single policy equation and to measure the relevance and effectiveness of all programs and activities against a truly coherent set of objectives in Asia.

We were able to avoid the question of priorities largely because during the first decades after World War II the new countries of Asia had such massive domestic problems of development that they quite understandably tended to turn inward and to ignore the problems of their neighbors, thereby allowing the United States to fall into the practice of providing bilateral aid and of treating the problems of each country separately. This tendency to treat development problems on a country-by-country basis minimized the need to deal with Asian problems as a whole. Although the Marshall Plan has been generally credited with establishing the principle of development aid, it is significant that when the scene shifted from Europe to Asia the focus also changed from regional planning to bilateral planning. During this period the problems of Asian development were seen in such a narrow national perspective that it was possible to talk about a development "race" between India and China that would of itself virtually determine the fate of Asia, without either country having to engage in any foreign-policy activities. At times we seemed to believe that most of the problems of Asia could be resolved if the free countries of the area would forego all foreign relations and single-mindedly concentrate each on its own internal development problems.

This benign and rather non-political view of the potency of economic development, enriched by our expectation as to what India might be able to represent to the whole developing world, was thrown into disarray, as were Indian policies themselves, by the shock effects of the Sino-Indian border conflict and by the growing war in Viet Nam. These and other recent fundamental changes have brought back into focus the inescapable fact that inter-state relations are going to be critical in determining the future of Asia. At the same time the Southeast Asian nations have gradually but significantly turned away from isolated concerns with domestic developments and have shown a growing interest in incipient forms of Asian coöperation. Not the least important reason for this trend is the fact that several of them are beginning to realize that there is an absolute ceiling on their prospects for economic development so long as they are limited to their small national markets. They have had to realize that their relatively small size and populations are not adequate for the creation of domestic markets large enough for setting up the heavy capital-goods industries requiring economies of scale. This new appreciation, which has come from the Asians themselves, is setting the stage for significant forms of regional coöperation.

This development can be profoundly significant in establishing the critically important mechanism of inter-state relations necessary if there is to be a balance of power in which the states of Southeast Asia supported by Japan, India and the United States can realistically find security. In fact, in looking ahead, it seems most likely that one almost certain consequence of any probable settlement of the Viet Nam War will be a massive infusion of American economic assistance to Southeast Asia which will spill over the boundaries of Viet Nam and provide a powerful stimulus for regional coöperation at a level which would have been inconceivable only a few years ago. In the light of what the United States did after previous Asian wars to rebuild and advance the economies of Japan, Korea and Taiwan, and given our intense emotional reactions to the Viet Nam War, we can expect that after the end of hostilities aid will be injected into Southeast Asia in quantities which will structurally change elements of the neutral economies involved and significantly advance regional development. As a result, economic development efforts in Southeast Asia will be based not on the earlier bilateral approach but rather on the broader foundations of multi-national markets.

In this respect Southeast Asian developments are likely to be less influenced in the future by the model of India and more by the realities of the Japanese economic contribution. Indeed, even limited coöperation among a few of the Southeast Asian states can provide the necessary formula for bringing Japan effectively into the process of supporting the Asian balance of power. As long as the countries of the region were dealing separately with their problems and as long as Japan was unsure of its role, there was no way of overcoming the residual feelings that trace back to World War II and the Japanese occupation of most of Southeast Asia.

In sum, it would appear not too unrealistic to see beyond the Viet Nam War the prospect of a considerably stronger and more integrated Southeast Asia in which Japan will be able to play an increasingly constructive role. Already Japan has taken the initiative in organizing the Asian Development Bank and in seeking more substantive ways of assuming a greater role in developing an Asian system of states.

III

Pronouncements about American policy which dwell mainly on optimistic possibilities for the economic development of Southeast Asia must seem to evade reality as long as no mention is made of Asia's central problem, Communist China. Has the time arrived to face more openly all the issues inherent in direct relations with China? As we observed at the outset, it seemed early in 1966 that a gradual but significant shift in American policy toward Communist China might take place which would lead to a broader range of relations. The Chinese, however, having plunged into their current self-destructive spiral of purge, succession crisis and teen-age rampage, are at present clearly in no position to talk soberly with anyone. They certainly cannot be expected at this time to engage in the delicate forms of communication which would have to precede any direct effort at improving United States-China relations.

Indeed, at a time when the Red Guards are producing the impression that the Chinese leaders have taken leave of their senses and when even Castro has concluded that Peking is "making a laughing stock of Socialism," an American effort to widen Chinese contacts with the outside world would appear to be merely a cynical act of psychological warfare. For the more people learn about the current realities of Communist China, the more they are likely to be shocked and distrustful of the ability of Peking to act responsibly in the international community. The fact is, however, that more direct and frequent forms of communication with the Chinese are not particularly central to the problem of American policy today. The real issues have little to do with human contacts but are deeply rooted in questions of military security and the future organization of Asia.

Indeed the key issue of policy toward China is the very basic judgment of what kind of a future force China is going to represent in Asia and the world. How powerful is China likely to become, and to what ends will the Chinese leaders direct this power?

Ever since the Korean War, security considerations have dominated American policy toward China. They bulked large in our overall policy at first because we were concerned about a China closely allied to the Soviet Union. Military planning with respect to China at that time had to include the possibility of general war against an extremely powerful enemy. Strangely, American security policies have not yet taken full account of the Sino-Soviet split and the consequent decline in Chinese power. The detonation of Chinese nuclear devices has helped to cover up Chinese weaknesses and has given a vague sense of justification for continuing to place a high priority on security considerations in the Western Pacific.

Looking ahead to the next stage in Asian developments, United States policy in general and security policies in particular will have to recognize the dramatic decline in what was once the Sino-Soviet combined threat and what is now only a nearly isolated Chinese threat. At present we are still uncertain as to how much weight should be given to Chinese military capabilities; and we have not only different judgments about Chinese capabilities but quite different policy deductions from similar evaluations. Thus it is possible to identify four influential views about the appropriate American attitude toward China, two of which stress China as a power and a threat and two of which emphasize the limits on Chinese capabilities.

First, there is the view reflected in some of Secretary McNamara's statements that China is a serious and growing military threat, and that therefore prudence demands a systematic increase in our security safeguards. And indeed

the remarkable pace at which the Chinese have made progress in both nuclear and missile development suggests that we must give most serious attention to projections of what the Chinese may be capable of doing in the next few years and by the end of another decade.

It is important to recognize, however, that the tremendous efforts being made by the Chinese in this field constitute a grotesque pattern of national development which still leaves China weak in conventional military forces. The only way that they can use their investment in nuclear and missile development to cover up their basic weaknesses is for others to believe that this can be done. A sober military appraisal of foreseeable Chinese gains in conventional forces deflates considerably the notion of spectacular advance in Chinese strength. It is hard to believe that forces which were once considered sufficient to deter China when it was closely supported by the Soviets should not be adequate for checking an isolated China. Indeed, the realization that China now stands alone and that Chinese power depends solely upon Chinese resources has encouraged a trend in Japan toward more realistic security policies. Combined with the Indian build-up after the border war, this development suggests the possibility of a greater Asian contribution to the balancing of China in non-nuclear respects. As long as American forces are employed to deter the Chinese nuclear threat, China does not appear to have the necessary conventional strength to disrupt the Asian balance. Therefore, in the meantime we would be playing the Chinese game if we allowed their militant language and rhetoric to exaggerate our estimate of their actual power.

A second influential American view also sees China as a rising power but counsels an exactly opposite response. Foreseeing ominous but unspecified dangers, the spokesmen for this position conclude that the only way the United States can get off a "collision course" with Communist China is to disengage gradually from the Asian mainland and retreat to offshore positions from which we can apply our advantages in air and sea power. The image of a powerful and dangerous China also reinforces vague anxieties that the United States may be overextended, particularly in Asia. This view is probably shaped more by reaction to the war in Viet Nam than to the realities of Communist China. Indeed, since much of the sense of urgency behind this view is inspired by concern over any form of escalation in the Viet Nam conflict, it is difficult to judge how significant it will be in the post-Viet Nam period. In the meantime, it has been considerably undermined by the contradictory arguments that China can be effectively contained by United States airpower but that the current air attacks can have no effect on Hanoi. Also, the very pace at which the Chinese have been developing their nuclear and missile programs, combined with our determination to prevent further nuclear proliferation, means that in time it will become increasingly difficult to consider any withdrawal of American nuclear force from Asia.

In contrast to these two viewpoints is the position of those who see a significant decline in Chinese military capabilities since the break with Russia. One influential group recognizes China's military weaknesses and argues that from our position of strength we can now follow a policy of "containment without isolation." It assumes that Peking's rule is firm, that the transfer of leadership will be relatively orderly and that China

will steadily become a more significant actor on the international stage. Therefore, in this view, the time has arrived to work toward more extensive and presumably more mutually satisfying relations with Peking.

Finally, there is a fourth view which also sees the weaknesses of the Chinese, but concludes that now is the time not to treat with Peking but rather to establish as firmly as possible the norms or standards of future international relations in Asia. And of course the critical principle to be established at this moment is the inadmissibility of indirect forms of aggression. Partisans of this view are convinced of the inability of the Chinese to intervene directly in Viet Nam, but are impressed with the Chinese potential for coaxing others into international mischief. More generally they hold that there is little to be gained from trying to establish a broader dialogue with Peking, that the mere effort can be frustrating and exhausting because even a weak China is hopelessly stubborn, and that therefore there is more to be gained by concentrating on the other dimension of American policy in Asia.

Any attempt to evaluate these points of view must be tempered by an appreciation of all the imponderables which will shape the prospects of Communist China. Current developments in that strange land, however, suggest that those who have taken the more qualified view of Chinese power are on firmer ground. This means that the serious debate about American policy will be between those who hold the third and fourth points of view and that some variation of these positions should provide the guiding principles for the next phase of American policy.

At this moment the upheavals in China make it exceedingly awkward for those who have pressed for finding ways to reduce Chinese isolation. Indeed, the proponents of this point of view, who deserve serious consideration precisely because they do appreciate the realities of Chinese weakness, run the danger of appearing to be rigidly doctrinaire if they cannot adjust to changing circumstances. Yet it would be quite improper to dismiss a policy approach for the longer run which seems absurd in the immediate context of the current Chinese fit of madness. Any strategy for maximizing the possibilities of moderation in China deserves sympathetic but rigorous analysis.

On the face of it, and taken solely as a slogan of policy, the recommendation that the United States should actively encourage the forces of moderation in China has considerable appeal. The problem, of course, is whether a gratifying posture can be an effective policy. Often the case for a "more relaxed and flexible posture" toward China is based on little more than an innocent faith in what might be called the pull of symmetry; if we display moderation and restraint the Chinese will gradually do likewise, but if we are rigid and hostile they will be the same. Thus the mere act of appearing to be more moderate is supposed to strengthen moderate forces in China, if not right away, at least in the next generation.

Leaving aside whether this proposition is valid, there is still the more limited question of its applicability to the Chinese Communists. Even if everyone agrees that the American objective should be to encourage a more moderate China, is this the best way of going about it? Is there any reason to believe that it is likely to be more effective than, say, the exact opposite approach — that of inhibiting and frustrating the Chinese until they are prepared to be more moderate and reasonable in international relations? Or is this a matter which cannot be appraised objectively, which means that the question is reduced to which approach is subjectively the most satisfying for Americans? After all, there are those who say that for some time we have been using China policy primarily to gratify our moralistic bent, and that the time has come to demonstrate the other side of our national character: pragmatic reasonableness.

Over the last few years there has been almost nothing in the record of Peking's behavior to suggest we can so easily influence Chinese attitudes. Indeed, it would be easier to make the case that the Chinese have tended to adopt postures directly opposite to those of the United States. For example, when we were being most rigid in opposition to Peking, the Chinese were enthusiastically joining in the benign spirit of Bandung and talking generally about good will among nations. More recently, the more we have tempered our criticism of China, the more intemperate the Chinese denunciations of the United States have become.

Those who advocate explicitly encouraging Chinese forces of moderation are generally realistic enough to recognize that it will be impossible to shake the fanaticism of the generation of the Long March, suggesting rather that our object should be to persuade the next generation of leaders that they can afford to be moderate and reasonable. The difficulty with this argument, of course, is that much of Mao's seeming madness stems precisely from the fact that he suspects this may be our game. Whatever the state of Mao's mind at this stage of his life may be, he certainly is sensitive to any signs that the spirit of his brand of Communism may be softening. More important, he has explicitly demonstrated that he makes the same deduction about the eroding effects of science and technology upon Communist ideology as Western analysts have done. Indeed, almost the essence of Mao's charge against "revisionism" is that Khrushchev allowed a technocratic class to come to positions of influence in the Soviet Union, and even worse, he allowed Russian scientists to meet their Western colleagues in situations which emphasized the universality of technical considerations and muted the importance of politics. A prime purpose of the "cultural revolution" is to drive out all vestiges of "bourgeois thought," which has increasingly come to mean any willingness to hold political considerations in abeyance. Therefore those qualities which we count on the most to produce moderation in the next generation, the technocratic approach to problem-solving and the apolitical spirit of science, are precisely those that Mao recognizes as the most dangerous.

In short, the Chinese are determined that what happened in the Soviet Union and in Soviet-American relations will not be repeated in their case, and they will certainly devise policies to thwart any American attempts to further such a development. Given this, any strategy explicitly designed to offer comfort to potential moderates in China is likely to be self-defeating, and, even worse, destructive of precisely the very individuals we would want to help. It is understandable that Americans would like to forget aspects of Stalin's Russia, but it is inexcusable to forget so soon the elementary principles of prudence called for in dealing with totalitarian systems and to compromise the safety of people who must live under the emotionalism of Mao's China. For American policy to take as its avowed goal the "encouragement of moderate elements" can be to make sus-

pect the very people we want to help. This is a very high price to pay, even though it gives us a sense of satisfaction at being eminently reasonable in the face of China's hate and hostility.

To gain a sense of perspective on what the United States can realistically hope to accomplish in influencing developments in China, it is helpful to keep in mind the difficulties others have had in trying to do the same thing. The Russians had far more intimate associations with the Chinese than the United States can possibly have in the foreseeable future, and were presumably anxious to influence the Chinese in the direction of moderation, yet clearly they not only failed but made matters worse for themselves. This despite the fact that they had the advantage of presumably sharing a common ideological framework with the Chinese and not being initially identified, as America is, as a sworn enemy. Likewise, it is difficult to see how the Indians, the Japanese, the British and the French, each in their quite different ways, have had any influence at all in reshaping Chinese developments in the direction of moderation.

It is of course true that other countries, in spite of their difficulties with China, have been exceedingly flattering of American influence by suggesting that a modest shift in American attitudes could produce profound changes in Chinese behavior. American policy-makers, however, cannot afford to confuse Chinese weaknesses and the basic inabilities of the Chinese to support materially their revolutionary pretensions throughout the underdeveloped world with an exaggerated view of what America can do to influence the evolution of Chinese society. The fact that China cannot effectively export her brand of revolution should not suggest that she is now vulnerable to the importation of American moderation.

None of this is to say that the ultimate trend of history is not in the direction of a steady moderation of the Chinese revolution. Although it is impossible to foresee the precise turn that events are likely to take in China, the general drift there is now fairly clear. Just as the Great Leap brought an end to the illusion that the Chinese Communists might have a magical solution to the problems of rapid economic development, the "Great Cultural Revolution" and the rampaging of the Red Guards have ended the remaining illusion about the magic of Chinese organizational abilities. The Chinese advances in economic development are never going to seem quite as impressive as they might have had there not been the pretensions of the Great Leap; and similarly, Chinese political development will be indefinitely compromised by the folly of using teenagers to purge both party and country. It is hard to imagine what could have caused Mao Tse-tung to set into motion a series of acts which can only destroy the precious mystique of party authority. From now on, government is going to be more difficult than before, and in spite of all the chanting of slogans it will be difficult to recapture its revolutionary élan.

What all this means, then, is that paradoxically the current upheavals will accelerate the day on which Chinese Communism will have to give up its pretensions and come to terms with the realities of Chinese resources and the basic facts of Chinese society. For American policy this means that we should have firm confidence that time will bring moderation in China and that the Chinese will be proved wrong in their forecast that "people's revolutions" will ignite the developing areas. This is now the basic issue which has in a sense replaced the earlier debate as to whether history is on the side of Capitalism or of Communism.

Precisely because we can have such confidence in our analysis of the eventual trend of events, it is we who should be prepared to settle for "peaceful competition" and not try to engage in small manipulations to "speed up the course of history." Specifically, this means that we should forego the temptation to engage in petty and marginal attempts to accelerate the processes of change by seeking "channels of communications" which can only be irritants to the Chinese. Just as we once learned that there was little to be gained and possibly much lost by trying to manipulate the weakening of Soviet Communism, so we should recognize that the same is true with Chinese Communism.

IV

In the next phase of the history of Asia, American policy is going to have to learn how to stand by while the Chinese go through the inevitable process of adapting and accommodating Communism to the real needs of their society. Until they have worked out for themselves what is to be the nature of Chinese, as opposed to Maoist, Communism, it is going to be exceedingly difficult to seek direct adjustment in American-Chinese relations. A counsel of patience should in the meantime replace the appeal of urgency which surrounded so much of the earlier discussion of the emergence of revolutionary Chinese power. To look back over the record of change in China in the last few years is to recognize the costs that would have been entailed in premature efforts to establish broader relations with China.

It is clear, for example, that China as it was before the Great Leap would have been more difficult to integrate into world politics than the later China. Similarly, a China that had experienced only the Great Leap and not the Red Guards would have been a more troublesome partner in international relations than the China that is going to emerge out of the current upheavals. Time has also given the rest of the world an increasingly clear appreciation of the pretensions and realities of Communist China. Indeed, it is precisely the need to understand better this gap between pretension and reality, between rhetoric and capability, that is a prerequisite of an improved China policy.

To counsel patience in finding possible ways of "communicating" with the Chinese is not to say that we should sit back and wait. On the contrary, the situation seems to call for far more significant action than such comparatively trivial matters as trying to arrange for exchange visits of newsmen and scholars. What is urgently needed is for America to apply again its classic approach of responding to the uncertainties of Asian developments — this time by directing attention to establishing a new Asian system of inter-state relationships in which Chinese power and interests will be appropriately recognized.

There are already a number of fundamental issues affecting the Asian balance of power which involve the structure of American bases and nuclear policies. These should be clarified in any comprehensive formulation of the future of Asia. And if we can assume a satisfactory outcome to the Viet Nam conflict, it will be urgently necessary to balance the Chinese sense of defeat with a constructive and very concrete statement of just what the United States means when it says that it is prepared to respect the "legitimate interests" of China.

The need is to make unmistakably clear what kind of Asia it is to which China must adjust, and to mobilize the rest of Asia to convince the Chinese that they can find security in such an Asia. In the past when we made our grand statements about Asia, such as in our enunciation of the Open Door, we did not have the capabilities we have now to affect Asian developments. What we lack now, however, is the grand formulation. This cannot be merely a matter of rhetoric; it must deal with such hard matters as the disposition of nuclear forces and the possibilities for trade and travel between parts of divided countries.

The reason that it is appropriate at this time, and would have been premature any earlier, is that at last much of the illusion about China has been stripped away and it is possible to discern fairly clearly the realities of Chinese power and the pace of Chinese progress. We can help to reduce the remaining gap between Chinese pretensions and reality by providing Chinese leaders, whether extremists or moderates, with a vivid sense of the kind of Asia they will have to live in.

With such large matters to be resolved in Asia in the immediate years ahead, it would be most unfortunate if the current American interest in discussing new approaches to China were to lead only to the examination of tactics for communicating with the Chinese and the old issue of United Nations membership. Only a slight raising of our sights might make it possible for us to reëstablish a true coherence in our policies by at last bringing together the two parts of what has been our bifurcated approach to Asia.

It may seem quixotic at a time when American forces are deeply involved in an ugly war in Viet Nam to call for discussion about what should follow after containment in Asia. Yet unfortunately so much of the discussion about Viet Nam has focused upon how we got there that we are in danger of once again fighting through a war without developing a vision of the political possibilities and necessities of the postwar period. The Viet Nam War itself and the advancing forces of regionalism in Southeast Asia will have demonstrated that China has been contained. Therefore many of the issues which have dominated debates on both China policy and the Viet Nam War should be put aside and vision should be directed to the far larger matter of the organization of a post-containment Asia.

III. THE FUTURE OF INTERVENTION: VIETNAM AND BEYOND

Robert A. Scalapino: WE CANNOT ACCEPT A COMMUNIST SEIZURE OF VIETNAM

Robert Scalapino is Chairman of the Department of Political Science at the University of California, Berkeley, and the author of many books and articles on Asian politics and American foreign policy. The following article is a defense of the case that "the peace of the world depends upon establishing some political equilibrium in Asia," and that such equilibrium in turn hinges on U. S. perseverance in Vietnam.

NO DOUBT, it was easier for the United States, two decades ago, to assume major responsibility for the defense and development of Western Europe than it is to undertake a similar role in Asia today. We were, then, fresh and idealistic — and, above all, "our world" was at stake.

"Europocentrism" and "spheres of influence" have been the two central elements shaping American foreign policy in the recent past. It is not surprising that many Americans, including a significant proportion of our intellectual community, find it difficult — even painful — to adjust to a rapidly changing world in which these themes are no longer sufficient.

We face a challenge in Asia similar in its proportions to that which we faced in Europe 20 years ago. In this sense, the Asia-Pacific area is unique. Only in this region are we confronted with the immediate necessity of joining with others to create a political equilibrium — participating in the establishment of a balance of power if peace is to be underwritten. Latin America and Africa present com-

plex problems affecting their peoples and the world, but neither continent contains the combination of factors which made Europe in its time — and Asia today — so crucial to global peace.

With this background in mind, let us look briefly at current trends in Asia. At the outset, I am prepared to make an embarrassing confession. In a period when being a fervent disciple of gloom is "in," I must admit to cautious optimism. I would assert that the broad events unfolding in Asia over the past several years warrant hope, and are themselves eloquent testimony to the importance of an American presence in Southeast Asia during the crucial times.

What are the most significant developments? First, a growing number of non-Communist Asian leaders are becoming alert to the responsibilities of this era — social, economic and political. In many Asian societies, one can detect a transition of major significance. Passing from the scene is a first-generation revolutionary elite that was strongly politicized, deeply ideological, and often possessed of striking charismatic qualities but very limited technical skills or interests. Emerging is a second-generation (or even third-generation) elite — more pragmatic than ideological, more administrative than charismatic, and infinitely more trained in, or committed to, the mechanics of social and economic engineering. If this transition continues and takes hold, it might well represent the most important development of this age.

Second, the economic progress achieved in certain parts of non-Communist Asia is impressive. The miracle of Japan has long been acknowledged, but recent economic trends in South Korea and Taiwan also deserve recognition. In Southern Asia, such states as Malaysia and Singapore, Thailand, and the Philippines — if political stability can continue — should be able to score striking economic gains in the years that lie ahead. Technical breakthroughs into population control, food production and industrial development, imaginatively used, could enable progress and freedom to go together in Asia. Meanwhile, non-Communist Asia can not only tolerate economic comparison with Communist Asia in many respects, but welcome it — a fact that shocks our die-hard pessimists.

Third, political trends can also be viewed as encouraging. A number of the small Asian states have not only survived the first critical years after their birth, but managed to gain legitimacy in an increasing measure. In Indonesia, moreover, a shift of far-reaching significance has taken place. The leftist swing and the alliance with Peking, so threatening to other Southeast Asian states, have been reversed, and a new effort to make moderate politics work is under way.

At the same time, the Communists of Asia have never before been so fragmented. Mainland China is in the midst of an upheaval involving top party and army circles. The party itself is split wide open. The Sino-Soviet cleavage, far from being healed as a result of the Vietnam conflict, as was predicted, has grown wider, partly because of that conflict.

Moreover, the small Communist states and parties of Asia have in some cases denounced *both* Moscow and Peking, seeking to form an alliance of the "small" against the "large" Communists. Currently, the North Koreans and the Japanese Communists are open members of that alliance, and some North Vietnamese are no doubt flirting secretly with the idea. Each of these parties, however, is split internally and, at least with the Korean and Japanese Communists, numerous purges have taken place.

Only the most rash man would attempt to predict the outcome of the Chinese internal struggle at this point, but its immediate impact upon the rest of Asia has been nothing less than disastrous for the Chinese Communist image. The purge of scores of intellectual, military and political leaders, together with the relentless pursuit of nuclear weapons, has drastically altered the "lovable China" myth so assiduously cultivated in the days of Bandung.

No leader in Asia today is unaware of the problem of China. And few non-Communist leaders — if any — fail to recognize the critical importance of building some balance of power, containing economic, political and military components, against the long-range threats confronting them. In this task, they assign the United States a vital but by no means exclusive role. The age of Western domination of Asia is ending. That of partnership may have just begun.

Some critics have argued that if the Communists were allowed to win in Vietnam, or possibly throughout the region known as Indochina, Ho Chi Minh would become another Tito. Ironically, at the moment, the chances for that seem far better if the Communists lose the struggle to conquer South Vietnam by force, and are caused to live in the midst of a true power balance, as was the case in Europe when Titoism emerged. Neither Chinese hegemony over continental Asia, nor an expanding Vietnamese Communist empire in the southeast (certain to be bitterly resisted and therefore heavily dependent upon external support) is a promising route for the real independence of Hanoi.

Vietnamese Communist independence will be meaningful only if Chinese power to the north is counterbalanced by some other power to the south, and if Hanoi is prepared to accept and work with a complex power relationship among Moscow, Peking and Washington. A pledge by the United States and its Asian allies to accept the sovereignty of North Vietnam and to allow Hanoi to benefit from broad economic developments with the Southeast Asia region, while receiving economic and technical assistance directly from the Soviet bloc, may be the only method of assuring Hanoi's independence from Peking in the long run. Surely, to count upon Peking's comradely benevolence in the absence of any balance of power in this area is naive, especially in view of China's attitude and actions toward other Asian Communist movements.

Naturally, there will be reverses in the future in Asia, as there have been in the past. Even where trends are broadly favorable, much progress will occur in a zigzag pattern. Some essential changes will come with painful slowness. Massive challenges lie ahead — particularly in societies like India and Indonesia. It is time, however, to demand that the pessimists at least face up to the evidence that contradicts their prognosis of unalleviated gloom and doom.

There are some Americans who believe that our decision to make a major commitment in Southeast Asia had nothing to do with these developments. I am not one of them; more important, neither are the overwhelming majority of non-Communist leaders in Asia. It is no exaggeration to assert that at present not a single non-Communist Asian government wishes the United States to withdraw from Southeast Asia or to be defeated in Vietnam. Cambodia's Norodom Sihanouk, in his famous letter to The New York Times of June 4, 1965, put the critical issue bluntly and in terms understandable to every leader of a small Asian state. "I have never had the slightest illusion," he wrote, "on the fate that awaits me at the hands of the Communists, as well as that which is reserved for 'my' government, after having removed from our region the influence, and especially the presence, of the 'free world,' and the U.S.A. in particular." Do we need stronger evidence, when such words can be written by one of our most bitter critics?

It is more meaningful to assert that our recent commitments in Asia have produced certain strains in our relations with Europe. Some articulate Europeans have feared that our preoccupation with the Pacific would reduce our interest in the Atlantic. Others have worried lest the Russians take advantage of the situation. Basically, however, non-Communist European leaders — Socialists included — have understood the reasons for our Vietnam policy, and supported it. Contrast their attitudes, for example, with those of Asian leaders two decades ago, when we were widely condemned throughout the non-Western world for upholding "rotten Western imperialist states."

A certain gap does exist between informed leaders and the common citizen in Europe. And this gap is produced in major part because the public, as in the United States, gets the TV-press treatment of the war in the American style. The Vietcong are notoriously uncooperative in allowing Western cameramen to shoot pictures of eye-gouging or throat-slitting ceremonies, or in permitting newsmen to attend briefings on marketplace terrorism. Most horror and sensationalism must thus be drawn from the non-Communist side.

To all of the above, France is a partial exception. Paraphrasing General de Gaulle, however, I think that old allies can afford to be frank with one another. Many French still harbor deep grievances against the United States for policies that appeared to them to abet the dismantling of the French Empire, and they suffer great anguish over the possibility that our policies might succeed in areas where French policies failed. Our understanding of these emotions does not require our acceptance of the judgments that flow from them.

In truth, our image in Europe and elsewhere will depend heavily upon one critical fact: can we succeed? It has been asserted by individuals who should know better, that we are big enough to accept defeat gracefully, and that our greatest contemporary problem is an arrogance of power. Such statements illustrate the powerful guilt complex that operates in some branches of American society, but they scarcely accord with the facts. The issue is not whether *we* can accept defeat but what the repercussions of our defeat would be for Asia and the world at this point. Our major problem in recent years, moreover, has not been an arrogance of power, but the uncertainty as to how best to use the massive power which we possess.

Our policy, and that of the South Vietnamese Government, must rest fundamentally upon two premises. First, the Vietcong movement is solidly controlled by the Communist party and that party in turn is dominated by the North. These points have now been virtually conceded by the Communists themselves (see, for example, the September, 1966, issue of Hoc Tap, the North Vietnamese party organ), so they should be removed from the debate. Any victory for the so-called National Liberation Front, therefore, would be a victory for the Communists — and, in the long run at least, for the *Northern* Communists. Korea provides an analogy. The Southern faction of the Korean Communist party was ultimately overwhelmed by the Northerners because they controlled the apex of power; indeed, the Southern leader, Pak Heun Yong, was executed by the Northerners during the Korean war, with his followers being relegated to obscurity.

The second essential premise must be that many elements currently in the National Liberation Front, especially those who are not hard-core Communists, may well have become disillusioned in recent months, and under the proper political circumstances might be separated from the movement. Concerning these crucial points and their policy implications, we shall have more to say later.

Neither of the above facts, to be sure, directly answers two questions advanced by certain critics. Granted that the National Liberation Front is largely a creature of the Communists, and that without Northern Communist leadership, organization and support this movement would not have been initiated in the form that it took, and might now collapse, is the Vietnamese conflict still not in essence a civil war? Moreover, is it not possible, despite their recent reverses, that the Communists have won the support of a majority of the South Vietnamese people, casting us in the role of thwarting the democratic will?

Of course, the Vietnamese struggle can be defined as a civil war in certain respects. Vietnamese are fighting against Vietnamese, and there are Northerners and Southerners on both sides of the conflict. To analyze the struggle merely in these terms, however, is profoundly to misunderstand the nature of our times. Divided states everywhere — Germany and Korea as much as Vietnam — represent a precarious balance involving regional and international interests as well as internal political divisions. In all cases, these divided states are a result of complex history and imperfect agreements. To attempt to change them by force at this point, however, represents far more than civil war. Whether in Europe or in Asia, it represents a direct challenge to the political equilibrium of the entire region, and hence to world peace.

There are good reasons to believe, moreover, that the attempt to bring South Vietnam under Communist control does not represent the desire of a majority of the Vietnamese people. On every recent occasion when the National Liberation Front has elected to test its political strength, it has suffered a major defeat. Its calls for general strikes in October and December, 1965, were almost completely ignored. Its attempts to block the municipal elections of 1965 and the Sept. 11, 1966, Constituent Assembly election were ignominious failures. And, perhaps of greatest significance, it was unable to seize control, or even play a commanding role, in the Hue and Danang uprisings of early 1966, when the authority of the central Government was at a low ebb.

None of this is to assert that the political problems are unimportant. On the contrary, the Vietnam struggle will ultimately be decided as much by political as by military considerations. A revolutionary movement dedicated to violence does not need to have majority support in order to be victorious. When even 10 per cent of the population is committed to such a movement, and able to neutralize the great majority of the people, most governments can be placed in grave jeopardy. Given our political culture, Americans naturally assume that threatening movements must have a majority on their side, but, in fact, deeply committed minorities prepared to employ any means to achieve power often hold the key to the politics of our times — unless they are resolutely and intelligently opposed.

A reasonable estimate of the broadest political divisions in South Vietnam would probably assign the N.L.F. some 15 to 20 percent support and opposition to the Communists 35 to 40 per cent, with the remaining citizens essentially apolitical, prepared to accept the winners. Any such bald assessment, of course, is misleading because it cannot measure the fragility and infinite gradation of political leadership. No objective observer would deny, moreover, that South Vietnamese politics constitute the Achilles heel of those attempting to prevent a Communist take-over, and pose the central challenge of the immediate future — *not* because the Communists are so strong, but because the opposition is so divided.

The politics of South Vietnam have been those of minority militance, majority disunity and public confusion. Serious regional, religious, political and personal differences — given considerable rein in an atmosphere where the Government does not, probably cannot, rule firmly — continue to plague the non-Communist cause. It is nonsense to define the present South Vietnamese Government as "Fascist." True, its efficiency has been low. It has been insufficiently representative. It has been unable, and often unwilling, to conduct badly needed reforms (and this is a crucial test that lies ahead, with improving security conditions now removing one major barrier). All of these problems are commonplace throughout the new world and naturally they are exacerbated when the Communists decide to inject terrorism and guerrilla warfare into the scene. The fact is, however, that a considerable amount of free expression — including strong criticism of the Government — takes place in South Vietnam every day — far more than is possible in Hanoi or, for that matter, in Rangoon.

It is also inaccurate to imply that the Communists have captured the Vietnamese national movement. Indeed, it is extraordinarily important that none of the prominent Buddhist, Catholic, Cao Dai, Hoa Hao or Dai Viet leaders — many of them fervent nationalists — have joined the N.L.F., whatever their grievances and divisions. They know the character of that organization, even if some foreigners do not.

The gulf between the Communists and ourselves is fundamentally over whether Vietnam shall be a unified Communist state or one divided into a Communist North and a non-Communist South. In this connection, the often-repeated thesis that the Communists could have won nationwide elections in 1956 should be closely scrutinized. What kind of elections? And won what? The Geneva agreement of 1954 was defective, if not fraudulent, in positing a Vietnam solution through "free elections." Every action of the Vietnamese Communists after 1950, including their assassination of scores of non-Communist nationalist leaders, made it clear that *their* concept of *"free elections"* did not include the right

of any real opposition to organize, or, indeed, to survive in areas where they had military control. The idea that an International Control Commission could establish freedom merely by supervising the mechanics of elections under these circumstances was scarcely worthy of world statesmen.

And if one chooses to believe in Utopia, what would truly free elections have demonstrated? Under no duress of any kind and with every group having full opportunities for campaigning, Vietnamese citizens in all probability would have voted overwhelmingly on the basis of religion, personalities and regional identifications. No political party would have come close to winning a majority of seats for a National Assembly. Undoubtedly, Ho Chi Minh would have been one of those elected, and quite probably he — as an individual — would have received the largest single number of votes. That would not have signified, however, that most Vietnamese wanted a dictatorship of the Communist party.

Up to date, the Vietnamese Communists have continued to demand unconditional surrender as the price for ending the war. The so-called Four Points of Hanoi and the Five Points of the National Liberation Front, together with the embellishments added to them, constitute precisely this demand: All military opposition to the Communists by us should cease, and all American and other non-Vietnamese forces should be withdrawn from South Vietnam. All equipment given by us to the South Vietnamese military forces should also be removed. The National Liberation Front should be recognized as the sole legitimate representative of the South Vietnamese people. Its program, based upon a step-by-step unification of Vietnam under Hanoi's

Communist regime, should be adopted.

The Communists are prepared today, as they have always been prepared, to negotiate with us on how these terms shall be carried out. Matters of timing and priority are open to discussion now as they were in 1964 and 1965, providing we accept their basic conditions. They are perfectly willing to help us save face, just as they sought to perform this service for the French at Geneva. Up to the present, however, they have not been prepared to accept any formula which would allow the non-Communists of Vietnam an alternative to Communist rule. When these facts are understood, much of the debate about our willingness to negotiate becomes irrelevant. The central issue is and always has been, are we prepared to accommodate ourselves to a total Communist victory?

Some critics insist that we too are demanding unconditional surrender, but this is not accurate. The United States does not insist upon a unified, non-Communist Vietnam, nor is it committed to a rollback of Communist governments elsewhere in Asia. Those individuals who want to live under Communism in Vietnam could have a Northern sanctuary. We are prepared, moreover, to withdraw American forces from South Vietnam when and if a political solution can be reached.

Indeed, there is nothing in the current American position that would bar the neutralization of the entire area under firm international security agreements. We are even prepared to see North Vietnam share in certain economic and political regional undertakings if the Hanoi Government chooses to do so. Are these the terms of unconditional surrender?

We are simply not prepared to accept a Communist seizure of power under the Hanoi-N.L.F. formula. Neither are the non-Communists of South Vietnam, who may be divided on many things, but who show unprecedented unity in rejecting current Communist terms.

Some observers believe that the Vietnamese Communists are being forced into a fundamental reconsideration of policy for the first time since 1959–60. Their heavy military losses, the growing disenchantment with Peking and increased Soviet influence in Hanoi, and the war weariness of the North are cited as key factors. The only evidence currently in the public domain is more ambivalent. French authorities have told us that Hanoi no longer believes that military victory is possible, but is prepared to conduct a holding operation rather than negotiate at this time.

Why? One might suppose that negotiations would now be extremely attractive, especially in view of our concessions. What if the Communists took advantage of all U.S. pledges with respect to military de-escalation in the event of negotiations, but entered the sessions intending to make absolutely no concessions? Could they not regroup and resupply their bone-weary, battered troops, and prepare them for future activities if necessary? It is legitimate to question whether our preparations for negotiations are adequate and whether our concessions in this connection have been wise.

Why have the opportunities not been tested by Hanoi? First, the North Vietnamese cannot rid themselves of the illusion that the United States is France, and that internal political crisis, combined with global pressures, will force an American surrender.

Hanoi also continues to count upon the political disintegration of South Vietnam, perhaps its most realistic hope. There is now evidence, moreover, that fairly intensive Communist efforts are under way to penetrate certain non-Communist groups, notably the so-called militant Buddhists.

The greatest barrier to negotiations, however, is probably a psychological one relating to the Communists themselves. For years, all Communist leaders beginning with Ho Chi Minh himself have ceaselessly proclaimed that they are prepared to settle for nothing short of total victory, even if the struggle takes 5, 10, or 20 years. Belief in total victory, indeed, has been made into an article of Marxist-Leninist faith, a touchstone of loyalty. Compromise, therefore, would be a traumatic experience for leaders and people alike, and possibly one with dangerous ramifications for the Communist party.

Thus, although the situation may change dramatically, the present prospects for negotiations are cloudy, and American policies for the immediate future must be based upon the assumption that the war will continue. Two related issues therefore continue to be of paramount importance. Are further concessions in an effort to induce negotiations in order, or should additional military escalation be undertaken for that purpose?

First, let us look very briefly at the past. Some critics charge the Johnson Administration with deliberately using peace overtures to camouflage its planned escalations. To me, this is a vulgarization of an enormously complex, difficult problem. The plot thesis upon which it rests is simple, psychologically satisfying — and incorrect. We are not ruled by diabolically wicked men. To imply this is to obscure the true issue: What policy is most appropriate in dealing with opponents who often mistake concessions for weakness and who have very different

rules for the political game? Is there a better method than a policy which simultaneously offers a broader set of opportunities for moderation and a set of rising penalties for extremism?

Earlier, we debated the enclave concept. As it was usually advanced, that concept had certain fatal weaknesses in my opinion, and it was correctly rejected. It would have destroyed all hope of any viable political alternative to Communism in South Vietnam. It thus would have separated us totally from the non-Communist Vietnamese nationalists, and supported the false thesis that our interests lay only in military bases and the retention of American power — or the saving of American face — in Asia. In sum, the charge of imperialism would have been underwritten by American policy itself.

Moreover, the enclave policy would have guaranteed no negotiations, because it would have given the Communists explicit indication of both the limits and the desperate nature of our commitment. Never have the Communists been willing to negotiate under such circumstances except to extract total surrender — and if that were our intent, there were less painful ways to effect it. Even from a military standpoint, the enclave proposal raised the gravest questions. The defense of fixed bases and separate garrisons, particularly if clogged with vast numbers of refugees, requires scarcely fewer men than a more mobile strategy, and it gives the enemy enormous psychological advantages.

The argument for unilateral American concessions currently centers on proposals for the cessation of Northern bombing. The issue of Northern bombing has always been a thorny one. Strong arguments against it were advanced at the outset — the effect on world opinion, the dangers of further escalation, the likelihood of increased Communist rigidity.

At least equally weighty considerations were advanced on the other side. Why should the Communists be able to transport men and equipment safely to the borders of the "enemy," enjoy the immunity of their own military facilities from attack, even be allowed to deny any involvement (as the North Vietnamese have consistently done)?

There is no question that the bombings have hurt the North, and hurt it badly. The Communists themselves have admitted this. They have acknowledged weariness, food shortages and even a creeping defeatism, which they insist is restricted to a small segment of the people. They have also admitted that some "counterrevolutionary" elements exist in the North, elements affected by recent developments. Southern morale was unquestionably bolstered by the knowledge that South Vietnam was not the sole target of a war in which Hanoi played such a critical role.

Moreover, the physical condition of Northern infiltrators and the amount of supplies they can bring with them are additional evidences of the effect of the bombings. Incidentally, the Northern bombings led the Soviet Union back onto the Vietnamese scene and served to reduce Chinese influence, because only the Russians could provide the sophisticated antiaircraft equipment needed once the bombings began.

These factors cannot be ignored, nor balanced by the simple assertion that the bombings have not stopped infiltration. We have stated that if there were signs — public or private — of an interest in negotiations or a willingness to engage in some reciprocal act of de-escalation, our bombing of the North would cease. Thus far, the campaign for an immediate, un-conditional, permanent cessation of these bombings on our part has failed to answer two related questions of major importance. Is there anything to indicate that a reduction of military pressure upon the Communists would induce compromises on their part, or would they merely take advantage of such a situation, as they have done on previous occasions? If so, how long could any Administration justify a return to the "privileged sanctuaries" position while American casualties mounted? To put it bluntly, is not a unilateral cessation of Northern bombing certain to lead to major escalation unless the Communists respond favorably within a matter of months at most, and does it not give to the Communists the real initiative in determining the escalation issue?

Sometimes it is asserted that South Vietnam cannot be saved if it is physically destroyed in the process. Such a statement conjures up a false image. There is no need to minimize the suffering and destruction taking place in Vietnam today in order to challenge terms like "annihilation" and "genocide." In fact, destruction in Vietnam at this point has not approached the level suffered by certain countries in World War II, nor that endured by Korea in the aftermath of an earlier "national liberation" effort by the Communists. Indeed, the major cities have been relatively untouched in physical terms and the Vietnamese population — both North and South — is currently rising, not falling. Moreover, in no other conflict in history has there been so much sensitivity to the suffering of innocent people. A number of Americans lie dead today because we have sought to reduce noncombatant casualties even at grave risks to our own men.

None of this is to indicate joy over this war nor is it to minimize the costs being borne by Vietnamese society. They are serious. It is time, however, to call a halt to emotional outbursts that grossly distort the facts. Furthermore, certain basic questions must be faced by those who imply that the responsibility for the killing lies with the non-Communists. Who is committed to the thesis that violence is an indispensable instrument of attaining power? Who categorizes all those opposing Communism as "enemies of the people" — legitimate targets for liquidation? And what would happen to those "enemies" if the Communists were to win in Vietnam? Does anyone seriously believe that an American withdrawal would end the killing or the suffering in Vietnam? If we ever reach a position where our legitimate concern about the miseries of war enables any aggressive force to use violence with impunity, will we then deserve to be called moral?

What course of action should now be pursued? First, if the arguments against unilateral de-escalation are powerful, so are the arguments against any massive escalation. To take steps, for example, that would threaten the obliteration of North Vietnam or involve us directly with either China or the Soviet Union would be to take actions unwise from any standpoint. Vietnam, above all, is a test of the American capacity to respond in measured terms to a threat that is important but not terminal. The Vietnam struggle must always be kept in its larger context, and to do so is to reject all extreme solutions.

With respect to the military arena, it is now time to define our function more specifically, and that act in itself can do much to prevent uncontrolled escalation. Our primary military task, and that of our non-Vietnamese allies, should be to prevent or to reduce to a minimum Northern infiltration into South Vietnam. No limit should be placed upon the number of troops necessary for this task, and the bombings of the North should be related specifically to this goal. Further escalation, thus, should not be contemplated unless the character of the infiltration changes.

We should make it clear, moreover, that we are prepared to reduce the level of our attacks as Northern infiltration declines, without any necessity for formal negotiations. Meanwhile, we, together with our allies (especially the Koreans), should concentrate upon the speedy training of new South Vietnamese officers and the revitalization of the South Vietnamese Army forces, so that they can ultimately take up the primary task of coping with the Vietcong.

It is impossible — and it would be unwise — to attempt any rigid line of demarkation at this point between the tasks of dealing with Northern infiltration and handling the Vietcong. The objective, however, and the policy thrust should be strongly in this direction.

Our task is that of providing a military umbrella under which the process of building a nation can take place. It is also clear, however, that we cannot afford to stand aloof from the vital socio-economic and political problems which South Vietnam faces. The so-called pacification program is not going well. The war cannot be lost militarily, but it can be lost politically. It can also be won — in the sense of seeing an evolution not dissimilar from that which has taken place in South Korea. Three basic conditions are necessary.

First, military security must be guaranteed, in order for villagers to have any confidence that their allegiance will not be their death warrants.

Second, a social revolution in the countryside must be sponsored by the South Vietnamese Government as its top political priority, with the full force of American influence being directed toward this end. In Japan, we conducted one of the most successful social revolutions ever undertaken in modern Asia. In Korea, we provided an environment for a much more modest evolution to take place. Vietnam demands an American policy between these two, but closer to the Japanese model. Corrupt and inefficient officials must go. Programs like land reform (on a much broader scale than previously attempted) must come — and now. This is more important — and more possible — than instant democracy, Western style.

Third, our general political support in Vietnam should be oriented less around a man, and more around a pattern of political evolution. The immediate thrust must be toward a mixed military-civilian Government, a working coalition of moderate elements from which can be drawn acceptable leaders and, eventually, a dominant party that can enlist support sufficient to allow both stability and some degree of openness. It is particularly essential to get more Southerners into the Government at all levels.

A formal coalition Government involving the Communists is neither wise nor feasible. It has not worked in Laos, Burma or any other nation of Asia, and it would not work in South Vietnam. A generous amnesty for ex-Vietcong elements, however, and the inclusion of some persons previously associated with the National Liberation Front in the Government as individuals may be both practical and desirable. The political evolution of South Vietnam is certain to be complex, with a number of crises lying ahead. Our stake in this evolution requires that our influence be felt.

Any Vietnam policy, to be effective, must be encased in a broader policy toward Asia that is at once subtle, flexible and forward-looking. With respect to the Communist states, we must advance policies that offer an extensive structure of opportunities for moderation, on the one hand, and a set of firm, explicit deterrents to extremism, on the other. Toward other Asian states, including our allies, we must increasingly solicit opinions and cultivate an atmosphere of partnership and mutual responsibility. Nothing is more important in this age of nationalism than the psychological relations between states, including the patterns of style and behavior that are established.

Vietnam is a major test of American institutions and American political behavior. Can our people endure a long, complicated, intricate game which must not be played at either 0 or 100? Can they adjust to playing at 46, and being willing to go to 63 — but no more? Or down to 8, but no lower?

In an age when the peace of the world depends upon establishing some political equilibrium in Asia, and fostering the type of socio-economic programs that will make that equilibrium viable, do we have the patience and the sophistication to take a leading (but not solo) role? And, finally, are our political, communications and intellectual elites capable of providing the blend of maturity, balance and wisdom that is essential if these challenges are to be met? Upon the answer to these questions hinges our future, and that of many other peoples.

W. W. Rostow: THE GREAT TRANSITION: TASKS OF THE FIRST AND SECOND POSTWAR GENERATIONS

As a member of the faculty at the Massachusetts Institute of Technology, Walt Whitman Rostow became widely known for his writing on the process of economic growth in some of the major nations of the world. He was brought into the State Department by President John F. Kennedy and is now serving as a special assistant to President Johnson. In the following lecture, delivered at the University of Leeds in February 1967, Mr. Rostow looks back over the postwar period and forward to the agenda for the next generation. In this context he sees the struggle in Vietnam — "if we have the common will to hold together and get on with the job" — as possibly "the last great confrontation of the postwar era."

IN HIS State of the Union address on January 10 of this year, President Johnson said:

We are in the midst of a great transition — a transition from narrow nationalism to international partnership; from the harsh spirit of the cold war to the hopeful spirit of common humanity on a troubled and a threatened planet.

It is this theme that I should like to elaborate today by looking backward over the two postwar decades and looking forward to the agenda which is emerging for the next generation.

History is rarely clean-cut in its lines of demarcation. Wars, revolutions, and other traumatic events do leave their mark on the calendar; but their clarity is sometimes illusory, distorting the timing of more profound changes they reflect. Nevertheless, I believe we are now — potentially — in a true watershed period. We can make some shape out of the major experiences through which we all have passed since 1945. We can define some of the dangers, challenges, and possibilities which are beginning to grip the world community and which will increasingly engage it in the years ahead. . . .

The postwar world was shaped by two quite arbitrary processes. First, there emerged *de facto* or *de jure* lines of demarcation between the Communist and non-Communist worlds. These lines resulted principally from the disposition of military forces at the end of the Second World War, although they were also affected by events in the early postwar years — notably Stalin's consolidation of his position in Eastern Europe and the Chinese Communist victory on the mainland.

Second, a series of new states emerged from the process of decolonization. Most of these were the product of colonial history; but in the Indian subcontinent, the Middle East, Southeast Asia, and elsewhere, the birth of new nations produced new lines on the map.

A great deal of the first postwar generation's history consists of efforts to frustrate those who sought to alter these international boundaries by force: Communists because they felt that they had the historical right and duty to move their power forward beyond them, certain new nations because they felt a sense

Reprinted from *Department of State Bulletin*, March 27, 1967, pp. 491–497, 500–504.

of grievance over the lines which had emerged. And at certain points the two efforts interwove, as Communists acted to exploit postcolonial ambitions, frictions, and discontents.

The postwar Communist offensive had a certain shape and rhythm. There was Stalin's thrust of 1946–51, in association with Mao from 1949; Khrushchev's of 1958–62; finally, the offensive conducted over the past 4 years by Mao and those who accepted his activist doctrines and policies with respect to so-called "wars of national liberation."

Starting in early 1946, Stalin consolidated into Communist states the countries of Eastern Europe where Soviet troop positions provided leverage, while pressing hard against Iran, Greece, Turkey; then via the Communist parties in Italy and France. His effort reached its climax in the Berlin blockade of 1948–49.

The West responded with the Truman doctrine, the Marshall Plan, and the creation of NATO. A stalemate developed after the success of the Berlin airlift in 1949.

As this duel in the west proceeded, Stalin, working through the Cominform, launched an offensive in the east. . . . It involved guerrilla warfare in Indochina, Burma, Malaya, Indonesia, and the Philippines. And after the Chinese Communists came to power in November 1949, the offensive in Asia reached its climax in the invasion of South Korea. It ended in May 1951 with the successful United Nations defense at the 38th parallel against a massive assault by the Chinese Communists, although costly fighting continued for 2 further painful years.

From the opening of truce talks in the summer of 1951 to the launching of the first Soviet Sputnik in October 1957, there emerged what passes in postwar history as a relatively quiet interval. It was, of course, interrupted by the Suez and Hungarian crises in 1956; but these resulted less from the tensions of the cold war than from the dynamics of change within the non-Communist world and within the Communist bloc, respectively. During this time, the Soviet Union was mainly engaged in its post-Stalin redispositions, political, economic, and military.

Meanwhile, Communist China turned primarily to tasks of domestic development. Only in Indochina did local conditions favor major Communist momentum; but the North Vietnamese settled in 1954 for half of the victory they had sought.

Khrushchev's domestic changes represented a significant softening of Stalin's harsh regime, and for Soviet citizens, historic gains. His foreign policy style, too, was different and, in its way, more flexible. Nevertheless, considerable ambitions remained embedded in Moscow's foreign policy.

And with the launching of Sputnik, a new phase of attempted Communist expansion got under way.

Khrushchev had consolidated by that time unambiguous control over the machinery of the Soviet Government as well as over the Communist Party. He looked to the exploitation of two new facts on the world scene: first, the emerging Soviet capacity to deliver thermonuclear weapons over long distances as a means of forcing the West to make limited diplomatic concessions; second, the marked acceleration of nationalism and modernization in Asia, the Middle East, Africa, and Latin America, yielding an environment of endemic turbulence on those continents.

It was in this post-Sputnik period that Moscow laid down its ultimatum on Ber-

lin; the Communist Party in Hanoi announced it would undertake to revive
guerrilla warfare in South Viet-Nam;
Castro took over in Cuba; and Soviet
military and economic aid arrangements
were extended to increase their leverage
not only in the Middle East, where the
process had begun earlier, but also in
Indonesia and elsewhere. It was then
that Mao announced: "The East Wind
is prevailing over the West Wind," and,
in that spirit, initiated in 1958 the crisis
in the Taiwan Straits.

There was a good deal of opportunistic
enterprise in all this rather than a majes-
tic grand design, but it was clearly a
phase of Communist confidence and attempted forward movement.

In 1961–62, Khrushchev's offensive was
met by the West as a whole at Berlin
and a further dramatic test of nuclear
blackmail was faced down in the Cuba
missile crisis by President Kennedy. For
the time being, at least, that latter crisis
answered a question which had greatly
engaged Khrushchev: whether the free
world would surrender vital interests
through diplomacy under the threat of
nuclear war.

The answer to the second question —
concerning the ability of the West to
avoid successful Communist exploitation
of the inherent vulnerability of the developing area — had to be given at many
points by many devices:

— In Laos, by an evident determination to frustrate a Communist takeover,
yielding the Geneva accords of 1962;

— In Viet-Nam, by President Kennedy's
decision in December 1961 to enlarge our
support for the South Vietnamese;

— In Africa, by the whole cast of European and American approaches to the
new African nations, and in particular,
support for the United Nations effort in
the Congo;

— In Latin America, by the isolation of
Castro's Cuba.

By the end of the Cuba missile crisis
in the autumn of 1962, the momentum
had largely drained out of Khrushchev's
post-Sputnik offensive; but Moscow's
move toward moderation, symbolized by
the negotiation of the atmospheric test
ban treaty in 1963, had no echo in
Peiping.

The Sino-Soviet split was gravely ag-
gravated after the Cuba missile crisis and
became increasingly overt as recrimina-
tions were exchanged and inter-Party
documents revealed.

The Chinese Communists sought to
seize the leadership of the Communist
movement, notably in the developing
areas, and to unite it with the radical
nationalists of Asia and Africa. They
thrust hard against Soviet influence
within Communist parties on every continent, fragmenting some of them; sought
to bring Castro aboard; moved boldly,
overplaying their hand, in Africa; probably played some role in triggering the
attempted Communist takeover in Indonesia; and postured aggressively during
the India-Pakistan war of 1965. As a
result of the problems they created, the
Afro-Asian conference at Algiers in 1965
never materialized.

At one point after another this Chinese
Communist offensive in the developing
world fell apart, leaving the war in Viet-
Nam perhaps the major stand of Mao's
doctrine of guerrilla warfare.

There is a certain historical legitimacy
in this outcome.

For the better part of a decade, an
important aspect of the struggle within
the Communist movement between the
Soviet Union and Communist China had
focused on the appropriate method for
Communist parties to seize power. The
Soviet Union had argued that the transit

of frontiers with arms and men should be kept to a minimum and the effort to seize power should be primarily internal. They argued that it was the essence of "wars of national liberation" to expand Communist power without causing major confrontation with the United States and other major powers. The Chinese Communists defended a higher risk policy, but they were militarily cautious themselves. Nevertheless, they urged others to accept the risks of confrontation with United States and Western strength against which the Soviet Union warned.

Although Hanoi's effort to take over Laos and South Viet-Nam proceeded from impulses which were substantially independent of Communist China, its technique constituted an important test of whether Mao's method would work even under the optimum circumstances provided by the history of the area. As General Giap [Vo Nguyen Giap, North Vietnamese Minister of Defense] has made clear, Hanoi is conscious of this link:

South Viet-Nam is the model of the national liberation movement in our time . . . if the special warfare that the United States imperialists are testing in South Viet-Nam is overcome, this means that it can be defeated everywhere in the world.

These Communist efforts to extend their power and influence beyond the truce lines of the cold war interwove, as I suggested earlier, with a second set of problems: the dissatisfaction of various ex-colonial nations with the frontiers — and other arrangements — which had emerged from the passing of colonialism. The list is long of conflicts based on real or believed grievances of this kind: the Arab-Israeli dispute; Suez; Somalia-Ethiopia; Algeria-Morocco; Kashmir; West Irian; the Indonesian confrontation of Malaysia; Cyprus; et cetera. In addition, older quarrels were exacerbated by the mood of rising nationalism which swept the developing world; for example, Peru-Ecuador, Thailand-Cambodia. The Communist powers sought to exploit a number of these conflicts in order to expand their leverage in the developing world via diplomacy, subversion, arms, and economic aid agreements. But their roots mainly lay in an extension of anticolonial attitudes and doctrines from the days of struggle to the early years of independence, in a continuity of policy from rebellion to government policy. It seemed easier for some leaders of the new nations to create a sense of nationhood by continuing to evoke the rhetoric and methods of anticolonialism — and xenophobic nationalism — than to turn immediately to the more mundane concepts and tasks demanded for the successful building of a viable nation.

Looking back over this whole sequence, certain general observations are possible.

First, the postwar international boundaries and truce lines have proved remarkably resistant to efforts to alter them by force. In this first postwar generation the non-Communist powers did not achieve a peaceful world community under law. But we did maintain the minimum condition for building such a community; namely, that aggression not be successful. And through persistent effort in the United Nations we have de-fused many small crises and choked off many episodes of violence which could have provoked major conflict.

Second, as the two postwar decades ended, some of the aggressive, romantic revolutionaries — Communist and non-Communist — were passing from the scene or entering a phase of protracted frustration, for the time being at least.

We have been dealing with leaders obsessed by ambitious maps of their region (or of the world) which they tried to bring to reality: from Mao's map of the area where China has, in the remote or recent past, wielded power or influence to Nkrumah's vision of a united black Africa led from Accra; from Castro's vision of the Andes as the Sierra Maestra of South America to Ho's image of the former French colonial empire in Asia run from Hanoi. Each has confronted both other people's nationalism, at the expense of which these maps would be fulfilled, and a more general resistance to changes in the territorial or political status quo by external violence. Resistance to the achievement of these visions, combined with the growing demand of people throughout the world for economic and social progress, has eroded both ideological and nationalist aggressive romanticism.

One sees this in the Soviet Union and throughout Eastern Europe; it is a central issue in the struggle within mainland China. This is the essence of the pragmatic tide rising through the developing nations, supplanting the slogans derived from Lenin's "Imperialism" and the struggle against colonialism with the more austere rhetoric of economic and social development. A new generation is emerging, skeptical of the expansionist and geopolitical concepts and visions that engaged their elders.

In an interesting leader of January 14, 1967, "The Last Revolution," The Economist recently advanced the proposition that the end of Mao would be the end of a line of romantic revolutionaries reaching back to 1789. I would put the proposition this way:

There have been three major types of war in modern history: colonial wars, wars of regional aggression, and massive wars to alter the Eurasian balance of power — the latter attempted by industrially mature powers. In the first post-war generation we have had to deal with the threat of the latter, as undertaken by Stalin and Khrushchev, under inhibitions set by the nuclear age. But we have also seen a good many acts of regional aggression arising from the dilemmas and the exuberance of newly formed national states, as they looked backward to past humiliation and forward to new opportunity, while confronting the choices open to them in the early stages of modernization. Despite their global pretensions, I would place Mao's efforts in the latter category.

Given the rhythm of modernization, with vast continents entering the early stages of modernization after the Second World War, it is natural that we should have seen a phase of regional aggression. From the record of history we should be in reasonably good heart about this phase. For these early, limited external adventures . . . appear generally to have given way to a phase of absorption in the adventure of modernizing the economy and the society as a whole. But, as I shall later emphasize, this underlying hopeful trend is potential, not inevitable, and it could be transitory.

If these aggressive impulses have diminished in the technologically mature Soviet Union and in most of the less developed nations, we should be able to go forward in the generation ahead from the frustration of aggression and the absence of major hostilities toward settlement, reconciliation, and cooperation. This, surely, should be the object of policy in Asia, the Middle East, and Africa; as it is already the object of policy in the West with respect to the Soviet Union, Eastern Europe, and mainland China.

We have had to allocate in the first

postwar generation an enormous amount of our energy, talents, and resources to the frustration of aggression and the avoidance of major war. Despite this environment of tension and to some extent because of it, the world community has also launched programs of economic and social development on an international basis which are truly revolutionary when compared to what was done during the interwar years or deeper in the past. . . .

It was in the post-Korea phase that thought and policy began to crystallize around the problem of accelerating economic growth in developing nations. In the early 1950's the best work on development by the United States was done in places in which we had major security commitments; for example, Turkey, Taiwan, and Korea. The substantial and sustained assistance provided for security purposes was gradually put to good advantage in terms of development. But toward the end of the 1950's, doctrines took hold and institutions emerged aimed at development itself — outside a narrow security context. . . .

[O]nly in the first half of the 1960's did the world community begin to bring development policy toward the center of the stage. . . . In the United States this transition assumed — putting aside Viet-Nam — the form of a shift from military to economic support and from generalized supporting assistance to purposeful development aid. Economic assistance of nations other than the United States rose by 18 percent from 1960 to 1965. . . .

One after another success story in development emerged in the sense that nations learned the trick of generating sustained and reasonably balanced growth at rates which substantially outstripped population increase. The list is now quite long: Greece, Turkey, Israel, Korea,

Taiwan, Thailand, Malaysia, Pakistan, Iran, Turkey, and nations in Latin America containing perhaps three-quarters of the population of that continent.

The problems of development are, of course, by no means solved. Large parts of Africa, for example, have not yet developed the human and physical infrastructure and sufficient political unity required for a sustained takeoff. And in each of the other developing regions some countries have not yet established the necessary and sufficient conditions — economic and political — for takeoff. . . .

In general, we have made great but uneven progress thus far in the 1960's. Many of the old contentious debates have subsided as men perceived their irrelevance; for example, arguments concerning private versus public enterprise, industry versus agriculture. They have given way to a pragmatic synthesis. New concepts, working methods, and institutions have emerged which should permit vigorous growth in the developing nations in the generation ahead.

But a lion stands in the path: the food–population problem. The solution to this problem will certainly be central to the agenda of the coming generation.

*   *   *

The central lesson we have drawn from our experience — and from the whole sweep of events since 1914 — is that our main task is the organization of a durable peace. We tend looking back, to share Churchill's judgment of the Second World War as "unnecessary." We are conscious that in a nuclear age the human race cannot afford another world war. Therefore, whatever the frustrations and difficulties, we are committed to look beyond the non-Communist islands of security, progress, and order to a settlement of the cold war itself and the shaping of something like a true global community.

The first condition for such a community is, I would say again, that alterations of the international status quo by force not be permitted to succeed. The status quo is, of course, not sacrosanct. It is always changing. And in the past two decades it has altered in major ways through changes within nations and by international agreement. We now have, for example, a fairly promising prospect before us in relations between the Soviet Union and Eastern Europe on the one hand and the West on the other. But we shall forget at our peril that this prospect was created mainly by the strength and unity of the West when confronted by the challenges of Stalin and Khrushchev.

* * *

In Communist China we are seeing one of the the great dramas of modern history. The Long March veterans, who worked for more than 30 years in what appeared to be remarkable unity, have now split and are engaged in an open struggle for power. Beneath the surface of the struggle for power is a debate on policy between revolutionary romantics and pragmatists. The resolution of this debate will shape mainland policy and Communist China's relations for many years ahead.

This judgment reaches back to the nature and roots of the Chinese crisis. It is clear that after their remarkable victory in 1949, Chinese Communist leaders made two grandiose errors.

First, they set in motion a pattern of economic development focused on heavy industry and the modernization of their armed forces which was historically inappropriate. They behaved as if they were at a stage similar to Stalin's Soviet

Union of 1930; in fact, they were closer to that of Japan near the turn of the century. Like Japan at that time, they needed to develop in modern China — as a foundation for industrialization — an agricultural system based on strong peasant incentives, combined with the massive application of chemical fertilizers. They chose collectivization and inadequate investment in agriculture. Despite some shift in recent years toward a higher priority for agriculture, the result is a food–population position which is incompatible with rapid economic development.

Second, they chose to move out onto the Asian and world scene with objectives that disregarded the realities of power in the world arena. They sought an expansion of control and influence beyond their capacity — and they failed.

In the face of these failures, the future of Chinese domestic and foreign policy is evidently now at stake as well as the future of the leaders engaged.

No one can confidently predict the timing and the sequence of the outcome. There is a decent hope, however, that soon or late, a mainland China will emerge which will accept as its primary task the modernization of the life of the nation and accept also the proposition that the international frontiers of the region shall not be changed by the use of force.

So far as the United States is concerned, President Johnson has made clear on a number of occasions that we look forward to that day and to welcoming that kind of mainland China into the community of nations.

* * *

President Johnson is conducting a policy which, in fact, is already at grips with many of what I have called second-generation tasks. I come from a Government which, contrary to a widespread view, is not overwhelmed and obsessed by the problem of Viet-Nam.

On the other hand, we are confident that what we are seeking to accomplish in Viet-Nam is right and essential if we are to move successfully through the great transition.

We are honoring a treaty which committed us to "act to meet the common danger" in the face of "aggression by means of armed attack" in the treaty area. And this commitment is also being honored by Australia, New Zealand, the Philippines, and Thailand — as well as by the remarkable action of South Korea, which was not bound by treaty in this matter.

We are also dealing with the gross and systematic violation of an agreement, signed in 1962, which committed all parties, including Hanoi, to withdraw their military forces from Laos, to refrain from reintroducing such forces, and to refrain from using the territory of Laos for interference in the internal affairs of other countries.

We are also encouraged by the efforts of the people of South Viet-Nam to make a transition to orderly constitutional government of the kind which the people of South Korea have accomplished with such notable success since 1961.

And we are answering, as we have had to answer on other occasions, the question: Are the word and commitment of the United States reliable? For the United States cannot be faithful to its alliances in the Atlantic and unfaithful to its alliances in the Pacific.

I know that some of the younger generation in the United States —and, I daresay, in Great Britain — believe that we in the American Government are old-fashioned in our approach to Viet-Nam. It is true that we recall often the lessons

of the 1930's; we recall experiences in Greece and Berlin and Korea which are not part of the living memory of those now in universities. That is, I think, because our experience has forced us to contemplate the chaos since 1914 and the reality of the task of building a durable peace. A new generation will, of course, decide what in its experience is to be remembered and set its own goals and priorities.

But in the perspective I have presented tonight, what is old-fashioned about Viet-Nam is the effort by the leaders in Hanoi to make their lifelong dream of achieving control over Southeast Asia come to reality by the use of force.

It is their concept of "wars of national liberation" that is old-fashioned. It is being overtaken not merely by the resistance of the seven nations fighting there but also by history and by increasingly pervasive attitudes of pragmatism and moderation.

History, I deeply believe, will show in Southeast Asia, as it has displayed in many other parts of the world, that the international status quo cannot be altered by use of external force. That demonstration is costing the lives of many South Vietnamese, Americans, Koreans, Australians, and others who understand the danger to them of permitting a change in the territorial or political status quo by external violence, who cherish the right of self-determination for themselves and for others.

If the argument I have laid before you is correct — and if we have the common will to hold together and get on with the job — the struggle in Viet-Nam might be the last great confrontation of the postwar era.

If the Cuba missile crisis was the Gettysburg of the cold war, Viet-Nam could be the Wilderness; for, indeed, the cold war has been a kind of global civil conflict. Viet-Nam could be made the closing of one chapter in modern history and the opening of another.

As befits a world in transition, then, we in the American Government, under President Johnson's leadership, are dealing with elements from the old agenda while doing what we can to define, grip, and move forward the new agenda.

President Johnson is honoring a treaty placed before the Senate by President Eisenhower in 1954 and overwhelmingly approved. He is insisting on compliance with an international agreement made in Geneva in 1962, by the administration of President Kennedy. But his thrust is forward. He has placed before the Congress a space treaty; proposals to expand East-West trade, to create the Asian Development Bank; a consular convention with the Soviet Union; a request for a resolution to multilateralize the American contribution to a sustained effort to win the race between food supplies and population increase.

It is clearly his hope to be able to pre-sent to the Senate a nonproliferation agreement; and we are prepared to put our best and most constructive minds to work in negotiations to head off, if possible, another major round in the arms race in strategic nuclear weapons.

In all this we are conscious that there is little we can accomplish by ourselves. The nation-state — whatever its size and resources — cannot solve the vast problems now before us or foreseeable. Nor is this any longer a bipolar world, despite the continued disproportionate concentration of nuclear power in the United States and the Soviet Union. The dynamics of the lively first postwar generation has yielded a world arena of diverse nations determined to take a hand in their own destiny.

We shall achieve arrangements of authentic partnership — based on mutual respect and acknowledgement of interdependence, or we shall not deal successfully with the new agenda.

America is now — and, I believe, will continue to be — ready to play its proper role in such partnerships.

John Kenneth Galbraith: THE MODERATE SOLUTION

A former U. S. Ambassador to India, and National Chairman of Americans for Democratic Action, Mr. Galbraith offers an alternative to the policy of the Johnson administration in Vietnam.

A SINGULAR and well-observed feature of war is for the view in retrospect to depart radically from that which attended the beginning. Dangers which at the outset of hostilities seemed to justify the most sanguinary steps in the perspective of years seem slight, some-times frivolous. And prospects which at the beginning of conflict seemed easy and brilliant come to measure only the depth of the miscalculation. The case of men who in the last thirty years have planned expeditions against Moscow, Pearl Harbor and Pusan not to mention Jerusalem

John Kenneth Galbraith, "Vietnam: The Moderate Solution," Washington: Americans for Democratic Action, 1967. Reprinted with the permission of John Kenneth Galbraith.

and Tel Aviv sufficiently establishes the point. At the same time war turns reason into stereotype. Acceptance of what in the beginning is an estimate of national interest becomes an article of faith, a test of constancy, a measure of patriotism. At least while it lasts, war has a way of freezing all participants in their original error.

The war in Vietnam, by various calculations, has now gone on for more than half a decade and with mounting intensity for three years. It has shown these classical tendencies. The march of history has massively undermined the assumptions which attended and justified our original involvement. No part of the original justification — I do not exaggerate — remains intact. More remarkable, perhaps, very few of the assumptions that supported our involvement are any longer asserted by those who defend the conflict. Yet the congealing intellectual processes of war have worked to the full. Action which is not defended is still adhered to as a dogged manifestation of faith.

Let me be fair. Those who are committed not to support of this venture but to opposition have also shown a tendency to become frozen in fixed positions. For the first time since 1815 we are engaged in a conflict to which a very large part of the population is opposed. The unanimity rule which has previously characterized our national conflicts does not exist. Those who defend and those who attack both have lost some of their capacity to accommodate their thoughts to new evidence.

My purpose here is to see if, however slightly, one can rise above these rigidities. I do not wish to pretend to view our situation in Vietnam with any special insight or wisdom. These I do not claim, and even if I did so, I would be cau-

tiously aware of our well-recognized and exceedingly valuable tendency to greet such pretension with something between skepticism and outright vulgarity. I would like merely to inquire how this conflict will look when minds, those of supporters and adversaries alike, are no longer subject to the congealing influences of war. And I would like then to propose the course of action — I venture even to call it the solution — that emerges from such a view.

Many will think that in labelling this a "Moderate Solution" I have made an unhappy choice of words. Moderation in these days is not in high repute. The term itself, in some degree, has come to imply pompous and comfortable and well-padded inaction. Thus, it rightly arouses suspicion. And increasingly men are divided between those who want the catharsis of total violence and those who want the comforts of total escape. Yet if our national mood opposes moderation, history favors it. It does not vouchsafe us sharp, well-chiselled solutions. It gives us blurred edges and dull lines. Whatever the ultimate bang or whimper, we can be sure that in between there will be only compromises.

Let me begin with the terrible treatment that history has accorded our original justification for this conflict.

II

No one can completely rationalize our involvement in Vietnam. We are there partly as a result of a long series of seemingly minor steps. Each of these steps, at the time, seemed more attractive — less pregnant with domestic political controversy and criticism — than the alternative which was to call a firm halt on our involvement. The aggregate of these individual steps — more weapons, more advisers, a combat role for our men, progressive increases in our troop strength, bombing of North Vietnam, a widening choice of targets — is larger by far than the sum of the individual parts. The resulting involvement on the Asian mainland is not a development that all who asked or acquiesced in the individual actions wished to see or even foresaw.

But back of these individual steps, and especially the earlier ones, was a political and military justification that once seemed compelling. And it is a justification which has since dissolved before our eyes. The justification was the assumed existence of a united, homogeneous and militantly evangelical Communism which has chosen South Vietnam as the weak point for a probe. Speaking to the National Press Club some six months after he assumed office, the Secretary of State gave an explicit formulation of the view of the world crisis in which Vietnam played a part. He said:

The central issue of the crisis is the announced determination to impose a world of coercion upon those not already subject to it . . . it is posed between the Sino-Soviet empire and the rest, whether allied or neutral; and it is posed on every continent . . .

This was an accepted view at the time. None thought Mr. Rusk's formulation other than commonplace. He and others repeated the thesis — the doctrine of a centrally controlled and disciplined power guided from Moscow — dozens of times. Implicit therein was a pattern of policy and of action. This had immediate relevance to Vietnam.

Thus, to assume a unitary and evangelical force was inevitably to urge a policy of resistance. And resistance would have to be everywhere on the Communist perimeter. To allow transgression in one place would, most plausibly, be to encourage it elsewhere. And here we have the foundation for the analogy to Munich which for a long time played such a dominant role in the Vietnam discussion. Given the assumptions, the analogy was persuasive.

The Sino-Soviet power being imperial and coercive, it was necessary also to assume that it would never be welcomed by those who might be subject to it. It could not reflect national aspiration; this was a flat contradiction in terms. Communist power might seek to exploit social grievance. But this, it was assumed, would only be a tactic designed to win subservience to the ultimate imperial and conspiratorial purpose. And this being so, no nation should yield to such tactics even when the grievance — as might often happen — was real. Far better that people stay in a less enduring state of exploitation than to pass forever into this all-embracing system of coercion. This meant, further, that we could not be particular as to whom we might support; even the most nauseous non-Communist dictator was preferable to the enduring Communist imperialism. And even if the Communists had seduced a majority of the population it was doubtful that we should yield. Rather we should try to win them back. The liberal strategist in this conflict set great store by ameliorative social action. Conservatives tended to place rather more reliance on a gun.

Given this view of the world struggle — and none I think will feel it an unfair summary of official attitudes in the early sixties — our intervention in Vietnam was wholly understandable. Let me go further and say that it was inevitable. It was unfortunate but not decisive that the governments we supported, in their commitment to democracy and humane and civilized values, left much to be desired. It was unfortunate but not decisive that our intervention was by something less than the popular demand of the people we aided.

Moreover, we had a right, given this view of the world, to expect two further and vital factors to be associated with our involvement. We had a right to expect that its necessity would be appreciated and supported by the American people — as our economic and political intervention in Turkey and Greece and Western Europe following World War II was supported or as our military intervention in Korea in 1950 was supported. And it was reasonable to expect that the most effective support would come not from those who automatically rally to the flag when the guns sound but from the more introspective, informed and deliberative community — those somewhat ambiguously styled the intellectuals — who would best appreciate the long run consequences of short run weaknesses and appeasement. People of this inclination had given strong support to the Marshall Plan and to the Korean intervention. A generation earlier they had been in the very forefront of the criticism of Munich, the agreed symbol of surrender. So their support could be expected now.

Finally, given this view of the world, there was every reason to expect that the American initiative in Vietnam would be welcomed by the rest of the non-Communist nations. Previous initiatives had attracted such applause. The closer a nation to the danger, the greater the prospective applause, for who could tell, after all, who was the next on the list. So the United States would both justify and enhance her claim to moral as well as economic and military leadership by assuming a commanding role in combatting the common menace in Indo-China.

III

Merely to state the assumptions which lie behind this conflict is to show how completely they, and the resulting expectations, have been dissolved. History may not vouchsafe us sharp edges but, obviously, it can be a very blunt instrument. We should perhaps remember, in this connection, that the assumptions which lay back of our Vietnam policy, including the concept of a unitary and all-embracing Communist imperialism, were never based on any very close knowledge of the subject. They were a formula, in some measure a theology, adopted by lawyers, businessmen, government officials and military men in the years of the Marshall Plan and NATO. Few of the authors had any first hand knowledge of Communism. Few had much experience of the political left. None had much experience of Asia. All were reacting to the current reality of Joseph Stalin. To some extent it was a doctrine recited to justify the political and legislative action — alliances, military appropriations, economic and military aid — which the proponents thought necessary. There is nothing especially remarkable in the discovery that a doctrine so contrived failed to stand the test of history. History is respectful of truth but not of official truth.

Since the basic decisions were taken to intervene in Vietnam the following has happened.

(1) The Communist world has come to pieces along national lines. The two great centers during the past years have, on occasion, been close to diplomatic breach.

(2) China, which the proponents of the Vietnam conflict for a while bravely pictured as the *deus ex machina* is rent within itself. Its assumed puppet in Hanoi, like its earlier puppet in North Korea, has publicly asserted its independence. Not even the most ardent defender of the war can now believe that Hanoi wants to be part of a Chinese-led empire.

(3) The people we fight in South Viet-

nam, it is now widely agreed, carry the banners of Vietnamese nationalism. They do this against former colonial officers whom we support. Gone, therewith, is the notion that people will rally to any alternative to Communism.

(4) Those we support, and Marshal Ky in particular, have by their burlesque of democratic and constitutional process reduced their American supporters and onetime defenders to an embarrassed silence. Gone is the notion that any alternative will be accepted in the United States. Marshal Ky's recently proclaimed view of the free elections which denies criticism to his opponents and promises military action against unwelcome winners was the *coup de grace*. I venture to think that he has now lost even his honorary membership in what are often called the forces of freedom.

(5) The assumption that we could count on the applause and support of the other countries has disappeared. No European or American nation has rallied to our side. Few leaders dare speak in our favor. In Asia, despite propinquity to the assumed danger, the most aggressive arm-twisting has not brought us allies, only a few clients.

But it is not that we have failed to win support that is our misfortune. We have aroused by far the most massive hostility in our national experience. There is an underlying implication, never quite vouchsafed, that much of this opposition has been manufactured by Communists. If this is so, it is the most drastic of all indictments of our Vietnam enterprise, for it shows what an unparalleled opportunity our enterprise has accorded the Communists for turning erstwhile friends into hostile critics. However, there is no reason to think that the Communists are this much involved. People have probably reacted in accordance with their own conclusions and their own conscience.

(6) Finally, with all else gone the assumption that Americans could be rallied more or less automatically, behind any war, however ill-considered, distant or cruel, provided only that Communists could be identified on the other side. Instead the American people have watched the collapse of the assumptions on which the Vietnam War was launched. In vindication of an intelligence none should mistrust, a very large number have reached the inevitable conclusion. The assumptions that took us there have been shown by history to be false. Therefore we should not be there. The reasons that took us into the conflict having disappeared, why do we remain?

We remain, as all know, because men are human and do not like to concede, even to themselves, that they were wrong. Those who urged our intervention were associated with what could one day be regarded as the greatest miscalculation in our history. They remain in command. They are naturally reluctant to admit that their view of the world — the view which counselled this vast effort — has been shown to be wrong. And so, aided by the military momentum of the event itself, they continue. That is why we are now at war.

It also counsels us on our course. Let us, as moderates, urge that when a change of direction comes as it must, there will be no recrimination. Let us counsel those that are persisting in error that they are far more likely to compound the damage to their reputation than to retrieve it. For that is what happens to men who persist in the face of fact.

IV

But there are stereotypes in the attitudes of those who are critics of our involvement in Vietnam. If one is detailing the miscalculations of those with whom he disagrees, it is salutary, also, to look for the errors of those with whom he agrees. It is most salutary of all, and in addition a trifle exceptional, to search for error in one's own past positions and attitudes.

One grave error of those who criticize our involvement in Vietnam is to assume that we are a small and heroic and perilously situated minority. We are nothing of the sort. In times past in the United States popular opinion and official persecution have dealt rather harshly with dissent. Lives have been ruined and men silenced. There has always seemed some special likelihood of this when the primitive emotions of war have been released. But this does not happen and will not happen when vast numbers, including an overwhelming proportion of the young and the articulate, are involved. One wonders, indeed, if under such circumstances one should speak of dissent. Certainly martyrs do not march by the millions. This tendency to appropriate their cloak serves only to give a highly erroneous impression of the weakness of the opposition to our venture in Vietnam.

If anything, reflection should be on the reverse. There is no community concerned with foreign policy in the United States where the critic of our involvement in Vietnam is not accorded a warm and even enthusiastic hearing. There are quite a few where it is not deemed tactful or discreet for an official defender to appear. For the first time in our history this spring the spokesman for our foreign policy found it necessary, in pursuit of this discretion, to avoid that fine old American folkrite, the commencement ceremony. Either too many students and too many faculty would be present or too many would unobtrusively decline to be

present. This is the situation on which we should reflect.

I think, also, that those who are critical of our involvement spend too much time worrying about the motives and tactics of those who share their goals. Second only to the fear that criticism will be suppressed is the fear of critics that they will be found in association with someone who, for whatever eccentric reason, has developed a latterday affection for Ho Chi Minh. This is silly. I do confess to wishing that all who are concerned about Vietnam would be more concerned with winning friends and influencing their fellow citizens in effective fashion.

I find myself also more than a little critical of those of my fellow critics who admit to a feeling of frustration and defeat in their efforts to influence the Administration on Vietnam. For one thing they have not been without influence. On the contrary, they have had a great deal. Even within the Administration there are far more people who share our honest doubts than is commonly imagined. There are more now, I venture to think, than ever before. And one has only to ask, had there been no criticism, no objection, for that matter no demonstrations, where would we be in Asia now? What would have happened had those who are committed to the old stereotypes met with no objection? Where would those whose reputation lies with a military solution now be? Can anyone doubt that we would be far more deeply and dangerously involved than now?

Next, as is said even of the President of the United States, the critics of our Vietnam involvement have been much too influenced by the polls. These I do not doubt show correctly the reaction of people to the war. They show the national, deeply-conditioned tendency to rally to the flag. But the polls do not show depth of feeling. They do not show ability to articulate feeling — to persuade. They do not show length of memory. They do not indicate who will write the history and draw the lessons. They do not always show where youth and thus the next generation stand. If those who feel deeply and remember long, those who can persuade others and who will be the next electorate are opposed, it may not matter too much that they are a minority. As noted, our wars in the past have been fought on something close to unanimity rule. And they have always had the part of the population that now opposes in full support. That it is wise to act in neglect of the informed, articulate and young — that they can be ignored as somehow morally as well as numerically inferior — is far from proven. On the contrary, it is likely to be remembered as one of the cardinal political errors of modern times. In American life, it has long been my observation that the intellectual, so-called, is fashionably dismissed as a serious factor in all the battles except the last.

The critics of our Vietnam involvement have also been too ready to imagine that the opposition in Hanoi is eager to oblige Americans of humane inclination by entering negotiations on whatever terms we believe convenient. This is unduly optimistic and also dangerous. Let me be clear on one thing. There is not the slightest doubt that overtures to negotiate have been made. And these have not involved the precondition of withdrawal. I urge all officials who may be tempted to deny this that credibility is not something lightly to be tossed away. But it is a mistake to base policy on any particular assumption as to the behavior and intentions of Hanoi or the leaders of the National Liberation Front. We do not know the enemy that well. Certainly

it is a mistake to imagine that they are only waiting to oblige Americans of goodwill. Such assumptions can be undermined by events. And it is very easy for those who are hostile to the idea of a negotiated settlement, those who want a military solution, so to handle our relations with Hanoi and the NLF and so to gauge and present their responses and non-responses that those who disagree — you and I and our friends — are left well out on a limb.

If we can have negotiations on equitable terms, that is much to be desired. But there must be something more. There must also be a policy that allows of stubbornness, suspicion, ill will, obtuseness and the waywardness of internal political struggle on the part of those with whom we are involved. No one, after all, would counsel Hanoi to repose high hopes in negotiations with Nguyen Cao Ky. Any policy which relies on negotiations is a policy that is at least partly at the mercy of others. We must also have a course of action which is within the scope of our own authority. We must invite negotiations. We must have a better policy than mindless escalation should negotiations prove not to be possible.

This brings me to my final point of criticism of my fellow critics. They exaggerate the difficulties in finding an alternative course of action to the one we have been following. This tragedy has continued so long that they have come to believe that the alternatives have now disappeared. "Perhaps something *could* have been done earlier. Now it is too late." This is wrong — as well as morally weak. Alternatives to continued and deepening involvement exist. They have even been made somewhat more feasible by the march of events.

Let me outline a feasible course of action which reduces our commitment in

Vietnam to sensible proportions, protects the larger peace, conserves our national interest and, what could perhaps be more important, reflects the interest of the sadly beset and tortured people of this part of the world. And it is a policy that does not depend on the cooperation of Hanoi and the NLF, although should that be forthcoming all would be much eased.

v

The first step is to accept in fact what many reasonable men have already conceded, which is that great areas of South Vietnam must remain indefinitely under the authority of the Viet Cong. They have been under this authority for years — sometimes ten or more. It was not the policy even in the most militant of the Cold War years to roll back the Communists from their established positions of power. Not even John Foster Dulles so urged. There is no indication that such policy is wanted by the people most immediately involved — there is no indication whatever that they would ask it at the price of the horrors of military liberation. None can say, in the context of rural Asia, that on the completion of this effort their liberties would be greater, their well-being enhanced. The men who defend these parts of the country — this is especially true of the Mekong Delta — are not foreigners but men who fight on their native soil.

Much of the country under Viet Cong control, the Delta apart, is wild and lightly populated. To invest American lives in so slight, improbable and subjective a gain as restoring these swamps and jungles to a Saigon administration is unthinkable. Nor do I honestly believe that even the militant friends of our involvement will defend it with much enthusiasm. In Laos we have reconciled

ourselves to continued control in the North by the Communist Pathet Lao. What was sensible there is sensible in Vietnam.

Next, having revised our strategic objectives, we should for the time being seek the maximum of security, tranquility and well-being in the limited but populous areas that we control. With our vast commitment of manpower to the area this broadly defensive strategy now becomes entirely feasible. This is not a matter of retiring to enclaves although the attack on that policy was less that it was militarily unwise than that it was militarily unwanted. Rather, it is simply a defensive policy which reflects the avowed absence of territorial ambition. I frankly do not think that the areas we defend can be very large — they will be in the main urban and populous areas which, by and large, have been difficult for or even immune to guerrilla operations. They will serve as a refuge for those who have committed themselves to our enterprise. They will be a position wherein to await negotiations. Should these be delayed and should the enemy continue to attack, an active defense will be necessary. There will be casualties. But these will be incomparably smaller than those resulting from any effort to secure and hold the whole country. Perhaps in this war-weary land we can expect stagnation and quiet — as in Laos or Korea. And one day there will be negotiations.

The next step, strongly dictated by our own interest, is to cease the bombing of North Vietnam. (The acceptance of the territorial status quo in South Vietnam will end, except for defensive purposes, the equally deadly and rather less publicized air attacks and expeditions there.) Our air attacks on the North have also, in their own way, dissolved a great many

*false assumptions — they have dissolved
the assumption that they could interdict
or even much handicap the movement of
men and supplies to the South, or that
they could force negotiation or that they
wouldn't affect our moral authority elsewhere in the world, or that because we
have airplanes, air power is pro tanto
always effective. They have shown that,
whatever the shortcomings of our politics, Americans are not so cynical that a
party can win an election by opposing
such use of air power and then turn
around and initiate such action all within
weeks.*

*Now and not surprisingly, given the
weight of our attack on a poor and primitive land, the supply of targets has been
exhausted. So it is clear that we should
now end these raids. With this action we
end the most reckless and sanguinary
aspect of our involvement in Vietnam
and the one that always carried with it
the temptation of yet more escalation, yet
greater involvement. We lose nothing.
And in the background are the repeated
suggestions that, if the bombing thus
ends, there can be negotiations. Rarely
in foreign policy is the path of wisdom
so clearly etched.*

Next we must begin to disengage ourselves from the political generals to whom
we have become committed in Saigon.
That commitment, no less than the belief
in a military solution, was the product of
assumptions that have thoroughly dissolved. It was part of the belief that
foreigners and Americans alike would
approve any alternative to Communism.
So far as one can tell from this distance,
it would seem that such detachment is
necessary if the elections, by which we
have set such store, are to be even marginally significant. If Marshal Ky and his
friends feel that they have the backing
or even the passive acquiescence of Amer-

icans in their unique view of democracy,
it is impossible to suppose that any internal morality will prevent them from per-
petrating an enormous fraud.

Finally, we must begin to put Vietnam
back in proper mental perspective. It
bulks large in our minds not because it
is a place where great issues are being
decided but because we have so often
said it is such a place. We must now
begin to live by the truth and not by our
own propaganda. Indo-China is not the
cross-roads of the world; no great issues
of strategy or security are involved. Earlier statements that to fight there is to
avoid fighting in Hawaii or Santa Monica
are now recalled only with amusement.
The countries so far that have lived in
the greatest security in that part of the
world have not been those, like Thailand,
which we defend but those, like Burma,
which we do not defend. The collapse
of Israeli democracy would have been a
tragedy for all mankind — and partly because it was a democracy it did not collapse. No serious person will suggest that
any government of the last decade in
Saigon should evoke a similar passion.
Our best judgment must now be that, on
the other side, we are involved with one
of the many forms of national Communism with which we have learned that
we can live and with which, as a practical matter, we now know that we must
live.

The steps I have just outlined — the
abandonment of the goal of territorial
conquest and pacification, de-escalation
and a defensive strategy, the ending of
the air attacks, political detachment, an
escape from our own propaganda, negotiation if this proves possible — are not
very dramatic. Nor do they bring our
history in Indo-China to an end — even
if the ending of the air attacks do not
bring negotiations, we can be sure that

some day negotiation will occur. But this is the nature of the moderate program. Violence and death do not lack in drama; as all who are experienced in Washington have long been aware, it is always the men of least moral courage who are the loudest in recommending sanguinary action and the mailed fist. But the moderate path I have outlined is one we can adopt and one that will see us clear. It is the one for which the largest measure of agreement can be won. Our task, the one to which we dedicate ourselves today, is to win that agreement.

Robert L. Heilbroner: COUNTERREVOLUTIONARY AMERICA

Robert Heilbroner is the author of many books and articles on economic theory and economic history. In the following article, Mr. Heilbroner considers the revolutionary demands of the underdeveloped world and argues that communism, however retrogressive it may be in the developed West, "may nonetheless represent a progressive movement in the backward areas, where its advent may be the only chance these areas have of escaping misery."

IS THE UNITED STATES fundamentally opposed to economic development? The question is outrageous. Did we not coin the phrase, "the revolution of rising expectations"? Have we not supported the cause of development more generously than any nation on earth, spent our intellectual energy on the problems of development, offered our expertise freely to the backward nations of the world? How can it possibly be suggested that the United States might be opposed to economic development?

The answer is that we are not at all opposed to what we conceive economic development to be. The process depicted by the "revolution of rising expectations" is a deeply attractive one. It conjures up the image of a peasant in some primitive land, leaning on his crude plow and looking to the horizon, where he sees dimly, but for the *first time* (and that is what is so revolutionary about it), the vision of a better life. From this electrifying vision comes the necessary catalysis to change an old and stagnant way of life. The pace of work quickens. Innovations, formerly feared and resisted, are now eagerly accepted. The obstacles are admittedly very great — whence the need for foreign assistance — but under the impetus of new hopes the economic mechanism begins to turn faster, to gain traction against the environment. Slowly, but surely, the Great Ascent begins.

There is much that is admirable about this well-intentioned popular view of "the revolution of rising expectations." Unfortunately, there is more that is delusive about it. For the buoyant appeal of its rhetoric conceals or passes in silence over by far the larger part of the spectrum of realities of the development process. One of these is the certainty

Robert L. Heilbroner, "Counterrevolutionary America," *Commentary*, April 1967, pp. 31–38. Reprinted with the permission of Washington Square Press, Inc. and of Robert L. Heilbroner.

that the revolutionary aspect of development will not be limited to the realm of ideas, but will vent its fury on institutions, social classes, and innocent men and women. Another is the great likelihood that the ideas needed to guide the revolution will not only be affirmative and reasonable, but also destructive and fanatic. A third is the realization that revolutionary efforts cannot be made, and certainly cannot be sustained, by voluntary effort alone, but require an iron hand, in the spheres both of economic direction and political control. And the fourth and most difficult of these realities to face is the probability that the political force most likely to succeed in carrying through the gigantic historical transformation of development is some form of extreme national collectivism or Communism.

In a word, what our rhetoric fails to bring to our attention is the likelihood that development will require policies and programs repugnant to our "way of life," that it will bring to the fore governments hostile to our international objectives, and that its regnant ideology will bitterly oppose capitalism as a system of world economic power. If that is the case, we would have to think twice before denying that the United States was fundamentally opposed to economic development.

But is it the case? Must development lead in directions that go counter to the present American political philosophy? Let me try to indicate, albeit much too briefly and summarily, the reasons that lead me to answer that question as I do.

I begin with the cardinal point, often noted but still insufficiently appreciated, that the process called "economic development" is not primarily economic at all. We think of development as a campaign of production to be fought with budgets and monetary policies and measured with indices of output and income. But the development process is much wider and deeper than can be indicated by such statistics. To be sure, in the end what is hoped for is a tremendous rise in output. But this will not come to pass until a series of tasks, at once cruder and more delicate, simpler and infinitely more difficult, has been commenced and carried along a certain distance.

In most of the new nations of Africa, these tasks consist in establishing the very underpinnings of nationhood itself — in determining national borders, establishing national languages, arousing a basic national (as distinguished from tribal) self-consciousness. Before these steps have been taken, the African states will remain no more than names insecurely affixed to the map, not social entities capable of undertaking an enormous collective venture in economic change. In Asia, nationhood is generally much further advanced than in Africa, but here the main impediment to development is the miasma of apathy and fatalism, superstition and distrust that vitiates every attempt to improve hopelessly inefficient modes of work and patterns of resource use: while India starves, a quarter of the world's cow population devours Indian crops, exempt either from effective employment or slaughter because of sacred taboos. In still other areas, mainly Latin America, the principal handicap to development is not an absence of national identity or the presence of suffocating cultures (although the latter certainly plays its part), but the cramping and crippling inhibitions of obsolete social institutions and reactionary social classes. Where landholding rather than industrial activity is still the basis for social and economic power, and where land is held essentially in fiefdoms rather than as productive real estate, it is not surprising that so much of society retains a medieval cast.

Thus, development is much more than a matter of encouraging economic growth within a given social structure. It is rather the *modernization* of that structure, a process of ideational, social, economic, and political change that requires the remaking of society in its most intimate as well as its most public attributes. When we speak of the revolutionary nature of economic development, it is this kind of deeply penetrative change that we mean — change that reorganizes "normal" ways of thought, established patterns of family life, and structures of village authority as well as class and caste privilege.

What is so egregiously lacking in the great majority of the societies that are now attempting to make the Great Ascent is precisely this pervasive modernization. The trouble with India and Pakistan, with Brazil and Ecuador, with the Philippines and Ethiopia, is not merely that economic growth lags, or proceeds at some pitiable pace. This is only a symptom of deeper-lying ills. The trouble is that the social physiology of these nations remains so depressingly unchanged despite the flurry of economic planning on top. The all-encompassing ignorance and poverty of the rural regions, the unbridgeable gulf between the peasant and the urban elites, the resistive conservatism of the village elders, the unyielding traditionalism of family life — all these remain obdurately, maddeningly, disastrously unchanged. In the cities, a few modern buildings, sometimes brilliantly executed, give a deceptive patina of modernity, but once one journeys into the immense countryside, the terrible stasis overwhelms all.

To this vast landscape of apathy and ignorance one must now make an exception of the very greatest importance. It is the fact that a very few nations, all of them Communist, have succeeded in reaching into the lives and stirring the minds of precisely that body of the peasantry which constitutes the insuperable problem elsewhere. In our concentration on the politics, the betrayals, the successes and failures of the Russian, Chinese, and Cuban revolutions, we forget that their central motivation has been just such a war *à l'outrance* against the arch-enemy of backwardness — not alone the backwardness of outmoded social superstructures but even more critically that of private inertia and traditionalism.

That the present is irreversibly and unqualifiedly freed from the dead hand of the past is, I think, beyond argument in the case of Russia. By this I do not only mean that Russia has made enormous economic strides. I refer rather to the gradual emancipation of its people from the "idiocy of rural life," their gradual entrance upon the stage of contemporary existence. This is not to hide in the smallest degree the continuing backwardness of the Russian countryside where now almost fifty — *and formerly perhaps eighty* — per cent of the population lives. But even at its worst I do not think that life could now be described in the despairing terms that run through the Russian literature of our grandfathers' time. Here is Chekhov:

During the summer and the winter there had been hours and days when it seemed as if these people [the peasants] lived worse than cattle, and it was terrible to be with them. They were coarse, dishonest, dirty, and drunken; they did not live at peace with one another but quarreled continually, because they feared, suspected, and despised one another. . . . Crushing labor that made the whole body ache at night, cruel winters, scanty crops, overcrowding, and no help, and nowhere to look for help.

It is less certain that the vise of the past has been loosened in China or Cuba. It may well be that Cuba has suffered a considerable economic decline, in part due to absurd planning, in part to our refusal to buy her main crop. The economic record of China is nearly as inscrutable as its political turmoil, and we may not know for many years whether the Chinese peasant is today better or worse off than before the revolution. Yet what strikes me as significant in both countries is something else. In Cuba it is the educational effort that, according to the New York *Times*, has constituted a major effort of the Castro regime. In China it is the unmistakable evidence — and here I lean not alone on the sympathetic account of Edgar Snow but on the most horrified descriptions of the rampages of the Red Guards — that the younger generation is no longer fettered by the traditional view of things. The very fact that the Red Guards now revile their elders, an unthinkable defiance of age-old Chinese custom, is testimony of how deeply change has penetrated into the texture of Chinese life.

It is this herculean effort to reach and rally the great anonymous mass of the population that is *the* great accomplishment of Communism — even though it is an accomplishment that is still only partially accomplished. For if the areas of the world afflicted with the self-perpetuating disease of backwardness are ever to rid themselves of its debilitating effects, I think it is likely to be not merely because antiquated social structures have been dismantled (although this is an essential precondition), but because some shock treatment like that of Communism has been administered to them.

By way of contrast to this all-out effort, however short it may have fallen of its goal, we must place the timidity of the effort to bring modernization to the peoples of the non-Communist world. Here again I do not merely speak of lagging rates of growth. I refer to the fact that illiteracy in the non-Communist countries of Asia and Central America is increasing (by some 200 million in the last decade) because it has been "impossible" to mount an educational effort that will keep pace with population growth. I refer to the absence of substantial land reform in Latin America, despite how many years of promises. I refer to the indifference or incompetence or corruption of governing elites: the incredible sheiks with their oildoms; the vague, well-meaning leaders of India unable to break the caste system, kill the cows, control the birthrate, reach the villages, house or employ the labor rotting on the streets; the cynical governments of South America, not one of which, according to Lleras Camargo, former president of Colombia, has ever prosecuted a single politician or industrialist for evasion of taxes. And not least, I refer to the fact that every movement that arises to correct these conditions is instantly identified as "Communist" and put down with every means at hand, while the United States clucks or nods approval.

To be sure, even in the most petrified societies, the modernization process is at work. If there were time, the solvent acids of the 20th century would work their way on the ideas and institutions of the most inert or resistant countries. But what lacks in the 20th century is time. The multitudes of the underdeveloped world have only in the past two decades been summoned to their reveille. The one thing that is certain about the revolution of rising expectations is that it is only in its inception, and that its pressures for justice and action will steadily mount as the voice of the 20th century penetrates to villages and slums where it is still almost inaudible. It is not surprising that Princeton historian C. E. Black, surveying this labile world, estimates that we must anticipate "ten to fifteen revolutions a year for the foreseeable future in the less developed societies."

In itself, this prospect of mounting political restiveness enjoins the speediest possible time schedule for development. But this political urgency is many times compounded by that of the population problem. Like an immense river in flood, the number of human beings rises each year to wash away the levees of the preceding year's labors and to pose future requirements of monstrous proportions. To provide shelter for the three billion human beings who will arrive on earth in the next forty years will require as many dwellings as have been constructed since recorded history began. To feed them will take double the world's present output of food. To cope with the mass exodus from the overcrowded countryside will necessitate cities of grotesque size — Calcutta, now a cesspool of three to five millions, threatens us by the year 2000 with a prospective population of from thirty to sixty millions.

These horrific figures spell one importunate message: haste. That is the *mene mene, tekel upharsin* written on the walls of government planning offices around the world. Even if the miracle of the loop is realized — the new contraceptive device that promises the first real breakthrough in population control — we must set ourselves for at least another generation of rampant increase.

But how to achieve haste? How to convince the silent and disbelieving men, how to break through the distrustful glances of women in black shawls, how to overcome the overt hostility of landlords, the opposition of the Church, the petty bickerings of military cliques, the black-marketeering of commercial dealers? I suspect there is only one way. The conditions of backwardness must be attacked with the passion, the ruthlessness, and the messianic fury of a jehad, a Holy War. Only a campaign of an intensity and singlemindedness that must approach the ludicrous and the unbearable offers the chance to ride roughshod over the resistance of the rich and the poor alike and to open the way for the forcible implantation of those modern attitudes and techniques without which there will be no escape from the misery of underdevelopment.

I need hardly add that the cost of this modernization process has been and will be horrendous. If Communism is the great modernizer, it is certainly not a benign agent of change. Stalin may well have exceeded Hitler as a mass executioner. Free inquiry in China has been supplanted by dogma and catechism; even in Russia nothing like freedom of criticism or of personal expression is allowed. Furthermore, the economic cost of industrialization in both countries has been at least as severe as that imposed by primitive capitalism.

Yet one must count the gains as well as the losses. Hundreds of millions who would have been confined to the narrow cells of changeless lives have been liberated from prisons they did not even know existed. Class structures that elevated the flighty or irresponsible have been supplanted by others that have promoted the ambitious and the dedicated. Economic systems that gave rise to luxury and poverty have given way to systems that provide a rough distributional justice. Above all, the prospect of a new future has been opened. It is this that lifts the current ordeal in China above the level of pure horror. The number of human beings in that country who have perished over the past centuries from hunger or neglect, is beyond computation. The present revolution may add its dreadful increment to this number. But it also holds out the hope that China may finally have been galvanized into social, political, and economic attitudes that for the first time make its modernization a possibility.

Two questions must be answered when we dare to risk so favorable a verdict on Communism as a modernizing agency. The first is whether the result is worth the cost, whether the possible — by no means assured — escape from underdevelopment is worth the lives that will be squandered to achieve it.

I do not know how one measures the moral price of historical victories or how one can ever decide that a diffuse gain is worth a sharp and particular loss. I only know that the way in which we ordinarily keep the books of history is wrong. No one is now toting up the balance of the wretches who starve in India, or the peasants of Northeastern Brazil who live in the swamps on crabs, or the undernourished and permanently stunted children of Hong Kong or Honduras. Their sufferings go unrecorded, and are not present to counterbalance the scales when the furies of revolution strike down their victims. Barrington Moore has made a nice calculation that bears on this problem. Taking as the weight in one pan the 35,000 to 40,000 persons who lost their lives — mainly for no fault of theirs — as a result of the Terror during the French Revolution, he asks what would have been the death rate from preventable starvation and injustice under the *ancien*

regime to balance the scales. "Offhand," he writes, "it seems unlikely that this would be very much below the proportion of .0010 which [the] figure of 40,000 yields when set against an estimated population of 24 million."

Is it unjust to charge the *ancien regime* in Russia with ten million preventable deaths? I think it not unreasonable. To charge the authorities in pre-revolutionary China with equally vast and preventable degradations? Theodore White, writing in 1946, had this to say: . . . "some scholars think that China is perhaps the only country in the world where the people eat less, live more bitterly, and are clothed worse than they were five hundred years ago."

I do not recommend such a calculus of corpses — indeed, I am aware of the license it gives to the unscrupulous — but I raise it to show the onesidedness of our protestations against the brutality and violence of revolutions. In this regard, it is chastening to recall the multitudes who have been killed or mutilated by the Church which is now the first to protest against the excesses of Communism.

But there is an even more terrible second question to be asked. It is clear beyond doubt, however awkward it may be for our moralizing propensities, that historians excuse horror that succeeds; and that we write our comfortable books of moral philosophy, seated atop a mound of victims — slaves, serfs, laboring men and women, heretics, dissenters — who were crushed in the course of preparing the way for our triumphal entry into existence. But at least we are here to vindicate the carnage. What if we were not? What if the revolutions grind flesh and blood and produce nothing, if the end of the convulsion is not exhilaration but exhaustion, not triumph but defeat? Before this possibility — which has been realized more than once in history — one stands mute. Mute, but not paralyzed. For there is the necessity of calculating what is likely to happen in the absence of the revolution whose prospective excesses hold us back. Here one must weigh what has been done to remedy underdevelopment — and what has not been done — in the past twenty years; how much time there remains before the population flood enforces its own ultimate solution; what is the likelihood of bringing modernization without the frenzied assault that Communism seems most capable of mounting. As I make this mental calculation I arrive at an answer which is even more painful than that of revolution. I see the alternative as the continuation, without substantial relief — and indeed with a substantial chance of deterioration — of the misery and meanness of life as it is now lived in the sinkhole of the world's backward regions.

I have put the case for the necessity of revolution as strongly as possible, but I must now widen the options beyond the stark alternatives I have posed. To begin with, there are areas of the world where the immediate tasks are so far-reaching that little more can be expected for some decades than the primary missions of national identification and unification. Most of the new African states fall into this category. These states may suffer capitalist, Communist, Fascist, or other kinds of regimes during the remainder of this century, but whatever the nominal ideology in the saddle, the job at hand will be that of military and political nation-making.

There is another group of nations, less easy to identify, but much more important in the scale of events, where my analysis also does not apply. These are countries where the pressures of population growth seem sufficiently mild, or the existing political and social framework sufficiently adaptable, to allow for the hope of considerable progress without resort to violence. Greece, Turkey, Chile, Argentina, Mexico may be representatives of nations in this precarious but enviable situation. Some of them, incidentally, have already had revolutions of modernizing intent — fortunately for them in a day when the United States was not so frightened or so powerful as to be able to repress them.

In other words, the great arena of desperation to which the revolutionizing impetus of Communism seems most applicable is primarily the crowded land masses and archipelagoes of Southeast Asia and the impoverished areas of Central and South America. But even here, there is the possibility that the task of modernization may be undertaken by non-Communist elites. There is always the example of indigenous, independent leaders who rise up out of nowhere to overturn the established framework and to galvanize the masses — a Gandhi, a Marti, a pre-1958 Castro. Or there is that fertile ground for the breeding of national leaders — the army, as witness Ataturk or Nasser, among many.

Thus there is certainly no inherent necessity that the revolutions of modernization be led by Communists. But it is well to bear two thoughts in mind when we consider the likely course of non-Communist revolutionary sweeps. The first is the nature of the mobilizing appeal of any successful revolutionary elite. Is it the austere banner of saving and investment that waves over the heads of the shouting marchers in Jakarta and Bombay, Cairo and Havana? It most certainly is not. The banner of economic development is that of nationalism, with its promise of personal immortality and collective majesty. It seems beyond question that a feverish nationalism will charge the atmosphere of any nation, Communist or not, that tries to make the Great Ascent — and as a result we must expect the symptoms of nationalism along with the disease: exaggerated xenophobia, a thin-skinned national sensitivity, a search for enemies as well as a glorification of the state.

These symptoms, which we have already seen in every quarter of the globe, make it impossible to expect easy and amicable relations between the developing states and the colossi of the developed world. No conceivable response on the part of America or Europe, or for that matter, Russia, will be able to play up to the vanities or salve the irritations of the emerging nations, much less satisfy their demands for help. Thus, we must anticipate an anti-American, or anti-Western, possibly even anti-white animus from any nation in the throes of modernization, even if it is not parroting Communist dogma.

Then there is a second caution as to the prospects for non-Communist revolutions. This is the question of what ideas and policies will guide their revolutionary efforts. Revolutions, especially if their whole orientation is to the future, require philosophy equally as much as force. It is here, of course, that Communism finds its special strength. The vocabulary in which it speaks — a vocabulary of class domination, of domestic and international exploitation — is rich in meaning to the backward nations. The view of history it espouses provides the support of historical inevitability to the fallible efforts of struggling leaders. Not least, the very dogmatic certitude and ritualistic repetition that stick in the craw of the Western observer offer the psychological assurances on which an unquestioning faith can be maintained.

If a non-Communist elite is to perse-

vere in tasks that will prove Sisyphean in difficulty, it will also have to offer a philosophical interpretation of its role as convincing and elevating, and a diagnosis of social and economic requirements as sharp and simplistic, as that of Communism. Further, its will to succeed at whatever cost must be as firm as that of the Marxists. It is not impossible that such a philosophy can be developed, more or less independent of formal Marxian conceptions. It is likely, however, to resemble the creed of Communism far more than that of the West. Political liberty, economic freedom, and constitutional law may be the great achievements and the great issues of the most advanced nations, but to the least developed lands they are only dim abstractions, or worse, rationalizations behind which the great powers play their imperialist tricks or protect the privileges of their monied classes.

Thus, even if for many reasons we should prefer the advent of non-Communist modernizing elites, we must realize that they too will present the United States with programs and policies antipathetic to much that America "believes in" and hostile to America as a world power. The leadership needed to mount a jehad against backwardness — and it is my main premise that only a Holy War will begin modernization in our time — will be forced to expound a philosophy that approves authoritarian and collectivist measures at home and that utilizes as the target for its national resentment abroad the towering villains of the world, of which the United States is now Number One.

All this confronts American policymakers and public opinion with a dilemma of a totally unforeseen kind. On the one hand we are eager to assist in the rescue of the great majority of mankind from conditions that we recognize as dreadful and ultimately dangerous. On the other hand, we seem to be committed, especially in the underdeveloped areas, to a policy of defeating Communism wherever it is within our military capacity to do so, and of repressing movements that might become Communist if they were allowed to follow their internal dynamics. Thus, we have on the one side the record of Point Four, the Peace Corps, and foreign aid generally; and on the other, Guatemala, Cuba, the Dominican Republic, and now Vietnam.

That these two policies might be in any way mutually incompatible, that economic development might contain revolutionary implications infinitely more far-reaching than those we have so blandly endorsed in the name of rising expectations, that Communism or a radical national collectivism might be the only vehicles for modernization in many key areas of the world — these are dilemmas we have never faced. Now I suggest that we do face them, and that we begin to examine in a serious way ideas that have hitherto been considered blasphemous, if not near-traitorous.

Suppose that most of Southeast Asia and much of Latin America were to go Communist, or to become controlled by revolutionary governments that espoused collectivist ideologies and vented extreme anti-American sentiments. Would this constitute a mortal threat to the United States?

I think it fair to claim that the purely *military* danger posed by such an eventuality would be slight. Given the present and prospective capabilities of the backward world, the addition of hundreds of millions of citizens to the potential armies of Communism would mean nothing when there was no way of deploying them against us. The prospect of an in-

vasion by Communist hordes — the specter that frightened Europe after World War II with some (although retrospectively, not too much) realism — would be no more than a phantasm when applied to Asia or South America or Africa.

More important, the nuclear or conventional military power of Communism would not be materially increased by the armaments capacities of these areas for many years. By way of indication, the total consumption of energy of all kinds (in terms of coal equivalent) for Afghanistan, Bolivia, Brazil, Burma, Ceylon, Colombia, Costa Rica, Dominican Republic, Ecuador, El Salvador, Ethiopia, Guatemala, Haiti, Honduras, India, Indonesia, Iran, Iraq, Korea, Lebanon, Nicaragua, Pakistan, Paraguay, Peru, Philippines, U.A.R., Uruguay, and Venezuela is less than that annually consumed by West Germany alone. The total steel output of these countries is one-tenth of U.S. annual production. Thus, even the total communization of the backward world would not effectively alter the present balance of military strength in the world.

However small the military threat, it is undeniably true that a Communist or radical collectivist engulfment of these countries would cost us the loss of billions of dollars of capital invested there. Of our roughly $50 billions in overseas investment, some $10 billions are in mining, oil, utility, and manufacturing facilities in Latin America, some $4 billions in Asia including the Near East, and about $2 billions in Africa. To lose these assets would deal a heavy blow to a number of large corporations, particularly in oil, and would cost the nation as a whole the loss of some $3 to $4 billions a year in earnings from those areas.

A Marxist might conclude that the economic interest of a capitalist nation would find such a prospective loss insupportable, and that it would be "forced" to go to war. I do not think this is a warranted assumption, although it is undoubtedly a risk. Against a Gross National Product that is approaching ¾ of a trillion dollars and with total corporate assets over $1.3 trillions, the loss of even the whole $16 billions in the vulnerable areas should be manageable economically. Whether such a takeover could be resisted politically — that is, whether the red flag of Communism could be successfully waved by the corporate interests — is another question. I do not myself believe that the corporate elite is particularly war-minded — not nearly so much so as the military or the congressional — or that corporate seizures would be a suitable issue for purposes of drumming up interventionist sentiment.

By these remarks I do not wish airily to dismiss the dangers of a Communist avalanche in the backward nations. There would be dangers, not least those of an American hysteria. Rather, I want only to assert that the threats of a military or economic kind would not be insuperable, as they might well be if Europe were to succumb to a hostile regime.

But is that not the very point?, it will be asked. Would not a Communist success in a few backward nations lead to successes in others, and thus by degrees engulf the entire world, until the United States and perhaps Europe were fortresses besieged on a hostile planet?

I think the answer to this fear is twofold. First, as many beside myself have argued, it is now clear that Communism, far from constituting a single unified movement with a common aim and dovetailing interests, is a movement in which similarities of economic and political structure and ideology are more than outweighed by divergencies of national interest and character. Two bloody wars have demonstrated that in the case of capitalism, structural similarities be-

tween nations do not prevent mortal combat. As with capitalism, so with Communism. Russian Communists have already been engaged in skirmishes with Polish and Hungarian Communists, have nearly come to blows with Yugoslavia, and now stand poised at the threshold of open fighting with China. Only in the mind of the *Daily News* (and perhaps still the State Department) does it seem possible, in the face of this spectacle, to refer to the unified machinations of "international Communism" or the "Sino-Soviet bloc."

The realities, I believe, point in a very different direction. A world in which Communist governments were engaged in the enormous task of trying to modernize the worst areas of Asia, Latin America, and Africa would be a world in which sharp differences of national interest were certain to arise within these continental areas. The outlook would be for frictions and conflicts to develop among Communist nations with equal frequency as they developed between those nations and their non-Communist neighbors. A long period of jockeying for power and command over resources, rather than anything like a unified sharing of power and resources, seems unavoidable in the developing continents. This would not preclude a continuous barrage of anti-American propaganda, but it would certainly impede a movement to exert a coordinated Communist influence over these areas.

Second, it seems essential to distinguish among the causes of dangerous national and international behavior those that can be traced to the tenets of Communism and those that must be located elsewhere. "Do not talk to me about Communism and capitalism," said a Hungarian economist with whom I had lunch this winter. "Talk to me about rich nations and poor ones."

I think it *is* wealth and poverty, and

not Communism or capitalism, that establishes much of the tone and tension of international relations. For that reason I would expect Communism in the backward nations (or national collectivism, if that emerges in the place of Communism) to be strident, belligerent, and insecure. If these regimes fail — as they may — their rhetoric may become hysterical and their behavior uncontrolled, although of small consequence. But if they succeed, which I believe they can, many of these traits should recede. Russia, Yugoslavia, or Poland are simply not to be compared, either by way of internal pronouncement or external behavior, with China, or, on a smaller scale, Cuba. Modernization brings, among other things, a waning of the stereotypes, commandments, and flagellations so characteristic of (and so necessary to) a nation engaged in the effort to alter itself from top to bottom. The idiom of ceaseless revolution becomes less relevant — even faintly embarrassing — to a nation that begins to be pleased with itself. Then, too, it seems reasonable to suppose that the vituperative quality of Communist invective would show some signs of abating were the United States to modify its own dogmatic attitude and to forego its own wearisome clichés about the nature of Communism.

I doubt there are many who will find these arguments wholly reassuring. They are not. It would be folly to imagine that the next generation or two, when Communism or national collectivism in the underdeveloped areas passes through its jehad stage, will be a time of international safety. But as always in these matters, it is only by a comparison with the alternatives that one can choose the preferable course. The prospect that I have offered as a plausible scenario of the future must be placed against that which results from a pursuit of our present

course. And here I see two dangers of even greater magnitude: (1) the prospect of many more Vietnams, as radical movements assert themselves in other areas of the world; and (2) a continuation of the present inability of the most impoverished areas to modernize, with the prospect of an eventual human catastrophe on an unimaginable scale.

Nevertheless, there *is* a threat in the specter of a Communist or near-Communist supremacy in the underdeveloped world. It is that the rise of Communism would signal the end of capitalism as the dominant world order, and would force the acknowledgement that America no longer constituted the model on which the future of world civilization would be mainly based. In this way, as I have written before, the existence of Communism frightens American capitalism as the rise of Protestantism frightened the Catholic Church, or the French Revolution the English aristocracy.

It is, I think, the fear of losing our place in the sun, of finding ourselves at bay, that motivates a great deal of the anti-Communism on which so much of American foreign policy seems to be founded. In this regard I note that the nations of Europe, most of them profoundly more conservative that America in their social and economic dispositions, have made their peace with Communism far more intelligently and easily than we, and I conclude that this is in no small part due to their admission that they are no longer the leaders of the world.

The great question in our own nation is whether we can accept a similar scaling-down of our position in history. This would entail many profound changes in outlook and policy. It would mean the recognition that Communism, which may indeed represent a retrogressive movement in the West, where it should continue to be resisted with full energies, may nonetheless represent a progressive movement in the backward areas, where its advent may be the only chance these areas have of escaping misery. Collaterally, it means the recognition that "our side" has neither the political will, nor the ideological wish, nor the stomach for directing those changes that the backward world must make if it is ever to cease being backward. It would undoubtedly entail a more isolationist policy for the United States *vis-à-vis* the developing continents, and a greater willingness to permit revolutions there to work their way without interference. It would mean in our daily political life the admission that the ideological battle of capitalism and Communism had passed its point of usefulness or relevance, and that religious diatribe must give way to the pragmatic dialogue of the age of science and technology.

I do not know how to estimate the chances of affecting such deepseated changes in the American outlook. It may be that the pull of vested interests, the inertia of bureaucracy, plus a certain lurking fundamentalism that regards Communism as an evil which admits of no discussion — the antichrist — will maintain America on its present course, with consequences that I find frightening to contemplate. But I believe that our attitudes are not hopelessly frozen. I detect, both above and below, signs that our

present view of Communism is no longer wholly tenable and that it must be replaced with a new assessment if we are to remain maneuverable in action and cogent in discourse.

Two actions may help speed along this long overdue modernization of our own thought. The first is a continuation of the gradual thawing and convergence of American and Russian views and interests — a rapprochement that is proceeding slowly and hesitantly, but with a discernible momentum. Here the initiative must come from Russia as well as from ourselves.

The other action is for us alone to take. It is the public airing of the consequences of our blind anti-Communism for the underdeveloped world. It must be said aloud that our present policy prefers the absence of development to the chance for Communism — which is to say, that we prefer hunger and want and the existing inadequate assaults against the causes of hunger and want to any regime that declares its hostility to capitalism. There are strong American currents of humanitarianism that can be directed as a counterforce to this profoundly anti-humanitarian view. But for this counterforce to become mobilized it will be necessary to put fearlessly the outrageous question with which I began: is the United States fundamentally opposed to economic development?

Suggestions for Additional Reading

The best comprehensive source on the evolution of American policy in Vietnam is the daily newspaper: chiefly *The New York Times* and the French *Le Monde.* For consistently well-informed periodic evaluations of the conflict the reader might most usefully consult *The New Yorker,* particularly Robert Shaplen's occasional "Letter from Saigon" and Richard Rovere's "Letter from Washington." Of special merit is Mr. Rovere's essay, "Reflections: Half Out of Our Tree," *The New Yorker,* October 28, 1967. See also the annual volumes published by the Council on Foreign Relations, *The United States in World Affairs* and *Documents on American Foreign Relations.*

Joseph Buttinger's first book on earlier Vietnamese history, *The Smaller Dragon* (New York, 1958), and his more recent two-volume study, *Vietnam: A Dragon Embattled* (New York, 1967), together constitute the richest historical source. Briefer, and perhaps the most valuable single study of Vietnam since World War II, is Bernard B. Fall's *The Two Vietnams* (New York, 1964). Fall has also published a collection of excellent articles: *Viet-Nam Witness, 1953–66* (New York, 1966).

Other useful general studies and collections include Marvin E. Gettleman, ed., *Vietnam: History, Documents, and Opinions on a Major World Crisis* (New York, 1965); George McTurnan Kahin and John W. Lewis, *The United States in Vietnam* (New York, 1967); Jean Lacouture, *Vietnam: Between Two Truces* (New York, 1966); Marcus G. Raskin and Bernard B. Fall, *The Viet-Nam Reader* (New York, 1965); Robert Scigliano, *South Vietnam: Nation Under Stress* (Boston, 1963); and Robert Shaplen, *The Lost Revolution* (New York, 1965).

For an excellent study of American and Chinese perspectives on Vietnam during the important years 1953–54, see Melvin Gurtov, *The First Vietnam Crisis* (New York, 1967). For the Kennedy years, there are three revealing volumes by members of the administration: Roger Hilsman, *To Move a Nation* (Garden City, 1967); Arthur M. Schlesinger, Jr., *A Thousand Days* (Boston, 1965); and Theodore C. Sorensen, *Kennedy* (New York, 1965). Consult also a small book by a former assistant to Presidents Kennedy and Johnson, Richard N. Goodwin, *Triumph or Tragedy* (New York, 1966).

The most interesting sources of more recent events, apart from the periodicals cited above, are the volumes of hearings before various committees of the U.S. Congress inquiring into various facets of American policy. See especially the hearings on Vietnam and China in early 1966 before the Senate Foreign Relations Committee, and the annual "military posture" testimony of the Secretary of Defense before the Armed Services and Appropriations Committees. Many official U.S. statements and addresses on Vietnam may be found in the *Department of State Bulletin.*

An important source of insight into the many dimensions of the Vietnam war is the general literature on insurgency and counterinsurgency, including Edgar S. Furniss, Jr., *Counterinsurgency: Some Problems and Implications* (New York, 1966); W. W. Rostow, "Guerrilla Warfare in Underdeveloped Areas," in *View From the Seventh Floor* (New York, 1964); George K. Tanham, *Communist Revolutionary Warfare* (New York,

1962); Sir Robert Thompson, *Defeating Communist Insurgency* (New York, 1966); and Charles Wolf, Jr., "Insurgency and Counterinsurgency," in *United States Policy and the Third World* (Boston, 1967).

Two interesting essays by an analyst of the U.S. Central Intelligence Agency with considerable experience in Vietnam are George A. Carver, "The Faceless Viet Cong," *Foreign Affairs*, April 1966, pp. 347–372, and "The Real Revolution in South Viet Nam," *Foreign Affairs*, April 1965, pp. 387–408.

On North Vietnam, the reader should consult P. J. Honey's periodic reports in the Hong Kong journal *China News Analysis*, as well as Mr. Honey's books, *North Vietnam Today* (New York, 1962) and *Communism in North Vietnam* (Cambridge, 1963). See also Hoang Van Chi, *From Colonialism to Communism* (New York, 1964); James Cameron, *Here Is Your Enemy* (New York, 1966); Harrison E. Salisbury, *Behind the Lines — Hanoi: December 23, 1966–January 7, 1967* (New York, 1967); and Denis Warner, "How Hanoi Sees the War," *The Reporter*, August 10, 1967, pp. 17–20.

Chinese foreign policy as it relates to Vietnam and the rest of Southeast Asia is discussed from a variety of perspectives in *U.S. Policy with Respect to Mainland China*, Hearings before the Committee on Foreign Relations, U.S. Senate (Washington, 1966). See also John K. Fairbank, *China: The People's Middle Kingdom and the U.S.A.* (Cambridge, 1967); Edwin O. Reischauer, *Beyond Vietnam: The United States and Asia* (New York, 1967); and Donald Zagoria, *Vietnam Triangle: Moscow, Peking, Hanoi* (New York, 1967).

The general literature critical of U.S. policy in Vietnam is very large. Particularly worthy of mention are Theodore Draper, *Abuse of Power* (New York, 1967); J. W. Fulbright, *The Arrogance of Power* (New York, 1966); Eugene J. McCarthy, *The Limits of Power* (New York, 1967); Arthur M. Schlesinger, Jr., *The Bitter Heritage* (Boston, 1966); Ronald Steel, *Pax Americana* (New York, 1967); and Edmund Stillman and William Pfaff, *Power and Impotence* (New York, 1967). For a contrasting view, see Maxwell D. Taylor, *Responsibility and Response* (New York, 1967).